Prime Ministerial Anecdotes

Roger Mason

Prime Ministerial Anecdotes

ROGER MASON

Fonthill Media Language Policy

Fonthill Media publishes in the international English language market. One language edition is published worldwide. As there are minor differences in spelling and presentation, especially with regard to American English and British English, a policy is necessary to define which form of English to use. The Fonthill Policy is to use the form of English native to the author. Roger Mason was born and educated in the UK; therefore British English has been adopted in this publication.

Fonthill Media Limited
Fonthill Media LLC
www.fonthillmedia.com
office@fonthillmedia.com

First published in the United Kingdom and the United States of America 2018

British Library Cataloguing in Publication Data:
A catalogue record for this book is available from the British Library

ISBN 978-1-78155-654-2

Typeset in Mrs Eaves XL Serif Narrow
Printed and bound in England

Preface

MY AIM IN writing this book is to give a very brief account of each of the country's fifty-four Prime Ministers. This does not just cover their time in that office, but also includes information about such things as their origins, education, other political offices, and activities outside politics. For each one, I also include a number of anecdotes. These are very wide-ranging. Some are factual, some are inspiring, some are funny, some are poignant, some are revealing, some are surprising, and a few are shocking. I hope that all are interesting. Space limitations only permit a very brief record of each of the Prime Ministers, which is frustrating, but inevitable.

Like everyone, I have views and prejudices about politics and Prime Ministers, but I have tried to be fair and suppress my prejudices and most of my views. It was not easy, but I hope that I have succeeded. If you think that you can detect them and you are right, then I have failed. If you think that you can detect them and you are wrong, then I have also failed. This is because I will have overcompensated.

I already knew that some of the stories about Prime Ministers are not true, and that some are of doubtful provenance. I have not included anything that I know or believe not to be true. In some cases, I have included things with a suitable warning; you will see such phrases as 'some people claim that'.

I have greatly enjoyed writing this book and I hope that it shows. I hope that you enjoy reading it.

Roger Mason
Leighton Buzzard, England
May 2018

A cartoon by Jame Gillray, published 24 February 1801. A group of resigning ministers, led by Pitt who holds a document entitled 'Justice of Emancipating ye Catholicks', leaving through an arched gateway inscribed 'Treasury.' Following Pitt are Dundas, Grenville, Spencer and Loughborough. From the left, represented by a plebeian rabble, is the Opposition, led by Sheridan and Tierney. Behind are Jekyll, Bedford, Nicholls, Tyrhwitt Jones, Norfolk and Burdett. The Opposition is held at bay by a sentry with G.R. on his bearskin. The sentry stands near his sentry-box with the placard: G.R. Orders for keeping all improper Persons out of the Public Offices.

Contents

1

Sir Robert Walpole

1721–1742

Sir Robert Walpole (1676–1745), portrait by Arthur Pond (1705–1758). *National Portrait Gallery*

NEARLY ALL HISTORIANS identify Sir Robert Walpole as Britain's first Prime Minister, but he was never formally appointed as such. The position of the monarch's first minister evolved, and, of course, continues to do so. Walpole's exact period of governmental dominance is a matter of debate, but he was appointed First Lord of the Treasury on 4 April 1721 and held the position until 11 February 1742. His period of office lasted twenty years and 313 days, which makes him the longest-serving Prime Minister. Pitt the Younger was the second longest. His two periods of office totalled eighteen years 346 days, the longest lasting for seventeen years and eighty-eight days.

Families in the eighteenth century were often very large, though the survival rate of children was often appalling. Walpole was one of nineteen children born to Robert Walpole MP and his wife Mary. He was the third son and destined for the church, but instead, he entered politics due to the death of his two older brothers.

In 1800, Walpole married Catherine Shorter, who brought a dowry of £20,000, and together they had three sons and two daughters.[1] It was not a happy marriage, and after a while, they led almost separate lives. He took a wealthy mistress, Maria Skerritt, who bore him a daughter and they openly lived together. He married Maria in 1738, shortly after his wife's death, and thus legitimised his daughter. Maria died following a miscarriage in 1739, leaving him devastated.

Walpole was born on 26 August 1676 and was educated at Eton and King's College, Cambridge. He was elected to the Commons at the age of twenty-four. Like his father, he was a Whig and soon became a leading member of the party. In 1708, he was appointed Secretary at War, and for a short time, he was also Treasurer of the Navy. His career came to a shuddering halt in 1712, when he was accused of corruption. He was impeached by the House of Commons and found guilty by the House of Lords, and as a consequence, he was imprisoned in the Tower of London for six months and expelled from Parliament. Shortly after his release, he was re-elected an MP and his career again blossomed. He became a Privy Councillor and Paymaster to the Forces. Starting in 1715, he spent eighteen months as First Lord of the

Treasury and Chancellor of the Exchequer, and he subsequently held the latter position for almost all his time as Prime Minister.

Walpole's assumption of the supreme government position was precipitated by the collapse of the 'South Sea Bubble'. The scandal badly damaged the standing of the King and the Whig Party. There had been very considerable parliamentary incompetence and corruption, and a large number of Peers and MPs had speculated in the stock. So too had several people very close to King George I. Walpole had speculated, but he had sold out shortly before the crash, making a large profit. He competently did his best to defend his colleagues and the King and he was appointed to sort out the mess.

In almost all writing about Robert Walpole's time as Prime Minister, and indeed about his life, the words bribery and corruption feature. There is no hiding the fact that he was very corrupt, though, of course, he was by no means alone in that. His actions in this field were both skilful and generally successful. It was the way that he operated and got things done. He paid attention to detail, chose his favours carefully, and explained his policies well. He was able to take knocks as well as render them, and he often displayed a surprising absence of rancour.

The Prime Minister's aims can best be summed up with the time-honoured words 'peace and prosperity'. Peace should take first place, and he did prevent his country becoming entangled in wars, something that was not easy to accomplish, but his authority finally drained away, one reason being that the King and many others wanted a war. They finally got one—the so-called War of Jenkins' Ear. His resignation came after a parliamentary defeat on a relatively minor issue.

Walpole retained just a little influence after his resignation and advised his colleagues and the King. He had been made a Knight of the Garter in 1726, and after his resignation, he was raised to the peerage as the Earl of Orford. He should perhaps be judged by the standards of his time and many consider him to have been a successful Prime Minister. At the age of sixty-eight, he died on 18 March 1745.

The Two Georges

During the first half of the eighteenth century, the monarch exercised great power, and part of Walpole's success depended on his ability to gain and keep the confidence of the two Kings who ruled between 1721 and 1742, George I and George II. The first one turned to him to save reputations threatened by the South Seas Bubble scandal. Walpole enjoyed his confidence and kept it until the King's death in 1727. The King's dependence on Walpole was partly caused by the fact that he spent a lot of the time in Hanover. Furthermore, his command of the English language was poor. He conversed with his Prime Minister in dog-Latin.[2]

Walpole overcame a potentially dreadful problem when the King died in 1727. George II disliked his father and distrusted the man that he had chosen to be his Prime Minister. The new King swiftly told Walpole that he should take instructions from Spencer Compton, the man who would eventually succeed him. However, Compton was not up to the job and Walpole had to help draft the King's Speech for the opening of the new parliamentary session. He inserted an increase of £100,000 in the Civil List to support the King's expenditure.[3] Walpole's position was promptly restored and he retained the confidence of the second George for more than another decade.

Cock Robin

Many nursery rhymes and similar songs have their origins in real events. A well-known example is 'Ring a ring o' roses', which is believed to have been inspired by the plague. It includes the chilling words

Political cartoons are not new. In this rude depiction one has to kiss the buttocks of Walpole if one hopes to get anywhere in society. Here he is blocking access to St James's Palace, the official residence of the king.

'Atishoo atishoo we all fall down'. It is not certain, but many believe that the same is true of 'Who killed cock robin?' Robin is a diminutive form of Robert and the words may refer to the attempts of Walpole's enemies to bring him down.

Retirement

Many Prime Ministers struggle to find satisfaction in retirement, Margaret Thatcher being a well-known example. It seems that Walpole suffered in this way. The following is taken from Mrs Piozzi's memoirs:

> When Sir Robert Walpole was dismissed from all his employments he retired to Houghton and walked into the Library; when, pulling down a book and holding it some minutes to his eyes, he suddenly and seemingly sullenly exchanged it for another. He held that about half as long, and looking out a third returned it instantly to its shelf and burst into tears. 'I have led a life of business so long,' said he, 'that I have lost my taste for reading, and now—what shall I do?'[4]

The Queen's Opinion of his Mistress

Queen Caroline was a big supporter of Walpole and her death was a factor in his loss of office, but she did not feel the same about his mistress, Maria Skerrett, who was twenty-six years his junior. The following was her reply when told that Walpole was in low spirits because his mistress was suffering from pleurisy:

> She was very glad he had any amusement for his leisure hours, but could neither comprehend how a man could be very fond of a woman he only got for his money, nor how a man of Sir Robert's age and make, with his dirty mouth and great belly could ever imagine any woman would suffer him as a lover from any consideration or inducement but his money. 'She must be a clever gentlewoman,' continued

> the Queen, 'to have made him believe she cares for him on any other score; and to show you what fools we all are in some point or other, she has certainly told him some fine story or other of her love and her passion, and that poor man—*avec les gros corps, ces jambes enflées, et ce villain ventre*—believes her. My God! What is human nature!'[5]

The Queen was probably being unfair. Maria paid a dowry of £30,000 when she married Walpole. One might also question Caroline's own motivation in marrying George II. She came from the small German state of Brandenburg-Ansbach, and at the time of her marriage, George was third in line to the British throne and heir apparent to the Electorate of Hanover. It puts one in mind of Mrs Merton's famous question to Debbie McGee: 'what first attracted you to the millionaire Paul Daniels?' This too was unfair because Daniels was not a millionaire at the time and Debbie had a successful career in her own right.

Two Worthy Quotations

'They now ring the bells, but they will soon wring their hands'—on the declaration of war with Spain in 1739.

'The balance of power'—to the House of Commons on 13 February 1741.

And an Unworthy Quotation

'All men have their price'—like many famous remarks, the words were probably never uttered exactly as they have been attributed. They are, though, believed because he might well have said them. According to George Malcolm Thomson, he pointed to a group of men and said, 'Those men have their price.'[6] This is different and does not slander the entire human race.

10 Downing Street

During his career, Walpole acquired and spent enormous wealth. It almost all came to him dishonourably, but as L. P. Hartley memorably wrote in *The Go-Between*: 'The past is a foreign country. They do things differently there'. What he did should be criticised, indeed heavily criticised, but let us remember at least one honourable action. George II offered 10 Downing Street to him as a personal gift. Walpole accepted, but only as the official residence of the First Lord of the Treasury. It has been used by Prime Ministers ever since.

2

Spencer Compton

EARL OF WILMINGTON

1742–43

Spencer Compton, Earl of Wilmington (*c.* 1673–1743), portrait probably by, or after, Godfrey Kneller (1646–1723).

BRITAIN'S FIRST TWO Prime Ministers were very different in nearly all respects. Walpole's period of office lasted nearly twenty-one years, whereas Wilmington's was less than a year and a half. Walpole dominated his long ministry and is remembered as an effective Prime Minister, neither of which can be said of Wilmington. The latter was weak and ineffectual. Walpole's aims were peace and prosperity, both of which were to some considerable extent achieved. It is hard to know what Wilmington's aims were. He did, however, share two similarities with Walpole. He was a gourmet eater and had a number of mistresses.

Spencer Compton, the third son of the 3rd Marquess of Northampton, never married. He was born in 1673 and was elected to Parliament as a Whig in 1698. He was Paymaster of Pensions from 1707 to 1713, and from 1715, he was not out of office for the rest of his life. His positions included Speaker of the House of Commons for twelve years. From 1725, he was Lord Privy Seal in Walpole's Government and later Lord President of the Council.

The last chapter tells how George II favoured Wilmington and on his accession wanted him to lead his government. It also tells how he missed the opportunity and was outmanoeuvred by Walpole. The latter retained his rival in office, but in 1728, arranged for him to go to the House of Lords as the Earl of Wilmington. This was to neuter his influence in the Commons. It was by no means the last time that Prime Ministers adopted this tactic.

Wilmington in office was a nonentity and is often said to be one of the country's very worst Prime Ministers. He was merely a figurehead and much of the power was wielded by the Secretary of State, Lord Carteret. Wilmington was sixty-eight when he ascended to the highest position, and thereafter, his health and powers declined until he died in office. If we are feeling charitable, this should be taken into account.

Lord Hervey's Quatrain

Among many other things, Lord Hervey was a wittily malicious writer. He wrote the following, which is supposed to be spoken by Lord Carteret to the King:

The Countess of Wilmington, excellent nurse,
I'll trust with the Treasury, not with the purse,
For nothing by her I've resolved shall be done;
She shall sit at that board as you sit on the throne.

A Memorable Phrase

When Speaker, Wilmington once said to a Member who complained of being interrupted: 'No Sir, you have a right to speak, but the House have a right to judge whether they will hear you'.

A Modest Approach to the Office of Speaker

When appointed to the role of Speaker, he insisted to the King that 'he had neither memory to retain, judgment to correct, nor skill to guide the debates'.[1]

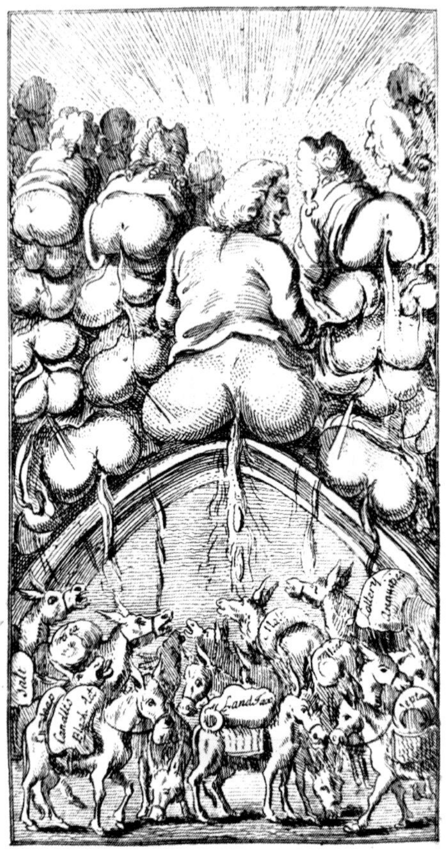

Henry Pelham's 1744 'broad-bottomed' coalition government allegedly abandoned their own opposition principles in exchange for wealth and honours. Here in this extremely vulgar cartoon—far more vulgar than anything today—exceptionally large and flabby bottoms are defecating onto several donkeys lurking anxiously below. The donkeys are symbolically burdened with labelled loads, ranging from 'Land Tax', the infamous 'Black Act', and 'Lottery annuities'

3

Henry Pelham

1743–54

Henry Pelham (1694–1754), portrait by John Shackleton (d. 1767), *c.* 1752. *National Portrait Gallery*

It took George II fifty-eight days to fill the vacancy created by the death in office of the Earl of Wilmington. This is the longest period in which the office of Prime Minister has been unfilled and it compares with eleven days taken by Queen Victoria after the death of Lord Palmerston. Henry Pelham was appointed on 27 August 1743, and he served until his death on 6 March 1754. He was the second (with Wilmington) of Britain's first three Prime Ministers to die in office, and the second (with Walpole) to serve for a lengthy and continuous period. According to various accounts, he was the third of the three to have a very large appetite.

Pelham came from one of the great Whig families. Born in 1696, he was the second son of Thomas, Lord Pelham, and the younger brother of Thomas Pelham-Holles. His older brother, who later succeeded him as Prime Minister, when still in his teens acquired the title Duke of Newcastle and the wealth that went with it on the death of his uncle. The brothers had closely linked political careers.

Pelham had an income of £5,000 a year settled on him by his father, and his wife, Catherine, brought a dowry of £30,000. Unlike many of his contemporaries, Walpole prominent among them, he did not gain financially from his offices, something that was noted and respected. He did, however, corrupt others.

Due to the influence of his brother, Pelham became an MP at the tender age of twenty-one. He was close to Robert Walpole, both personally and politically, throughout the latter's career, and this benefited his advancement. So close was the attachment that some parliamentarians dubbed him 'Walpole's Chief Clerk'. He became Secretary at War in 1724 while still in his twenties, and Leader of the House and Paymaster of the Forces in 1730. This office gave him considerable opportunities to acquire wealth, but he did not take them. He was Chancellor of the Exchequer throughout his time as Prime Minister.

Pelham is regarded as one of the country's accomplished Prime Ministers, not outstanding, but competent. He operated in a measured and moderate way, and effectively managed his colleagues and the Commons in this manner. He was a pragmatist. His policies were much the same as Walpole's and can be summed up as peace and prosperity. He had to deal with the War of the Austrian Succession, and he was successful in managing the economy. A kind epitaph might be that he brought stability.

Relationship with the King

The power of the Monarch relative to that of the Prime Minister declined during the reign of George II, but it was still very considerable. The fifty-eight days taken to appoint him is an indication that the relationship had to be worked on, and this Pelham did. He managed the King with skill and patience. When his health began to fail, he wanted to retire, but George persuaded him not to. When he died, the King said: 'Now I shall have no peace'. It was a prescient comment.

Relationship with his Brother

Pelham was personally close to his brother, the Duke of Newcastle, and they worked together throughout his career. They were a potent combination, and Newcastle was very prominent in his cabinet. They sometimes disagreed violently, and Newcastle sometimes resented Pelham's increasing dominance, but it did not affect their personal relations.

A Ferocious Cost Cutter

For more than ten years, Pelham was both Prime Minister and Chancellor of the Exchequer, and the success of his fiscal policies stand as his greatest achievement. Most of the recent incumbents of these offices should be envious of his record. In 1748, after a period of war, the national debt stood at £76 million. Over the next two years, government expenditure was reduced from £12 million to £7 million. His economy measures included cutting the Navy from 51,550 men to just 8,000.[1] It was just as well that there was no war.

A Gift to the Cartoonists

At one time, Pelham's cabinet included politicians of different parties and views. It was dubbed the broad-bottomed ministry, which cartoonists gleefully linked to the amply proportioned Prime Minister's appearance.

The Jacobite Rebels

Pelham was a firm supporter of the Hanoverian Succession, and in 1715, with his brother, he raised a troop of cavalry and took it to fight the Jacobite rebels at Preston.

Bravery and a Hot Temper

On one occasion, Pelham drew his sword to protect Walpole who was being threatened by a mob. On another, the Speaker had to forbid a duel when he clashed with another MP in the Commons.

Two Tragic Deaths

Both his sons died in 1739 of a sore-throat condition that became known as 'Pelham's Disease'.

4

Thomas Pelham-Holles

DUKE OF NEWCASTLE

1754–56; 1757–62

BRITAIN'S FOURTH PRIME Minister was a somewhat curious man, eccentric and with character weaknesses. However, he did hold major political office for almost four decades and he was twice Prime Minister, so it is right to recognise some strengths as well. His career benefited from two major advantages: he was very well connected and he was very rich.

Thomas Pelham-Holles was the son of Thomas Pelham, 1st Baron Pelham. His mother was the sister of John Holles, 1st Duke of Newcastle upon Tyne. At the age of twenty-one, he acquired the title of Duke of Newcastle upon Tyne and took his seat in the House of Lords. His younger brother served as Prime Minister for more than ten years and preceded him in that office. His brother-in-law, Charles Townshend, was married to the sister of Robert Walpole and held high political office.

Henry Pelham (1694–1754), portrait by John Shackleton (d. 1767), *c.* 1752. *National Portrait Gallery*

Newcastle inherited very large sums of money from both his father and his uncle, and while still in his teens, he became one of the richest persons in the kingdom. He was profligate with his money, something that annoyed his brother, and at the end of his life, his wealth had decreased by £300,000. It hardly needs saying that in the eighteenth century this was an enormous sum. Some of his money went on personal expenditure, but much went on buying political influence. By spending his money in this way, he managed to control many parliamentary constituencies.

Horace Walpole, son of Sir Robert Walpole, said that 'he was a Secretary of State without intelligence and a minister hated and despised by his master'.[1] Lord Waldegrave said that 'he was confused and rambling, in parliamentary debate, his manner was ungraceful and his language barbarous; he was neither a reliable friend nor a bitter enemy'.[2] However, the same man also said that 'it cannot be denied that he possesses some qualities of an able minister'.[3] Fussiness is a word much used about him. Many thought that he was more effective supporting Walpole and his brother than he was in the top job. When Prime Minister, he was inclined to appoint less able people, which was indicative of insecurity on his part.

Newcastle was appointed Lord Chamberlain in 1717 at the tender age of twenty-three, holding this office for the next seven years. He developed an interest in foreign affairs, and in 1724, he was made Secretary of State for the Southern Department in Walpole's Government. He often deferred to Charles Townshend, the other Secretary of State, who was more senior, but Townshend was forced out in 1729. Newcastle was then the senior Secretary of State and continued to be so until he took the top position in 1754.

During his first period as Prime Minister, Newcastle played a part in precipitating the Seven Years' War with France. It initially went badly, and after thirty-two months in office, he was replaced by the Duke of Devonshire, but after an interlude of just eight months, he resumed the office. Britain was a great deal more successful during his second term, though much of the credit should go to the Secretary of State and future Prime Minister William Pitt.

George II died in October 1760 and was replaced by his twenty-two-year-old grandson. The new King George III did not like Pitt nor did he like Newcastle. The former resigned and Newcastle was forced out in May 1762. A few years later, Newcastle was for a short time Lord Privy Seal in the first administration of the Marquis of Rockingham.

Newcastle died at the age of seventy-five. Fittingly, he was buried next to the man who preceded him as Prime Minister, his brother.

Trouble with the King

As recounted in the last chapter, George II greeted the news of the death of the previous Prime Minister with the words 'Now I shall have no peace'. The King and the Duke of Newcastle did not have a happy relationship. George once said that he thought that his Prime Minister's intellectual powers fitted him to be the chamberlain of some minor German principality.[4] During one altercation, George's poor command of the English language led Newcastle to believe that he had challenged him to a duel.

Hypochondria

Robert Parker states that Newcastle was an extreme hypochondriac and that he exhibited an almost neurotic fear of catching colds. He had a tendency to faint and break down into public fits of weeping, gaining him an almost comical reputation among most observers.[5]

A Shouting Match in Bed

Newcastle visited William Pitt at a time when he was ill in bed. It was cold so that Newcastle, fully clothed, climbed into an adjoining bed. An Under Secretary entered the room to find the government's two most senior ministers sitting up in bed shouting at each other.[6]

Deserted by the Bishops

Newcastle hung on as power slipped away at the end of his second ministry. Eventually, even the bishops, some of whom he had appointed, deserted him. 'Even fathers in God sometimes forget their maker,' he said.[7]

A Demonstrative Man

The Duke of Grafton lay in bed covered in bandages. Newcastle burst into the room hugging and kissing him. The alarmed Grafton shouted, 'Get Away, Get Away.'[8]

The Opinion of the Earl of Wilmington

Britain's second Prime Minister stated: 'He always lost half an hour in the morning, which he was running after for the rest of the day without being able to overtake it'.[9]

5

William Cavendish

4TH DUKE OF DEVONSHIRE

1756–57

DURING THE EIGHTEENTH and early part of the nineteenth century, the Whig Party was dominated by a relatively small number of Whig families. At times, they wielded very considerable power and there was a marked tendency for marriages to take place between them. Antonia Fraser perceptively called them 'the cousinhood'.[1] The Cavendish family was at the summit of this small number of families, and it provided the 4th Duke of Devonshire, Britain's fifth Prime Minister. He was the great-great-great-great grandfather of Queen Elizabeth II, and the father-in-law of William Cavendish-Bentinck, 3rd Duke of Portland and future Prime Minister.

William Cavendish 4th Duke of Devonshire (1720–1764). *Chatsworth House, west gallery*

The 4th Duke of Devonshire was born in 1720. He was Lord Cavendish until 1729, Marquess of Hartington until the death of his father in 1755, then the Duke of Devonshire. By all accounts, he was a modest and decent man, with a pronounced sense of duty. He was one of the youngest of the Prime Ministers, being only thirty-six when appointed, and his term of office was one of the shortest, lasting only 222 days. He did not thrust himself forward to gain the position, and he told the King that he would only serve on the understanding that it was just for the duration of the parliamentary term.

Like many leading Whigs, Cavendish was elected to the Commons while very young. Family influence secured him a seat at the tender age of just twenty-one. He was an MP for six years then moved to the House of Lords. In his early years in Parliament, he was a firm supporter of Walpole, Pelham, and the Duke of Newcastle. Devonshire was Lord Lieutenant of Ireland from 1754, and in 1755, he was made one of the Lord's Justices of the Realm during the King's absence in Hanover.

In 1756, the Seven Years' War with France had started and it was going badly, and furthermore, the King felt that the trial and forthcoming execution of Admiral Byng was badly handled. He therefore asked Newcastle to resign. Devonshire, who took his placc as Primc Minister, was the figurehead and administrator, but much of the power was with William Pitt. The quarrel between Newcastle and Pitt had been a cause of Newcastle's resignation, but before long, they patched it up, Devonshire resigned, and Newcastle started his second ministry.

After his short time as Prime Minister, Devonshire became Lord Chamberlain and held this position until 1762. He died at Spa in what is now Belgium, the only Prime Minister to die while out of the country. At forty-four years and 147 days, he was the shortest-lived Prime Minister of them all.

A Brief but Happy Marriage

At the age of twenty-seven, Devonshire married Lady Charlotte Elizabeth Boyle, 6th Baroness Clifford, and the union produced four children. At the time of the wedding, Lady Charlotte was not long past her sixteenth birthday and she died at the age of twenty-three. The marriage was brief, but very happy. Lady Charlotte was very rich and, consequently, the already considerable wealth of the Cavendish family increased significantly.

'Capability'

The Duke's main residence was the magnificent Chatsworth House in the Derbyshire Dales. He commissioned the renowned landscape gardener Lancelot 'Capability' Brown to transform the estate. It is open to the public and it can be seen that he did a splendid job. Brown's numerous assignments included Luton Hoo, the estate of the future Prime Minister, the 3rd Earl of Bute. He acquired the sobriquet 'Capability' because he would tell landowners that their estates were capable of improvement.

A Bitter Farewell

George III succeeded to the throne in October 1760 at the age of twenty-two, and he had an uneasy relationship with his Prime Minister (Newcastle) and his Lord Chamberlain (Devonshire). In October 1762, the King wrongly thought that Devonshire was about to resign and refused to see him. The King later wrote: 'I ordered the page to tell him I would not see him'. As Devonshire left, he said to the page, 'God bless you. It will be very long before you see me here again.' At a meeting of the Privy Council four days later, the King personally struck out Devonshire's name from the list of Privy Councillors.

6

John Stuart

3rd EARL OF BUTE

1762–63

John Stuart, 3rd Earl of Bute, portrait by Allan Ramsay (1713–1784). *The National Trust for Scotland, Hermiston Quay*

It is probably correct to say that the 3rd Earl of Bute was the last person to hold the highest political office because he was a favourite of the monarch, something that partially accounted for the fact that he was possibly the most vilified of the country's Prime Ministers. He was the first Tory to hold the position and the first of seven to be born in Scotland. He was the second of nineteen to attend Eton College and he continued his education at the University of Leiden in the Netherlands, where he graduated with a degree in civic and public law.

Bute, who was born in Edinburgh in 1713, inherited his title at the age of ten on the death of his father. Following this, he was brought up by his uncles. In 1737, he was elected a Scottish representative peer, but he did very little in the Lords and was not re-elected in 1741. He moved to London at the time of the Jacobite Rebellion, and in the circumstances of the time and later, his Scottish origins caused problems for him.

Bute met Frederick, Prince of Wales, in 1747 and became a friend and associate. Following the Prince's premature death four years later, he continued a close friendship with his widow, Augusta of Saxe-Gotha, the Dowager Princess of Wales. The friendship and mutual respect resulted four years later in him being appointed tutor to Prince George, the heir apparent, and to his brother, Prince Edward. Bute took his responsibilities seriously and had considerable success. George referred to Bute as 'his dearest friend'.[1]

The Prince succeeded to the throne as George III at the tender age of twenty-two. Bute expected that his rise to power would be swift and he was not disappointed. When the Prime Minister, the Duke of Newcastle, called on the King with a draft of the King's Speech to Parliament, George told him to 'take it to my Lord Bute, who will tell you my thoughts'.[2] In 1760, Bute was again elected a Scottish representative peer. He was named to the Privy Council just two days after George's accession, and he became Secretary of State for the Northern Department. The King replaced Newcastle as Prime Minister in 1762, but Bute's period of office only lasted 317 turbulent and unhappy days.

The major event during his premiership was the ending of the Seven Years' War with France. This had started badly, but later, in no small part to the efforts of William Pitt, Britain had done very well. The war was, however, a massive drain on the treasury, and both Bute and the new King wanted it over. Peace was achieved, but in the opinion of Pitt and some others, the terms were much too favourable to the French. Prodigious bribery secured the acceptance of the treaty by Parliament. The strain and unpleasantness took its toll on the Prime Minister.

During his brief premiership, Bute managed to weaken the power of the Whig families. He was always very unpopular in the country and this culminated in violent opposition to a new cider tax. The Government needed the revenue and Bute managed to get the tax on the statute book, but suffering from strain and poor health, he could not take any more of the vicious hostility and he resigned a few days later. However, he did retain the respect of the King, and for a while, he continued to influence events, much to the disgust of his successor. Eventually, George agreed to break off contact with him. Despite Pitt's hostility, some at least count the ending of the war an achievement, but he was not sufficiently robust to keep his job. Bute's long retirement was not particularly happy, and he died in London in 1792, twenty-eight years after ceasing to be Prime Minister. He was buried on the Isle of Bute.

A Happy and Fruitful Marriage

At the age of twenty-three, Bute married Mary Wortley Montagu, who was eighteen at the time. The marriage very considerably increased Bute's estates and wealth, and it was by all accounts a happy one. The couple had eleven children in the course of the next eighteen years.

A Fine Leg

Bute was tall, slim, and acknowledged to be a good-looking man. Contemporary accounts refer to the fact that he had a 'fine leg', an attribute that was much valued at the time.

An Eventful Shower

A life-changing event for Bute was his meeting with Frederick, Prince of Wales. The Prince took shelter from a shower while attending Egham races. He fancied a game of whist, but was short of a fourth player. A companion was despatched to find someone of suitable rank. He returned with Bute and the rest, as they say, is history.

A Possibly Adulterous Affair

Following the death of the Prince of Wales, Bute maintained a long and very close friendship with his widow, the Dowager Princess. So close was the friendship that it was widely believed to be adulterous. There was an assumed scandal and allegations were published in scurrilous pamphlets. There was no evidence and the allegations may well not have been true. They did, though, seriously damage him.

The Threat of Violence

Bute went about his business in fear of physical violence directed against him. He suffered a number of attacks and his coach was smashed while taking him to the Guildhall. A jack-boot and a petticoat (representing himself and the Dowager Princess of Wales) were burnt in the streets and hung from gallows. He was forced to use the services of prize fighters to secure his protection.

Considerable Education and Wide Interests

Bute was a man of considerable education and wide interests, something for which he deserves credit. The interests were pursued over lengthy periods and included the study of botany, architecture, and agriculture. His achievements included the publication in 1785 of *Botanical Tables Containing the Families of British Plants*.

7

George Grenville

1763–65

George Grenville (1712–1770), portrait by William Hoare (1707–1792). *Christ Church, University of Oxford*

George Grenville came from a group of very influential, interrelated Whig families—the Temples, Pitts, Lyttletons, and Grenvilles. They were powerful politically and mainly wealthy. They occasionally fell out, but, by and large, they helped one another. George Grenville was not only the son of an MP, all his four brothers were MPs. His sister married William Pitt and this made him the brother-in-law of the statesman and future Prime Minister. It also made him the uncle of another Prime Minister, William Pitt the Younger.

Grenville was born in 1712 and entered Parliament in 1741. He quickly associated himself with a group known as 'Cobham's Cubs', named after his relative Richard Temple, 1st Viscount Cobham. They opposcd Sir Robert Walpole in his later days as Prime Minister. His rise was steady and he held offices as Treasurer of the Navy, Leader of the Commons, Speaker, First Lord of the Admiralty, and Northern Secretary.

When Bute resigned, he recommended Grenville as his successor. The King did not like him, but he accepted the advice, something that he later regretted. Bute and the King intended that Bute would act as the King's adviser, but Grenville resented it and eventually he got the King to promise not to consult Bute.

Historians have generally not been kind to Grenville, but several things can be said in his favour. For a start, he was a man of integrity, and that should count for a lot. He was strong on detail and had a talent for administration. He was a master of parliamentary procedures, something that stood him in good stead when he was Speaker and when he was Prime Minister. He worked towards putting the country's finances back on a sound footing after the ruinous expense of the Seven Years' War against France.

On the debit side, Grenville suffered from a lack of eloquence, a lack of imagination, and a lack of finesse. He was often long-winded and rather charmless. He bored the King, which was, to say the least, unfortunate, and like Margaret Thatcher, he had few, if any interests outside politics.

Grenville's period of office is remembered for the use of general warrants for the arrest of John Wilkes and the prosecution of Wilkes on a charge of seditious libel. It is also remembered for the Stamp Act. This was a tax placed on the American colonies. It caused riots and outrage in America, and was a significant step towards the American War of Independence.

George III finally removed Grenville from office following a perceived slight over the Regency Bill. After the King had suffered a bout of illness, it was intended that a Regency Council be established to act if and when he was unable to do so. Grenville refused to name the King's mother as part of the Council. This was because she was widely believed, perhaps wrongly, to be conducting an adulterous affair with the Earl of Bute, Grenville's predecessor as Prime Minister.

A Happy and Successful Marriage

At the age of thirty-six, Grenville married Elizabeth Wyndham, who was twenty-eight at the time. Her face was badly marked by smallpox and she looked very much older than her years. It was a successful marriage and they had eight children together. Elizabeth was a great help to her husband's career. A friend said that 'she was the first prize in the marriage lottery of our century'.[1]

Father and Son

Britain has had two pairs of father and son Prime Ministers. George Grenville's son, William, held the position in 1806–07. The other pair were their relatives, Pitt the Elder and Pitt the Younger.

Gentle Shepherd

Grenville acquired this nickname in 1763 after speaking in the Commons on the Cider Bill. Over and over again, he asked that someone tell him 'where to lay the new tax if it was not to be put on cider'. Pitt whistled the air of the popular tune 'Gentle shepherd, tell me where'. Honourable members laughed and the name stuck.

Boring the King

It is not good when a monarch finds the Prime Minister boring. Queen Elizabeth II has probably found some of her Prime Ministers boring, and we may be able to guess which ones, but we shall probably never know. It was much more serious in the 1760s because the King had very real power. George III did find Grenville boring. This is quite apart from personal dislike and policy differences. The following remarks have been attributed to the King:

> When he has wearied me for two hours, he looks at his watch to see if he may not tire me for an hour more.
>
> I would rather see the devil in my closet than Mr Grenville.
>
> His opinions are seldom formed from any other motives than such as may be expected to originate in the mind of a clerk in the counting house.

Pocket Borough

Grenville represented the constituency of Buckingham for twenty-nine years. This so-called pocket borough returned two MPs and had just thirteen electors. It was in the control of his uncle Richard Temple, Viscount Cobham.

8

Charles Watson Wentworth

2nd MARQUESS OF ROCKINGHAM

1765–66; 1782

THE 2ND MARQUESS of Rockingham is one of the less-remembered Prime Ministers. He held the position twice, though for short periods each time, and he deserves credit for integrity and the consistency with which he held his views. He was a poor speaker and did not enjoy good health. He was the country's second youngest Prime Minister, having taken office shortly after his thirty-fifth birthday. He only ever held two offices, Prime Minister and Leader of the House of Lords.

The expression 'born with a silver spoon in his mouth' came into common usage shortly before Rockingham was born in 1730, and its use in his case is apt. His father was an MP before his elevation to the Lords, and the 2nd Marquess was his fifth, but only surviving son. He inherited the title at the age of only twenty. At that time, his estates yielded an annual income of £20,000, and a couple of years later his marriage made him richer still.

Charles Watson Wentworth, 2nd Marquess of Rockingham (1730–1782), portrait by Joshua Reynolds (1723–1792). *Royal Collection*

At such a young age, Rockingham controlled three parliamentary seats, together with twenty-three livings and five chaplaincies in the Church of England. A few weeks after his twenty-first birthday, he was appointed Lord Lieutenant and *custos rotulorum* of both the West Riding of Yorkshire and York city and county. The *custos rotulorum* was the keeper of records and the highest civil officer in the county. Before his twenty-second birthday, he joined White's (the prestigious gentleman's club), the Jockey Club, and the Royal Society.

Rockingham gradually emerged as the leader of a group of Whigs not reconciled to the policies of Bute or Grenville. On the resignation of Grenville, the King took the advice of his uncle, the Duke of Cumberland, and appointed Rockingham as Prime Minister. His brief period in office was dominated by the issue of the American colonies. He secured the repeal of the Stamp Act, which had so upset the King's American subjects. This pleased them, but they did not at all like the Declaratory Act, which asserted that the British Parliament had 'the right to legislate for the American colonies in all cases whatsoever'. After just over a year in office, dissent within his cabinet led to his resignation.

The Marquess was then out of office for nearly sixteen years. During this time, he led a parliamentary group known as the 'Rockingham Whigs', which opposed the American war. He spoke up for constitutional rights in Britain and the colonies and against the excessive power of the King.

Following the resignation of Lord North, Rockingham again became Prime Minister in 1782. To put it mildly, the King was not pleased to make the appointment, but the strength of Rockingham's position in Parliament compelled him to do so. Rockingham's conditions for accepting the post included that George would accept all his nominations for office, that he would approve all the ministry's legislation, and that he would accept American independence.[1] The King reluctantly had to accept the terms. Rockingham embarked on a programme of reform, but he succumbed to influenza and died in office after only fourteen weeks. He was only fifty-two and had more to offer.

A Courageous and Committed Teenager

Rockingham was fifteen in 1745, when Charles Edward Stuart (Bonnie Prince Charlie) landed in Scotland and led the Jacobite Rebellion. His father organised volunteers to serve the Hanoverian cause and help defend the country. He made his teenage son a colonel and the fifteen-year-old future Prime Minister joined the King's uncle, the Duke of Cumberland, in his campaign to crush the rebellion. Cumberland was impressed with him and later played an important part in making him Prime Minister.

Early Royal Approbation

In his latter teenage years, Rockingham made an extended grand tour of Europe, and while visiting Hanover, he met George II. This was the man on whose behalf he had recently campaigned during the Jacobite Rebellion. The King afterwards said that 'he had never seen a finer or more promising youth'.

A Badly Received Maiden Speech

Rockingham's maiden speech in the House of Lords was in support of a Bill that disposed of lands confiscated in the aftermath of the 1745 Jacobite Rebellion. He was very outspoken and his speech was not well-received. Horace Walpole, the son of the former Prime Minister, criticised him for 'venturing into a debate so much above his force'.

A Passion for Horse Racing

During the eighteenth and nineteenth centuries, a number of Prime Ministers had a great interest in horse racing. Rockingham, the 14th Earl of Derby, and the 5th Earl of Rosebery come particularly to mind. Rockingham devoted considerable time and money (which he could afford) to gambling and breeding race horses. In 1776, the first running of the St Leger, said to be the world's oldest classic horse race, was won by one of his horses.

9

William Pitt

EARL OF CHATHAM

1766–68

Most Britons would struggle to name many or indeed any of their country's early Prime Ministers. Those that could would most probably include the first, Sir Robert Walpole, and the ninth, William Pitt. Frederick the Great of Prussia said: 'England has been a long time in labour, but she has, at last, brought forth a man'. As the saying goes, it takes one to know one, and they were both great men. The man in question was born in 1708, and for most of his life, he carried the name William Pitt. During this period, he was often respectfully and affectionately known as 'The Great Commoner'. On becoming Prime Minister in 1766, he went to the House of Lords with the title of Earl of Chatham. Posterity has accorded him the sobriquet William Pitt the Elder in order to distinguish him from his son and future Prime Minister William Pitt the Younger.

William Pitt, Earl of Chatham (1708–1778), portrait from the studio of William Hoare (between *c.* 1707 and *c.* 1792). *National Portrait Gallery*

At the late age of forty-six, Pitt married thirty-three-year-old Lady Hester Grenville, daughter of the 1st Countess Temple and sister of the future Prime Minister George Grenville. It was a very happy union, which in its first seven years was blessed with five children. The fourth of these was the man who would be Britain's fourteenth Prime Minister, William Pitt the Younger. The elder Pitt was a devoted husband and father. He suffered badly from gout for most of his life and at times from severe mental disability. This was manifest during much of his time of slightly more than two years as Prime Minister. He had an imperious manner and was something of a loner. He was a leader rather than a team player. This sometimes antagonised his parliamentary colleagues and also the two monarchs under which he served.

Pitt, who was a Whig, was noted for his oratory, his devastating debating skills, and for his mastery of the House of Commons. He was greatly respected and admired by the people of his country. One reason was that, unlike many of his contemporaries, he was not corrupt and did not profit from the offices that he held. Another was that he was self-evidently a patriot who loved his country.

Much of his career was spent in opposition and he was a thorn in the flesh of various governments. He opposed corruption in the 1730s, Hanoverian subsidies in the 1740s, the terms of the peace treaty with France and Spain in the 1760s, and the policy towards the American colonies in the 1770s. He even managed for a time to oppose a government while serving in it.

Pitt's greatest period was from December 1756 to October 1761. With an interlude of just a few weeks in 1757, he served as Secretary of State and leader of the House of Commons, first under the Duke of Devonshire and then under the Duke of Newcastle. It was the time of the Seven Years' War with France and Spain, which had started badly for Britain. Then, the fortunes of his beloved country improved enormously and Pitt could justly claim a lot of the credit. He was both indefatigable and successful. In particular, he directed British forces against French colonies, including Canada. There were great victories and it drew the French away from the war in Europe. The Treaty of Paris that ended the war was concluded while he was out of office. He considered it far too lenient to the French and the Spanish and that it left them with the option of rekindling the war later.

Pitt, as the Earl of Chatham, was Prime Minister from 30 July 1766 to 14 October 1768. The King gave him a free hand to choose his ministers, but he was ineffective and very often absent. Not surprisingly, his colleagues went their separate ways and there were almost no successes worth mentioning. His reputation rests firmly on what he did while not holding the position of Prime Minister. The problem was that for much of this time, he was in very poor health and suffered both physically and mentally. In fact, some say that his mental state almost amounted to insanity. Thomas Whateley wrote to George Grenville:

> He sits most part of the day leaning his head down upon his hands, which are rested on the table. Lady Chatham does not continue generally in the room; if he wants anything he knocks with his stick; he says little even to her if she comes in; and is so averse to speaking, that he commonly intimates his desire to be left alone, by some signal rather than by any expression. The physicians, however, say there is nothing in his disorder which he may not recover, but do not pretend to say there is any prospect of its being soon.[1]

His eventual resignation was on the grounds of ill health.

After leaving office, his health improved somewhat and his last great campaign was for generous treatment of the American colonists who were in dispute with Britain. Had his views been heeded, there might have been a better outcome from the British point of view. He was not, however, in favour of conceding independence. 'The Great Commoner' died on 11 May 1778 at the age of sixty-nine. He was granted the rare distinction of burial in Westminster Abbey with the honours of a public funeral.

Was he Really Prime Minister Three Times?

Almost all authorities say that Pitt was Prime Minister just once, from 30 July 1766 to 14 October 1768, but there is another view. No less a person than the forty-sixth Prime Minister, Harold Wilson, says that although he was never First Lord of the Treasury, it is right to recognise him as three times Prime Minister.[2] This is because as twice Leader of the Commons, he was so dominant that the acknowledgment is justified.

'Diamond Pitt' and a Political Family

Thomas Pitt, William's grandfather, served as governor of Madras, and he enriched himself in the process. Not least, he purchased an extremely large and very fine uncut diamond for £20,400 and subsequently sold it to Phillipe II, Duke of Orléans, for £135,000. The coup was the cause of his acquiring the soubriquet 'Diamond Pitt'. It is now owned by the French state and is on display in the Louvre. His son, William's

The Collapse of the Earl of Chatham in the House of Lords, 7 July 1778 by John Singleton Copley (1738–1815), painted *c.* 1779-81. *National Portrait Gallery*

father, was an MP and so were two of William's uncles. More political connections were secured by marriages made by female members of the family. William Pitt was well-placed for a career in politics.

Eton and Oxford

Like eighteen other Prime Ministers, Pitt was educated at Eton. Like some of them, especially the 3rd Marquess of Salisbury, he did not particularly enjoy the experience. He later remarked: 'A public school might suit a boy of turbulent disposition but would not do where there was any gentleness'. His lifelong affliction of gout started while he was at the school and it was the reason that he left Oxford without completing his degree.

Old Sarum

The Old Sarum constituency returned two Members of Parliament, and prior to 1832, it was the rottenest of the rotten boroughs. There were seven empty plots and the landowner had the right to nominate seven tenants who were not required to live there. These were the voters, so effectively, just one man chose two MPs. William Pitt's grandfather (Diamond Pitt) used some of his considerable wealth to purchase control of the constituency, and for many years, it was in the control of the Pitt family. William became one of its two MPs at the age of twenty-six, and he represented the constituency for the first twelve years of his parliamentary career.

A Short Military Career with a Controversial Ending

In his early adult years, Pitt embarked on a military career and obtained a commission in the King's Own Regiment of Horse (later 1st King's Dragoon Guards). He was still a serving officer after his election to Parliament in 1735, but George II and Sir Robert Walpole were so offended by his criticism that Walpole arranged for his dismissal from the Army. This caused much feeling against Walpole because it was seen as a threat to the freedom of speech enjoyed by Members of Parliament, something protected by parliamentary privilege. Pitt was not, however, reinstated into the Army.

Hereditary Mental Instability

Pitt suffered several periods of acute nervous depression, at times very seriously, and there must be at least a suspicion that the malady was hereditary. According to William Douglas Home, the same disability afflicted his brother and four of his five sisters.[3] It did not pass to his son, William Pitt the Younger.

Three Quotations

> The atrocious crime of being a young man ... I shall neither attempt to palliate nor deny.

Speech to the House of Commons
27 January 1741

> You cannot conquer America.

18 November 1877

> Unlimited power is apt to corrupt the minds of those who possess it.

Speech to the House of Lords
9 January 1770

The last of these predates Lord Acton's famous dictum, 'Power tends to corrupt and absolute power corrupts absolutely', by 117 years.

An Inconsiderate Master

When Secretary of State Pitt would not, according to Shelburne, allow his Under-Secretaries to sit in his presence.[4]

No Longer 'The Great Commoner'

Until 1766, Pitt refused to accept a title, hence the sobriquet 'The Great Commoner'. When he finally did so, the decision caused public sadness and affected his popularity. In anticipation of his appointment to the position of Prime Minister, the City of London had planned a banquet and a general illumination, but the celebrations were cancelled when news of the title became known.

Pittsburgh

The great American city of Pittsburgh was named after William Pitt the Elder after it was captured from the French in the Seven Years' War.

Financial Extravagance

William Pitt's grandfather was very rich, but his money was spread around many descendants and not very much came his way. This was unfortunate because Pitt was inclined to be extravagant, rather like Winston Churchill—another great wartime leader.

The Dower Duchess of Marlborough left him £10,000 when she died in 1744, and this helped a lot. Her motivation was her disapproval of Sir Robert Walpole and her admiration for the way that Pitt opposed him. After his resignation in 1761, George III granted him a pension of £3,000 a year. In 1765, an admirer, Sir William Pynsent, left his entire estate to Pitt and this yielded an income of £3,000 a year. The family finances were not in good order when he died in 1778, but his admirable wife was very competent and good with money. She managed to put them on a sound footing.

Troubled Relationship with his Monarchs

Pitt served under George II and George III. His relationship with them fluctuated, but generally it was not good. In fact, it was bad. As already recounted, the problems started when he annoyed George II soon after his election to Parliament. Things deteriorated further in the early 1740s when he opposed the Hanoverian subsidies. These were payments to assist Hanover, which feared an invasion by France. The King had spent the first thirty years of his life in Hanover and he took Pitt's opposition very badly. George had to accept him in government in 1746, but continued to resent him. In 1756, he stopped him being Prime Minister, but accepted his having a dominant cabinet position. The King died in 1760 and was succeeded by George III, aged just twenty-two.

The new King had his own ideas and this was one of the reasons that Pitt's power did not last. However, George arranged a pension for him. He also offered a title, which was refused. He accepted him as Prime Minister in 1766, together with very wide authority to select his ministers. Pitt died in 1778 and the House of Lords voted to attend his funeral as a body. It was held in Westminster Abbey and a sum was voted for the erection of a monument over his grave. A shockingly ungracious King wrote: 'I am surprised at the vote of a public funeral and monument, an offensive measure to me personally'.[5]

10

Augustus Henry Fitzroy

3rd DUKE OF GRAFTON

1768–70

Four dukes served as Prime Minister in the sixty-one years following the resignation of Sir Robert Walpole. A duke holds the highest rank in the peerage, and for the whole of this time, there were fewer than forty non-royal ones. To serve in high political office was to a considerable extent expected of them. It could be said to be 'noblesse oblige'. Not all the dukes were highly regarded and this is most certainly true of the 3rd Duke of Grafton. He was not esteemed at the time and the verdict of history has been no kinder. He entered the Commons as a Whig at the tender age of twenty-one, but within a year, he assumed the title of Duke on the death of his grandfather.

Augustus Henry Fitzroy, 3rd Duke of Grafton (1735–1811), portrait by Pompeo Batoni (1708–1787). *National Portrait Gallery*

Grafton aligned himself with William Pitt and was part of a group that opposed Lord Bute, and due to Pitt's influence, he became Secretary of State in the Marquis of Rockingham's brief first government. When Pitt, as Earl of Chatham, became Prime Minister in 1766, Grafton was appointed First Lord of the Treasury. Very unusually, this position was separate from the position of Prime Minister. However, after a while, the decline in Chatham's physical and especially mental health left him in practice leading the government. Chatham was almost always unavailable and it was extremely difficult for him. Nevertheless, he was inadequate and made a poor job of it.

Following Chatham's resignation, Grafton, just turned thirty-three, became Prime Minister on 14 October 1768, and he held the position for just one year and 106 days. He was regarded as lazy, and he devoted far too much time to racing and foxhunting. He was weak and did not effectively lead his cabinet colleagues. A very important instance of this was his failure to prevent the so-called Townshend Acts, named after his Chancellor of the Exchequer, Charles Townshend. These raised taxes on the American colonies and were a step towards the forthcoming rebellion. Another failure was his ineffectiveness in dealing with the crisis caused by the very damaging crusade for parliamentary reform conducted by the controversial rake John Wilkes. To make matters worse, Grafton suffered repeated and anonymous devastating press attacks.

The weary Duke did not want the job and quite possibly never had done, and he eventually persuaded the King to let him retire. He served as Lord Privy Seal under Lord North from 1771 to 1775, and in the same position under the Earl of Shelburne in 1782. He resigned from Lord North's Government because he could not accept its policy towards the American colonies. He died in 1811 at the age of seventy-five.

The Stuart Connection

Uniquely among the Hanoverian Prime Ministers, Grafton had a known connection with the deposed Stuart dynasty. His great-grandfather, the 1st Duke, was the illegitimate son of Charles II by his mistress Barbara Villiers. The nickname of the 3rd Duke was 'Black Harry', and it has been noted that he looked rather like his royal ancestor.[1]

Women and Children First

At the age of twenty-one, Grafton married Anne Liddell, daughter of the Earl of Ravensworth. They had five children, but it was not a happy marriage and they separated in 1764. At the time of the separation, he was conducting a scandalously public relationship with the low-born Nancy Parsons, known as Mrs Horton because she had lived in the West Indies with a man of that name. Grafton had even flaunted her at the opera in the presence of the Queen. A contemporary rhyme had it

From fourteen to forty, our provident Nan
Has devoted herself to the study of man.[2]

In 1769, his separated wife became pregnant by the Earl of Upper Ossary, and an Act of Parliament granted Grafton a divorce. Three months later, and while Prime Minister, he married Elizabeth Wrottesley, the niece of the Duke of Bedford. They had nine children and appear to have lived happily ever after.

According to Robert J. Parker, Grafton fathered more than a dozen illegitimate children.[3] He was the first Prime Minister before Sir Antony Eden to be divorced and the second, after Sir Robert Walpole, to be married in office.

Racing and Hunting

Several Prime Ministers have had a passion for racehorses and Grafton is prominent among them. His achievements included breeding three Derby winners. Unfortunately, his interest was sometimes pursued at the expense of business. A cabinet meeting was twice postponed, once because he had visitors at home and on the second occasion to let him attend a meeting at Newmarket.[4]

He loved hunting, and George III once said: 'Pretty occupations for a man of quality ... to be spending all his time tormenting a poor fox that is generally a much better beast than any of those that pursue him'.[5]

Religion

In his later years, Grafton became, like Neville Chamberlain, a Unitarian. He took his religion seriously, was a regular worshipper, and wrote on theological matters. In 1773, he supported a bill to release Anglican clergy from the obligation to subscribe to the Thirty-Nine Articles. In time, he took to advocating more moral behaviour by the upper classes. As it says in the Holy Bible: 'I say unto you, that likewise joy shall be in heaven over one sinner that repenteth, more than over ninety and nine just persons, which need no repentance'.[6]

11

Frederick, Lord North

1770–82

LORD NORTH IS remembered as 'the man who lost the American colonies', and is generally believed to have been a poor Prime Minister. Many go further and say that he was a bad one or even a dreadful one. Modern Prime Ministers have sometimes been vitriolically castigated as 'the worst Prime Minister since Lord North'. The man certainly had his faults, but many historians believe that the judgment is too harsh.

Frederick, Lord North (1732–1792), portrait by Nathaniel Dance (later Sir Nathaniel Holland). *The History of Parliament*

The main reason for his poor reputation is the country's failure in the American War of Independence. In his defence, North said: 'I found the American war when I became minister. I did not create it. It was the war of the country, the Parliament and the people'.[1] He might have added that it was very much the war of the king, George III. Nevertheless, North was head of the government that prosecuted the war, so he must take his fair share of the blame.

Frederick was the son of the 1st Earl of Guilford and was born in 1732. He used the courtesy title Lord North from 1752 and became the 2nd Earl of Guilford on the death of his father in 1790. Like many of the early Prime Ministers, he was elected to the Commons when very young, twenty-two in his case. He was returned unopposed as the member for the family controlled borough of Banbury, and he held the seat for thirty-six years.

North had administrative ability and an amiable disposition. He was liked and had the knack of criticising others without incurring their wrath. These attributes helped his ascent to the premiership and they helped him discharge his duties during his long occupation of it. At the age of only thirty-five, he became Chancellor of the Exchequer, and shortly afterwards, Leader of the Commons. He held both positions for fifteen years, up to and throughout his twelve-year period as Prime Minister. He was a prudent and reasonably successful Chancellor, though it can be argued that his eye on the costs hampered the prosecution of the war.

In 1770, at the tender age of thirty-seven, North succeeded the Duke of Grafton as Prime Minister. The respect of the Commons was a factor, but he was very much the choice of George III. The King liked him and knew him well. They had in fact played together as children. North accepted the appointment somewhat reluctantly, but felt that it was his duty to serve the Monarch.

The country was in a buoyant mood following victory in the Seven Years' War, and North enjoyed an early triumph when he forced Spain to abandon its attempt to take control of the Falkland Islands. He was not the only Prime Minister whose popularity was increased by success in these lonely islands in the South Atlantic. Regard for Margaret Thatcher was boosted in the same way.

North was Prime Minister in the six difficult years leading up to the American War of Independence. Feelings ran high, and in 1773, at the so-called Boston Tea Party, colonists dumped taxed tea into the harbour. His government sent troops to Boston and closed the harbour. It also introduced what became known as the Coercive Acts. The relationship between the colonies and the mother country slid into conflict, and in 1776, it led to war.

Things went from bad to worse, and the British defeat at the battles of Saratoga brought the French into the war on the side of the colonists. The country needed someone like William Pitt, but it had to make do with Lord North. The Prime Minister knew his limitations as a war leader and repeatedly asked the King to release him from office, but George would not accept his resignation. Eventually, the disastrous defeat at Yorktown convinced North that it was futile to continue. He pressed his resignation again and this time George, who was determined to continue and win, accepted it. The King was of course wrong, and the independence of the colonies was acknowledged in the treaty of Paris in 1783.

North had lost the confidence of the King and his standing in Parliament was greatly reduced, but he continued in active politics. For a few months, he served as Home Secretary in the so-called Fox-North coalition, which operated under the nominal leadership of the Duke of Portland. His acceptance of this office infuriated the King who detested Fox.

In 1786, North began to lose his sight and, in time, became totally blind. He died of dropsy at the relatively early age of sixty. He was by no stretch of the imagination a good Prime Minister: in fact, he was a poor one. His awful reputation is, however, unjustified.

An Uncanny Resemblance

Lord North had an uncanny physical resemblance to his monarch, George III, something that is evident in many portraits. Somc pcoplc havc wondered if they were half-brothers. North's mother and father were both active in the court of Frederick, Prince of Wales, never a king, but father of George III. This is the reason for the speculation. There is no evidence and it is generally believed to be a coincidence. DNA evidence could probably prove or more likely disprove it. The body of Richard III was discovered buried beneath a Leicester car park, and 527 years after his death, a DNA sample was taken from the son of his sixteenth-generation great niece in the direct maternal line: this proved that the body was indeed Richard.[2]

Affected Somnolence

North sometimes slept in Parliament or at least appeared to do so, which could be effective. On one occasion, a speaker who was attacking him stopped and complained that he was asleep. 'I wish to God I was,' he said.[3]

A Joke about his Family

At Covent Garden, a man said to North: 'Who is that plain-looking woman in the box opposite?' The conversation then went as follows:

A James Gillray cartoon of 5 May 1783 showing a carousel with Charles Fox, Lord North, Edmund Burke and Admiral Keppel. The carved beam at the centre is a depiction of George III.

That is my wife.

Oh, I don't mean her, I mean the lady next to her.

That sir, is my daughter: we are considered to be three of the ugliest people in London.[4]

Swayed by a Sermon

North listened to a sermon preached by a poor cousin of his wife, the Reverend William Speke. The chosen text was Psalm 75 verse 6: 'For promotion cometh neither from the east, nor from the west, nor from the south'. Soon afterwards, the Reverend Speke was appointed to a better living.[5]

Meeting an Old Political Enemy

Out walking towards the end of his life, North, who was blind, was told that an old political enemy was approaching. This was Colonel Barré, who was also blind. North stopped him and said: 'Though you and I have had our quarrels in the past, I wager there are no two men in England who would be happier to see one another today'.[6]

12

William Petty Fitzmaurice

2nd EARL OF SHELBURNE

1782–83

William Petty Fitzmaurice was born in Dublin in 1737 and entered the House of Lords as the 2nd Earl of Shelburne at the age of twenty-four. He had a rather unhappy childhood in Ireland and felt that he had been poorly educated.

It is to Shelburne's credit that his poor education did not hold him back. Throughout his life, he sought the company of people with first class minds. In his later years, he entertained many intellectuals and enjoyed his discussions with them. Drawing on his considerable wealth, he became a renowned collector of works of art and antiques, and he built up a very substantial library.

William Petty Fitzmaurice, 2nd Earl of Shelburne, (1737–1805), portrait by Jean-Laurent Mosnier (1743–1808). *Sothebys*

Unfortunately, he was a man easy to dislike and many did. His contemporaries considered him untrustworthy and his manner was often hectoring. In Parliament, he could be vituperative and he was something of a political loner. On the plus side, throughout his career, he persistently advocated free trade, religious toleration, and parliamentary reform. In respect of the last two of these aims, he could be said to be ahead of his time.

After a short period at Oxford University, Shelburne enlisted in the Army and served with distinction in the Seven Years' War. His engagements included the battles of Minden and Kloster-Kampen. This led to him becoming an aide-de-camp to George III.

The future Prime Minister's first office was as First Lord of Trade in 1763, but he resigned after just a few months. He was Southern Secretary for two years starting in 1766, but his conciliatory attitude towards the Americans led to his exclusion from the government. After that, he was in opposition for fourteen years, returning in March 1782 as Secretary of State for the Home Department in the short second government of the Marquess of Rockingham. He took this office with the understanding that the King was willing to accept the independence of the United States.

Shelburne became Prime Minister following the unexpected early death of Rockingham. His period in office only lasted 235 days and was dominated by the peace negotiations with the Americans. His terms were widely criticised for conceding too much land and being too generous. They were defeated in the House of Commons and he was forced to resign. He blamed the King as well as the lost vote. The

King, the Parliament, and the British people were reluctant to acknowledge the scale of their defeat and the concessions that had to be made. Despite this, Shelburne's rejected terms were very similar to those subsequently signed in the Treaty of Paris. Harold Wilson summed it up very well:

The Earl of Shelburne, who was Prime Minister from 3 July 1782 to 24 February 1783, was one of the most superb failures among eighteenth century statesmen. He failed because he reached the top at the precise moment when the peace negotiations with the victorious Americans reached the decisive stage—and since the Americans were in a position to dictate the terms and Britain's international standing was the lowest since the time of the Stuarts, no possible agreement stood any chance of being popular.[1]

Controversial Promotion

During his military service in the Seven Years' War, Shelburne was awarded the rank of colonel and became aide-de-camp to George III. His promotion was ahead of much more senior officers and caused considerable resentment. The Duke of Richmond resigned a post in the royal household in protest. Despite having no subsequent military career, Shelburne later received further promotions, finishing as general in 1783.

The Duel

Lieutenant-Colonel William Fullerton MP said that Shelburne had been corresponding with the enemy, meaning the Americans. He responded by challenging him to a duel and this took place in Hyde Park. Shelburne was slightly injured in the groin, but he made light of the injury. 'I don't think Lady Shelburne will be worse for it,' he said.[2]

Some Terrible Insults

Shelburne was greatly disliked and a cursory search will find details of numerous insults hurled at him. George III called him 'the Jesuit of Berkeley Square', which was where he lived.[3] He was widely derided as 'Malagrida'.[4] In case the name is not familiar, it might be helpful to explain that this was the name of a Jesuit prominent in Portugal. He was suspected of treason and executed as a blasphemer and heretic. The basis of these insults was that at the time Jesuits were held to be synonymous with deceit. Edmund Burke called him 'a Borgia, a Cataline and a serpent with two heads'.[5]

Most Modest of Graves

The graves of most British Prime Ministers are marked with some prominence, but Shelburne is an exception. He is buried in the High Wycombe parish church and there is no plaque or similar indication to mark his prominence.

13

William Cavendish-Bentinck

3rd DUKE OF PORTLAND

1783; 1807–9

William Cavendish-Bentinck, 3rd Duke of Portland, 1738–1809), portrait by Matthew Pratt (1734–1805), *c.* 1774. *National Gallery of Art, Washington DC*

The Duke of Portland is one of the seventeen prime Ministers who have served more than one non-continuous term of office. In Portland's case, the terms were nearly twenty-four years apart, which is by a considerable margin the longest interval. The nearest is the Marquess of Rockingham, whose two terms were separated by nearly sixteen years. It is a notable fact, but Portland is not remembered as a notable Prime Minister. In fact, he is remembered as being high in the ranks of the unnotable ones. For different reasons, he was not properly in charge of either of his ministries.

Portland was first Prime Minister in 1783 as the nominal head of a short-lived coalition. His role was necessary because of the two factions within it. The government became known as the Fox-North Coalition, which is a good indication of where the power lay. It is remembered for the signing of the Treaty of Paris, which ended the American War of Independence. This was ironic because the treaty's terms were almost the same as the rejected ones negotiated by Portland's predecessor the Earl of Shelburne. The government was dismissed by the King after the Lords, urged on by himself, defeated Fox's India Bill. The King had not wanted the government and he was delighted to see the back of it.

Portland's second ministry commenced in 1807 following the break-up of the so-called ministry of all the talents. The King asked him to serve and he unwisely agreed. It was a Tory-leaning administration. He was feeling his age and his health was failing. He should not have accepted the position because he was tired and unable to do the job. The situation worsened as time went on. Things were so bad that his cabinet operated without his guidance and control. It even met without his knowledge. He resigned in 1809 following a stroke and died two months later.

Although he was not a successful Prime Minister, he had some success in his long time at the forefront of politics. Being a duke counted for a lot, and he was a very well-connected one. He was elected to the Commons at the age of twenty-three and moved to the Lords on the death of his father a year later.

Portland was firmly associated with the Rockingham faction of the Whig party and he was Lord Chamberlain in Rockingham's first ministry. Although not required to do so, he resigned when it ended, and was in opposition for nearly the next sixteen years. He returned to government as Lord Lieutenant of Ireland in Rockingham's second ministry. Then, after the brief premiership of Shelburne, under whom he did not serve, he was the anodyne choice acceptable to the King to preside over the different factions in the Fox-North Coalition.

Following another period out of office, in 1794, he led the conservative Whigs into government under Pitt the Younger. He served as Home Secretary for seven years then as Lord President of the Council for another four.

Portland was not an eloquent speaker and he spoke in the Lords relatively infrequently. He was rather shy. He did, however, have principles and he worked long and hard. Despite his unfortunate spells as Prime Minister, he had quite a few successes. His virtues should not be overlooked.

A Grand and Well-Connected Man

Portland held a title of every degree of British nobility. He was a duke, marquess, earl, viscount, and baron. His mother was the daughter of the 4th Duke of Devonshire, and he was therefore the son-in-law of a former Prime Minister. He is the great-great-great grandfather of Queen Elizabeth II through her maternal grandmother.

Recognition of Problems to Come

Portland approached his second spell as Prime Minister with justified foreboding. He said: 'My fears are not that the attempt to perform this duty will shorten my life, but that I shall neither bodily nor mentally perform it as I ought'.

An Anonymous Contemporary Satire

He totters [jibed the opposition] on a crutch,
His brain, by sickness long depressed
Has lost the sense it once possessed,
Though that's not saying much.[1]

A Royal Row about Money

The first three King Georges had problems with their heirs, and from time to time, they had problems with their Prime Ministers. The two problems coalesced in 1783 during Portland's first term as Prime Minister. The Prince of Wales, the future George IV, turned twenty-one in that year and he was dissolute, exceedingly extravagant, and heavily in debt.

Portland proposed a financial settlement that gave the Prince twice the income that his father had received when he was the heir. The King violently objected and there was an angry confrontation with the Prime Minister. Afterwards, Parliament voted a sum to pay off the Prince's debts, and he received half the originally proposed annual sum plus the Duchy of Cornwall revenues.[2]

The Talent of Dead Silence

Portland was known for periods when he did not say much and times when he did not say anything at all. One writer commented as follows: 'The Duke of Portland, it was said, possessed in an eminent degree the talent of dead silence. In his case it was due to an almost pathological shyness'.[3]

14

William Pitt

THE YOUNGER

1783–1801; 1804–06

THERE HAVE BEEN two Prime Ministers called William Pitt. To differentiate them, we generally refer to them as Pitt the Elder and Pitt the Younger. This one was the fourteenth Prime Minister and he was the fourth child and second son of the ninth, William Pitt the Elder. It is something of an understatement to say that he was well-connected. He was the nephew of the seventh Prime Minister, George Grenville, and the cousin of Lord Grenville, who would later become the sixteenth Prime Minister. He also had other powerful political connections.

William Pitt the Younger (1759–1806), portrait by John Hoppner (1758–1810). *Bonhams, via Wikipedia*

It would also not be an understatement to say that he was a remarkable man, and like his father, he was regarded as one of the great Prime Ministers. Why remarkable and why great? For a start, he was Chancellor of the Exchequer at twenty-three and Prime Minister at twenty-four, making him by a large margin the youngest person to hold that office.

With a break of three years near the end, he was then Prime Minister for the rest of his life. He died at the early age of forty-six. Apart from Sir Robert Walpole, he held the position for longer than anyone. He was incorruptible and a patriot, and he left his mark on the country's system of government. He was a good administrator and a sound Chancellor. He presided over bringing Ireland into the United Kingdom, adopted firm policies during and after the French revolution, and led his country in the wars with the revolutionary French and in the early part of the Napoleonic wars.

Pitt the Elder groomed his son for greatness. The younger Pitt suffered from poor health as a child and was educated at home by a tutor. He then moved on to Pembroke College, Cambridge, at the precocious age of fourteen. That would be incredible now and it was incredible at the time. He then embraced his destiny by entering the Commons as the member for Appleby at a by-election. This was a rotten borough controlled by James Lowther, which was ironic because a few years later, he tried to curb the number of the rotten boroughs. After his maiden speech, Edmund Burke said: 'He is not a chip off the old block. He is the old block itself'.[1]

Pitt's appearance was easy to caricature. He was thin, with a long neck and a nose that was long and upturned. He exhibited a superior manner and had a glacial look, and to some extent, this matched his character. He worked exceptionally hard and exceptionally long, which left him little time for women and other interests.

He was something of a loner who lived for his work and his country. He died a bachelor, one of just four Prime Ministers who never married. He did have women friends, but they were not permitted to get close to him, something that no doubt disappointed some potential brides and their mothers. To badly misquote Jane Austen: 'It is a truth universally acknowledged that a single Prime Minister must be in want of a wife'. Inevitably, there has been speculation about his sexuality. If he did lean towards homosexuality, it must have been suppressed. There is no evidence of it—perhaps he was asexual.

Pitt became Chancellor of the Exchequer in Shelburne's Government, and he later held that position all the time that he was Prime Minister, something that increased his workload. When Shelburne resigned, the King asked him to be Prime Minister, but he declined because he knew that he did not have enough support in Parliament. The request was made again after the short government of the Duke of Portland, and this time, he felt in a position to accept. He was the only minister in the Commons and had to speak in that House on all topics of business.

He was widely expected to fail and after a month was defeated on a motion of no confidence. Controversially, he did not resign. He had the support of the House of Lords, the country, and, most importantly, the King. The problem was with his fellow MPs. In 1784, a general election was called and he triumphed with a majority of over a hundred. He was then firmly established in office and was to be Prime Minister for the next seventeen years.

In the year after the election, he tried and failed to get rid of thirty-six rotten boroughs. Electoral reform would have to wait until the 1832 Reform Act. He was a hard-working and successful Chancellor and administrator, and he made sound progress in restoring the public finances to order after the deprivations caused by the American war. This was a major achievement.

The French Revolution caused great concern in Britain. During its early days and before the terror, Pitt said to his guests at a dinner in Downing Street that 'things in England will go on as they are until the day of judgment'.[2] Burke, who was present, responded by saying 'very likely but it is the day of judgment that I am afraid of'. Pitt's lack of concern did not last long and his government moved in the direction of repression. Habeas Corpus was suspended in 1794, and his other measures included the Seditious Meetings Act and the Combination Acts. Pitt's liberal reputation was damaged.

He was in power during the wars with revolutionary France and for the first part of the Napoleonic Wars. Views differ about his effectiveness. French successes and the failure of the first and second coalitions left Britain facing France alone in 1800. If Germany is substituted for France, similarities with 1940 can be perceived.

William Pitt was Prime Minister of Great Britain from 19 December 1783 to 31 December 1800, and Prime Minister of the United Kingdom from 1 January 1801 to 14 March 1801. The distinction is made because the Act of Union joined Ireland with Great Britain. Pitt presided over it and it led to his loss of office. He pushed for the union because Irish nationalists had staged a rebellion in the belief that the French would come to their assistance. In order to get Irish agreement, he had rather ambiguously promised that Catholic emancipation would follow. In the event, he could not deliver on his semi-promise. The King said that it would violate his coronation oath and that it was not a matter for Parliament. Pitt resigned and gave his support to Henry Addington, his successor and friend.

The war with France was halted by the Treaty of Amiens in 1802, but it resumed a year later. Addington was not the right person to be a war leader and Pitt, in alliance with Fox, brought down his government.

A cartoon by Thomas Rowlandson, 'Billy Lackbeard and Charley Blackbeard playing at Football', published 7 February 1784. Pitt and Charles James Fox had argued in parliament over the regulation of the East India Company. Rowlandson mischievously shows them as contrasting characters, playing football with East India House.

Having promised the King that he would introduce no measure in support of Catholic emancipation, he resumed the office of Prime Minister on 10 May 1804.[3] His position in Parliament was weaker than during his first ministry. During this second period in office, he saw the founding of the third coalition and Nelson's stunning victory at Trafalgar.

The strain of being a war Prime Minister wore him out. He had always worked long and hard and he continued to do so. His health had never been robust and it deteriorated. He had always been a heavy drinker of port, and in this last period of his life, his consumption increased. He died in office on 23 January 1806, the probable cause being peptic ulceration of the stomach.

Pitt and his father were both rightly celebrated. They invariably figure in lists of the great Prime Ministers.

The Rolliad

This was a work of satire directed principally at the administration of William Pitt the Younger. It was published in 1784–85 in serial form in the *Morning Herald*. The following verse attacked Pitt for his consumption of port and for having no relationships with women:

Tis true, indeed, we oft abuse him,
Because he bends to no man;
But Slander's self dares not accuse him
Of stiffness to a woman.

Another verse ridiculed Pitt for his youth:

Above the rest, majestically great,
Behold the infant Atlas of the state,
The matchless miracle of modern days,
In whom Britannia to the world displays
A sight to make surrounding nations stare;
A kingdom trusted to a schoolboy's care.

A French cartoon, *c.* 1795. William Pitt is standing on the British crown, flattened by the weight of his authority; he is holding a flag that depicts implements of slavery, and in his left hand holds the chains of bondage that are connected to George III, in the foreground on the right, and members of Parliament or of the working class behind the king and on the left. *Library of Congress*

Any Port in a Storm

Pitt had an inherited susceptibility to gout, and when a young man, he had been recommended by his doctor to drink port. It was very mistakenly believed that this alleviated the symptoms. He followed the advice and did so for the rest of his life. His normal consumption was one to two 35-cl bottles a day, but towards the end of his life, it was up to three bottles a day.

The Pilot that Weathered the Storm

The future Prime Minister George Canning, using an alias, composed an eight-verse poem/song for a banquet to honour Pitt's birthday on 28 May 1802. Pitt, who was out of office, did not attend. The poem praised him for his success in weathering the storm of the war with France. He was the pilot that weathered the storm. The last verse warns that the country might need him again. It reads:

And Oh! If again the rude whirlwind should rise!
The dawning of peace should fresh darkness deform,
The regrets of the good, and the fears of the wise,
Shall turn to the Pilot that weather'd the storm.

The Duel on Putney Heath

George Tierney, a future cabinet minister, took exception to a remark made about him by Pitt in the House of Commons. Pitt refused to withdraw it and Tierney challenged him to a duel. Pitt accepted and it took place in front of a big crowd on Putney Heath on Sunday 27 May 1798. The duel increased Pitt's popularity, but he was criticised for desecrating the Sabbath. Each man fired twice into the air and honour was satisfied. There were no injuries.

Income Tax

Pitt is highly regarded for many things that he did, but many of us curse one of his measures. In 1799, he introduced income tax to help pay for the war with France. It was abolished by Addington's government in 1802, reintroduced in 1803, and abolished again in 1816. Sir Robert Peel brought it back in 1842 and it has been with us ever since.

A Man who could Withstand Pain

In 1786, a tumour developed on Pitt's face and a surgeon operated in Downing Street to remove it. This was in the pre-anaesthetic age. He would not let the surgeon tie his hands as was normally done, and assured him that he would not move. The surgeon said that it would take six minutes. The Prime Minister looked at the clock and sat impassively while the surgeon operated. When he had finished, Pitt told him that he had exceeded the time by half a minute.[4]

Words on Hearing of the Battle of Austerlitz

Napoleon decisively defeated the much larger combined Russian and Austrian armies on 2 December 1805. Pitt heard the news a few weeks before he died. In despair, he said: 'Roll up that map, it will not be wanted these ten years'.

His Last Speech in Public

At the Guildhall on 9 November 1805, he stated: 'England has saved herself by her exertions, and will, as I trust, save Europe by her example'.

Last Words

These were probably a despairing 'My country! How I leave my country', but they might have been 'I think that I could eat one of Bellamy's pies'. It would be nice to think that it was the latter and that he died with happy thoughts.

'The Plum Pudding in Danger'. A cartoon by James Gillray, 26 February 1805. Napoleon is busy carving off Europe while Pitt carves off half of the world.

15

Henry Addington

1801–04

HENRY ADDINGTON DID not seek the position of Prime Minister, but he reached what Disraeli later described as the top of the greasy pole. Furthermore, he did it despite some major handicaps. For a start, he came from the middle classes, not the aristocracy or landed gentry. His father was a successful doctor who specialised in mental illness, and who had treated William Pitt the Elder. This was the connection that led to Henry becoming friends with William Pitt the Younger. Very unfairly, his relatively modest background was held against him. As well as this, he was a poor speaker and noted for being rather humourless.

Henry Addington, 1st Viscount Sidmouth (1757–1844), portrait by Sir William Beechey (1753–1859), 1803. *National Portrait Gallery*

His term as Prime Minister was preceded and succeeded by the ministries of his friend William Pitt. Comparisons were bound to be unfavourable. He did achieve some things and to criticise him for not being Pitt was unfair. It was hardly his fault and it might be mentioned that he was not the only person who was not Pitt. Nevertheless, comparisons were made. George Canning, the very witty future Prime Minister said:

> Pitt is to Addington
> As London is to Paddington

He was not highly thought of at the time, or for a long time afterwards. His reputation is still not high, but it has improved with the perspective of time.

Addington was born in 1757 and elected to the Commons in 1784. Five years later, thanks partly to the offices of his friend William Pitt the Younger, he was made Speaker, and a good Speaker he was too. After twelve years in the job, Pitt resigned over the issue of Catholic emancipation. He wanted his friend to move to 10 Downing Street and the King was of the same opinion. Addington was reluctant, but he was persuaded.

Then, after a while, it all went wrong. He was not seen to be a good war leader and he could not command support in Parliament. Pitt joined others in opposing him, and although he had the support of the King, he resigned in May 1804.

Prime Ministers are nearly always most remembered for what they did in that office, but there was a lot more to come. Henry Addington, shortly to be ennobled as Viscount Sidmouth, was only forty-six and had more to offer. After a very short break, he served as Lord President in Pitt's last cabinet, and as Lord Privy Seal and Lord President in Lord Grenville's ministry of all the talents that followed. In 1812, he joined Lord Liverpool's cabinet for a few months as Lord President, then for nearly ten years as Home Secretary. From 1822, he served the following two years in the cabinet as Minister without Portfolio. He had served in six administrations. 'He is like smallpox. Everybody is obliged to have him once in their lives,' observed the witty Canning.[1]

Lord Liverpool served in turbulent times and his government had to deal with disaffection at home as well as the end of the Napoleonic Wars and what followed overseas. Those favourably inclined towards Addington (now Viscount Sidmouth) might say that as Home Secretary, he consistently took a firm line. Plenty of others said that he was reactionary and repressive. There were many challenges to the government's authority. The Luddites were smashing machinery and the so-called Peterloo massacre took place in 1819. In 1820, the Cato Street Conspiracy was a failed plot to murder the entire cabinet. Addington's response, and that of the government, included the suspension of *habeas corpus* in 1817 and the Six Acts in 1819. Among other things, these shackled radical newspapers and labelled any meeting advocating radical reform as an overt act of treasonable conspiracy.

Addington lived on to the age of eighty-six. He was a pious, kindly old gentleman who wrote occasional harmless poetry.[2]

A Lecture Received with Merriment

Addington is described above as a poor speaker, but many contemporaries would have considered that assessment much too generous. When Speaker, he lectured the Commons on the subject of the corn shortage and the beneficial effects of bran. To the merriment of Honourable and Right Honourable Members, he waxed lyrical about 'the rarefying warmth, the solvent moisture and the grinding action of the stomach'.[3] It was not his finest hour.

A Successful Chancellor

Like Pitt, Addington was Chancellor of the Exchequer while serving as Prime Minister, and despite his deficiencies as PM, he was a successful one. He inherited a poor financial position, but founded a tax base that could finance the resumed war. He presented four budgets and is credited with delivering the first one in the form that we recognise them today.[4] Previously, accounts of past performance and future prospects were scattered during a parliamentary session.

A Heavy Drinker?

Addington was said to be usually a sober figure, but was known to like wine. Joseph Farington, the landscape artist and diarist, recorded:

> He wants spirits and courage for his situation and though a temperate man, now drinks perhaps 20 glasses of wine at his dinner before he goes to the House of Commons to invigorate himself.

Surely this cannot be right. Twenty glasses is equivalent to three to four modern bottles—enough to cause severe health problems.

Amiens and Munich

Addington was responsible for the 1802 Treaty of Amiens that ended the war with France. He acted from a position of weakness and the terms were not favourable to the United Kingdom. Napoleon's aggression continued and Addington declared war a year later. It is not hard to see parallels with Neville Chamberlain's actions at Munich in 1938. To continue the analogy, both Addington and Chamberlain declared war within a year. Addington's position was by then stronger, and in 1940, Churchill did have the Spitfires—just.

His Sight of Future Prime Ministers

Addington was forty-six when he resigned as Prime Minister, and he lived for another forty years. In that time, he saw more new Prime Ministers than any of the fifty-three others who have held the position. There were nine—Lord Grenville, Spencer Perceval, the Earl of Liverpool, George Canning, Viscount Goderich, the Duke of Wellington, Earl Grey, Lord Melbourne, and Sir Robert Peel.

Henry Addington and Napoleon draw swords in James Gillray's 1803 print *Armed Heroes*.

16

William Wyndham

LORD GRENVILLE

1806–07

LORD GRENVILLE WAS Prime Minister for fourteen months following the death in office of his cousin, William Pitt the Younger. He led what is invariably known as the ministry of all the talents. It had the support of his own followers, the followers of Charles Fox, and the followers of Lord Sidmouth (formerly Henry Addington). Grenville's cousin, William Windham, and his younger brother, Thomas Grenville, were both in the cabinet, as were Fox and Sidmouth. The King loathed Fox, who had not been in government since 1783, so it was a compliment to Grenville that he accepted him. In the event, Fox died after seven months.

William Wyndham Grenville, 1st Baron Grenville by John Hoppner, *c.* 1800. *National Portrait Gallery*

The ministry of all the talents is remembered for the abolition of the slave trade, but otherwise was not a success. Efforts to make peace with France failed and the ministry ended when Grenville and other ministers wanted to make moves towards Catholic emancipation. This was still abhorrent to the King and Grenville resigned.

Lord Grenville was extremely well-connected and this greatly helped his political career. He was the son of the former Prime Minister, George Grenville, and the uncle of the 1st Duke of Buckingham and Chandos. His father's sister married William Pitt the Elder, which made him the cousin of his predecessor as Prime Minister, William Pitt the Younger. He himself married a Pitt—the Honourable Anne, daughter of Thomas Pitt, 1st Baron Camelford. The couple had no children.

Grenville did not hold office during his remaining twenty-seven years after resigning as Prime Minister, but he served almost continuously before it. Family connections secured his election to the Commons at the age of twenty-two, and he was almost immediately made Chief Secretary for Ireland. He was Paymaster of the Forces from 1784 to 1789, and then very briefly Speaker of the Commons. This was followed by two years as Home Secretary, and while holding this office, he moved to the House of Lords and was Leader of the Lords. In 1791 and for nearly ten years, he was Secretary of State for Foreign Affairs. He sat in the Lords during his brief period as Prime Minister.

His time at the Foreign Office was turbulent because he had to deal with revolutionary France. He believed that fighting on the continent was the key to victory, and he opposed the faction of Henry Dundas,

A cartoon by James Gillray, 23 March 1807, depicting the king kicking out the Grenville government. The Ministry of 'All the Talents' was a unity government formed by Grenville on his appointment as Prime Minister on 11 February 1806, following the death of Pitt the Younger.

which favoured war at sea and in the colonies. All this time, he was serving under his cousin, Pitt the Younger, and he resigned with him in 1801. He did not serve in Pitt's second ministry because he had become close to Charles Fox, Pitt's long-standing enemy. This soured the relationship between the cousins.

After leaving office, he opposed the Peninsular War of 1809–14. He supported free trade and opposed the passing of the corn laws. He suffered a stroke in 1823 and died in 1834.

His Manner and Manners

Grenville was not personally greatly liked—either by the people at large or by some of his contemporaries. Terms used by recent writers include:

His appearance was not prepossessing: his manners were shocking.[1]

As a politician he lacked one ingredient usually necessary for ultimate success: a sense of camaraderie. He was stiff, formal and, as George III thought, obstinate. Grenville was quite aware that he was no leader of men.[2]

Lord Liverpool, who followed him as Prime Minister, wrote in 1807:

Not an ill-tempered man but he has no feelings for others—in his outward manner, offensive to the last degree[3].

It was noted that his marriage, at the age of thirty-two to the Hon. Anne Pitt, was a help to both his manner and manners.

Dropmore House

Grenville was one of the nineteen Prime Ministers educated at Eton College, and during his schooldays, there he enjoyed extensive country walks. During these walks, he became familiar with some land near Burnham Beeches. Its attractions included views of Windsor Castle and of his school. Later, during his thirties, he had Dropmore House built on the site. It gave him great pleasure and, alongside the influence of his new wife, perhaps helped him be a nicer person.

He had around 2,500 trees planted, and by the time of his death, the estate had the biggest collection of conifer species in Britain. In doing this, he shared an affinity with Lord Heseltine, the former Deputy Prime Minister. Heseltine expressed his love of trees by building a famous arboretum at his home at Thenford in Northamptonshire.

The 10 Downing Street Postbag

When Prime Minister, Lord Grenville received around sixty letters a week.[4] Even his enemies conceded that he worked hard and it was possible for him to read every one and be personally involved in the replies. How different things are now. The Prime Minister of the day receives more than 10,000 letters and emails a week. Routine thanks and acknowledgments to most of them are inevitable.

Thoughts on Leaving Office

Many Prime Ministers hate the thought of losing office, and some have to be almost dragged from Downing Street. Margaret Thatcher is one that comes to mind. Others find it a relief, or at least say that they do. This is particularly true of some of the early ones who took the job feeling an obligation to be of service. Lord Grenville comes into this category. Shortly after his resignation, he wrote the following to his brother, Lord Buckingham:

> The deed is done and I am again a free man, and to you may I express what it would seem like affectation to say to others, the infinite pleasure I derive from my emancipation.

17

Spencer Perceval

1809–12

Spencer Perceval (1762–1812), portrait by George Francis Joseph (1764–1846). *National Portrait Gallery*

SPENCER PERCEVAL IS the only Prime Minister to have been assassinated. We must sincerely hope that there will never be another. No fewer than four Archbishops of Canterbury have suffered this fate, though the first person to hold this office was appointed in the year 597. The first Prime Minister was appointed in 1721.

Perceval was not wealthy, and before entering politics, he practised law as a barrister. Born in 1762, he became a King's Counsel in 1796, just before being elected to the House of Commons. He became Solicitor General in 1801 and then Attorney General the following year, a position he held throughout the remainder of Pitt's ministry and the ministry of Henry Addington. He declined to serve in Lord Grenville's ministry of all the talents, something that devalued its name because his was one of the talents not employed in it.

He was Chancellor of the Exchequer and Leader of the Commons under the Duke of Portland and was then Prime Minister. He remains the only Solicitor General who has served as Prime Minister and also the only Attorney General who has done so.

Throughout his political career, Perceval consistently opposed Catholic emancipation, which endeared him to George III, and he also opposed parliamentary reform. He enthusiastically supported the abolition of the slave trade. Firmly, and with some success, he waged war on Napoleonic France. As Prime Minister and against some opposition, he supported Wellington's ultimately successful campaign in the peninsula.

He was a very committed evangelical Christian and member of the Church of England, something that shaped his actions and behaviour. He led a moral life, opposed adultery, and was opposed to hunting and gambling.

Perceval's time as Prime Minister was difficult because he had a weak position in the House of Commons. He was his own Chancellor of the Exchequer and all but one of his ministers sat in the House of Lords. In 1810, George III finally descended into madness and Perceval played a critical part in establishing the Regency. The Prince Regent (the future George IV) had enjoyed poor relations with Perceval and it was expected that he would immediately sack him as Prime Minister, but he did not do so. He said that he did not wish to do anything that might upset his father's health.

Contemporary opinions on Perceval differed. He had some success and we should give credit for the consistency and strength of his principles. However, by no means all of the assessments were favourable. Although deploring his murder, Lord Holland, a political opponent and the nephew of Charles Fox, summed him up by stating: 'A very fortunate event for the glory, happiness and independence of my country'.[1]

The Assassination

Perceval was shot as he walked through the lobby of the House of Commons. The murderer was John Bellingham, who carried a burning grievance against the government and the Prime Minister. He had been imprisoned in Russia, wrongly he fervently claimed, and the government had not given him the support that he believed was his due. An attempt to get financial compensation from the government had failed.

After firing the fatal shot, Bellingham sat down and waited to be arrested. Five days later, he was convicted of murder, and two days after that, he was hanged in public. Justice could be very swift in those days—perhaps we have something to learn. Shockingly, news of the murder was not universally received with horror. The poet Samuel Taylor Coleridge heard of it on the street and was shocked to see that the lower orders were jubilant, as if a tyrant had been overthrown.[2]

His Country's Gratitude

Following his dreadful death, monuments were erected in Lincoln's Inn, Westminster Abbey, and Northampton, the constituency that he represented in Parliament. Perceval was not a wealthy man and he left a widow and twelve children. Parliament voted to settle £50,000 on his children, and additionally voted annuities for his widow and eldest son.

Something Unique

Perceval is the only Prime Minister to have lived his entire life within the reign of a single monarch. He was born in 1762 and died in 1812. George III came to the throne in 1760 and he died in 1820.

Generous with his Money

Pitt the Younger died with considerable debts. Perceval, who only had meagre financial resources, immediately contributed £1,000 to a fund to help pay them.

Elopement

Spencer Perceval and his brother fell in love with sisters. The girls' father had no objection to the marriage of one sister to his brother, but he balked at the prospect of Spencer marrying the other. He told her to wait three years until she was twenty-one. She did wait, but her father was still worried about Spencer's financial prospects and would not agree to the marriage. The couple then eloped and married by special licence.

The Sabbath

Perceval was a committed Christian. He tried hard to observe the Sabbath and he encouraged others to do the same. On one occasion, he put off the assembly of Parliament so that members would not have to travel on a Sunday.[3]

18

Robert Banks Jenkinson

2ND EARL OF LIVERPOOL

1812–27

LORD LIVERPOOL IS not ranked with the very good Prime Ministers, but he was most definitely not a failure. A Tour de France cycling analogy is that he was not near the yellow jersey at the front, but was well-placed in the pack behind. He was a skilled politician who for a long time held together the liberal and reactionary wings of the Tory party. This was something that his successors found very difficult.

Robert Banks Jenkinson, 2nd Earl of Liverpool (1770–1828), portrait by Sir Thomas Lawrence (1769–1830), 1793. *National Portrait Gallery*

Liverpool was forty-two years and one day old when he became Prime Minister. No subsequent one has been so young. He held the position for just under fifteen years and only resigned because he suffered a stroke. No later Prime Ministers have served for so long, and only two of his predecessors (Walpole and Pitt the Younger) did so.

He was elected to the House of Commons at the precocious age of twenty, but took his seat following his twenty-first birthday. He moved to the House of Lords at the age of thirty-three. Pitt the Younger appointed him to the Board of Control for India at the age of twenty-three, and apart from a period of fourteen months, he was in office until his resignation as Prime Minister thirty-four years later. During the fourteen months, he was leader of the opposition to Lord Grenville's ministry of all the talents.

He was Foreign Secretary for three years starting in 1801 and negotiated the Treaty of Amiens, which temporarily halted the war with France. He was Home Secretary (1803–06 and 1807–09) and Secretary for War and the Colonies (1809–12). When Pitt died in 1806, the King asked him to form a government, but he declined because he did not have sufficient support in Parliament. He later agreed to serve following the assassination of Spencer Perceval.

Liverpool did not have an easy ride as Prime Minister. He had to deal with the last three years of the Napoleonic Wars and with the 1812 war with America. That was the one in which British troops burned the White House. His government helped reshape Europe at the Congress of Vienna, and it controversially introduced the Corn Laws.

The country was in a restless state. The Luddites smashed machinery and the so-called Peterloo massacre took place in 1819. Liverpool and his government responded firmly with repressive measures.

Habeas corpus was suspended and the notorious Six Acts limited free speech and the right to gather for peaceful demonstration.

His merit is summed up in *The Biographical Dictionary of British Prime Ministers*:

Perhaps the true measure of Liverpool's modest merits as Prime Minister is the sorry history of the Tory party after he left office. In less than four years it had shattered into at least three feuding factions.[1]

The Railway Station

In London, Liverpool Street and Liverpool Street Station are named after him. This is the only London station named after a Prime Minister, but Waterloo is named after Wellington's greatest battle.

Fall of the Bastille

Liverpool was in Paris in July 1789, and he saw the unrest that led to the fall of the Bastille and the early stages of the French Revolution. The experience made him think that extension of the franchise in Britain could lead to destabilisation or even revolution.[2]

Marriage

When he was twenty-five, Liverpool married Louisa Hervey. She was the daughter of a notorious eccentric and did not bring a dowry. His father opposed the marriage and it took the combined efforts of the King and the Prime Minister to get him to give his support. It was an exceptionally happy marriage, but with no children.[3] Following her death in 1820, he married again. The second marriage was happy but short.

The Massacre of Tranent

In 1797, the people of Tranent in East Lothian, Scotland, protested at measures to conscript Scots into the British military. During an angry confrontation, the Cinque Ports Light Dragoons shot dead at least twelve people, some of whom were not involved in the protest. Liverpool was the commanding officer of the Dragoons, but he was not present. He was afterwards blamed for remaining at Haddington as his presence might have prevented the loss of control by his troops.

Strokes, Resignation, and Death

Liverpool suffered a severe cerebral haemorrhage on 17 February 1827. A few days afterwards, he could not speak and was paralysed on his right side. Despite this, his resignation was delayed, and in early March, George IV wrote a polite letter to his wife to say that he should not be upset by talk of resignation. He resigned on 9 April, fifty-one days after the stroke. He suffered a further stroke in July and a final, fatal one in December 1828. It was a prolonged and distressing death.

19

George Canning

1827

GEORGE CANNING HAS been called the Lost Leader. He was in poor health when he was appointed Prime Minister and died in office after just four months. He did very little in that time, so there is not much to report. There are enough things about his character and record to suggest that he might have been a great Prime Minister, but on the other hand, there are enough things to suggest that he might not. He could be abrasive and unpopular, and it would probably have been a bumpy ride. Several members of Lord Liverpool's cabinet refused to serve under him, and despite being a Tory, he was forced to appoint a number of Whigs to his government.

George Canning (1770–1827), portrait by Richard Evans (d. 1871). *National Portrait Gallery*

Canning had a flamboyant personality and a volcanic temperament. He had the unfortunate knack of irritating friends and upsetting enemies, but on the other hand, he had wit and great intelligence. He could be charming and was a man with convictions. He worked hard and was one of the greatest orators of his time. He could be jealous and was one of life's instinctive intriguers—something that made him enemies (Lord Castlereagh in particular). All this adds up to a combustible mix. The Lost Leader might have achieved great things, but his premiership might have been a short, sharp failure.

George Canning had Anglo-Irish origins. His father, who had great financial difficulties, abandoned his family and died on his son's first birthday. His Irish mother became a stage actress, an activity generally considered to be not respectable and which was sometimes held against the future Prime Minister. Canning was fortunate that a wealthy uncle took a hand in his upbringing and education, and as a consequence, he attended Eton College and then Christ Church, Oxford. He was a brilliant scholar and distinguished himself in many areas.

In 1793, he became an MP at the age of twenty-three. He was a follower of Pitt the Younger and held a number of positions, then resigned with Pitt in 1801. He was Treasurer of the Navy from 1804 to 1806 and President of the Board of Control from 1816 to 1821. However, he is best remembered for being Secretary of State for Foreign Affairs from 1807 to 1809, and again from 1822 until he became Prime Minister in 1827. He took the foreign office following the suicide of Lord Castlereagh and he was then concurrently Leader of the Commons until he became Prime Minister.

Many of his policies could be classed as liberal, which alienated the ultra-wing of the Tory party. He favoured Catholic emancipation and the abolition of slavery, but he opposed parliamentary reform.

A Critical Half Hour

According to A. J. P. Taylor, the Duke of Wellington recounted what Canning did when received by George IV.[1] He said that he stood with a watch in his hand and gave the King half an hour to make him Prime Minister.

Son of an Actress

Canning's mother did not live a conventional life, which was sometimes held against her son. She became an actress but did not achieve success. She lived with an actor who deserted her, and then with another man with whom she had several children. In 1827, Lord Grey said that 'the son of an actress is, *ipso facto*, disqualified from becoming Prime Minister'. Canning was largely brought up with his cousins.

Richard Brinsley Sheridan

Richard Brinsley Sheridan was a satirist, poet, playwright, and, for many years, owner of the London Theatre Royal, Drury Lane. For thirty-two years, he was also an MP. Despite his achievements and high income, he died in poverty. On the day of his funeral, a man dressed in mourning clothes called at the house and asked to pay his respects to an old friend. The coffin lid was raised and the man produced a bailiff's wand and arrested the corpse in respect of a debt of £500. As the funeral group assembled, Canning and Lord Sidmouth each wrote a cheque for £250 to discharge the debt. These were accepted by the bailiff and Sheridan was buried in Poets Corner at Westminster Abbey.[2]

Princess Caroline

In 1795, the future George IV married his cousin, Caroline of Brunswick. It was a disastrous union and the couple soon separated on bad terms. Canning became a close friend of Caroline, and although there is no evidence, it is possible that they had a brief sexual relationship. Whether or not this was the case, their friendship continued.

When he became King in 1820, a bitter George tried to divorce his wife. He failed and Caroline became his estranged Queen, but she died soon afterwards. Canning supported Caroline and resigned from his position as President of the Board of Control. Two years later, Castlereagh committed suicide and Canning was the obvious person to replace him as Foreign Secretary. The King resented Canning and was reluctant to make the appointment, but he was persuaded to do so.

A Talent for Verse

Canning had a talent for writing verse and enjoyed doing it. Examples have been given in this book in the chapters on Pitt the Younger and Henry Addington. The following was sent to the ambassador in The Hague in a cipher that he did not possess. When it was finally deciphered, the irritated ambassador read:

In matters of commerce the fault of the Dutch
is giving too little and asking too much;
With equal protection the French are content:
So we'll lay on Dutch bottoms just twenty per cent.

A cartoon of the Congress of Verona which met on 20 October 1822. The Duke of Wellington attended in place of Viscount Castlereagh who had committed suicide on 12 August of that same year. Wellington is shown in the background, Canning is depicted to the right in Greek costume.

The Duel with Lord Castlereagh

In 1809, Canning was involved in a series of disputes with his cabinet colleague, Lord Castlereagh. They affected the conduct of government business and Canning intrigued to have Castlereagh removed. In response, Castlereagh challenged Canning to a duel. Canning took it very seriously. He made his will and wrote a tender letter of farewell to his wife. He had never fired a gun in his life, so was at a disadvantage. Both men missed with their first shots. Then Canning missed again and suffered a minor wound in his thigh from Castlereagh's second shot. He was not seriously hurt. Duelling was illegal and caused some outrage. Both men felt obliged to resign from the cabinet.

Latin America and a Memorable Phrase

In his two spells as Foreign Secretary, Canning was closely involved in the affairs of Spain, Portugal, and Latin America. He worked towards the ending of the colonial power of the two countries in the region. His influence and British sea power were major factors. In 1825, Portugal recognised Brazil's independence, and in the same year, Mexico, Argentina, and Colombia were recognised by Britain. Speaking in the House of Commons, Canning stated: 'I resolved that if France had Spain it should not be Spain with the Indies. I called the new world into existence to redress the balance of the old'.

20

Frederick John Robinson

VISCOUNT GODERICH

1827–28

HE WAS BORN in 1782 and until 1827 was the Honourable F. J. Robinson. Shortly before becoming Prime Minister, he went to the Lords as Viscount Goderich, and in 1833, he became the Earl of Ripon. He is generally remembered as Viscount Goderich. He was an amiable man and a good administrator, but a disastrous Prime Minister. His period of office lasted just 144 days, which, apart from the term of his deceased predecessor, is the shortest of all the Prime Ministers.

Frederick John Robinson, Viscount Goderich (1782–1859), portrait by Sir Thomas Lawrence (1769–1830). *National Portrait Gallery*

The word disastrous is not misplaced, but it is only fair to mention that he was dealt a very difficult hand. Harold Wilson is not the only person to point out that he served in circumstances that would have tested a far greater statesman.[1] His Tory Party was split into four factions, divided over Catholic emancipation, parliamentary reform, and other matters, and he faced the enormously difficult task of getting his colleagues to pull together. To make matters worse, his cabinet, like Canning's, contained Whigs and they had their own opinions. They also had their own views on how many and which cabinet positions they should hold.

The King appointed Goderich in the hope and expectation that he would be malleable to royal wishes. Furthermore, he tried to impose his own views on who could hold cabinet positions. Goderich was not his own master. The situation required strong character, strong leadership, charisma, and determination. Goderich had his good points, but he was not the man to provide them. After a short time, the King turned to Wellington, who did not include Goderich in his cabinet. It is not clear whether the Prime Minister resigned or was dismissed, but in less than five months, he was gone.

At the age of twenty-two, Goderich was appointed private secretary to his mother's cousin, who was Lord Lieutenant of Ireland, and two years later, family connections via a pocket borough secured him a seat in Parliament. Under Lord Liverpool, he was Vice-President of the Board of Trade from 1812 to 1818, and he was then promoted to the cabinet as President of the Board of Trade and Treasurer of the Navy. Liverpool made him Chancellor of the Exchequer in 1823. He was a success in this position, but feeling under stress in January 1827, he requested and was granted a move to the Lords. In his very brief administration, Canning made him leader of the House of Lords and Secretary of State for War and the Colonies.

His dreadful period as Prime Minister was by no means the end of his career. He moved to the Whigs and served in Earl Grey's cabinet as Colonial Secretary, and then as Lord Privy Seal. Later, he moved back to the Tories and served Robert Peel as President of the Board of Trade and from 1843 to 1846 as President of the Board of Control. He then retired from politics.

Goderich was progressively a Pittite, a Canningite, a Whig, a Stanleyite, a Conservative, and a Peelite, and in addition, he was at one time close to Lord Castlereagh. Affiliations were then generally much looser than is the case now, but one is minded to think of the song 'The Vicar of Bray'. The 'facts' on which the song is based are dubious in the extreme, but it tells the story of a clergyman who more than once adapted his religious principles in order to keep his living at Bray in Berkshire.

We should give Goderich credit for his good nature and his administrative ability. His record in various offices was no worse than that of many others, but he is mainly remembered for being a very poor Prime Minister. Disraeli summed him up with the words 'a transient and embarrassed phantom'.[2]

A Unique Distinction

Goderich was the only Prime Minister never to face Parliament.

Nicknames

During his career Goderich acquired no fewer than four nicknames.

Blubberer

Goderich was a man easily moved to tears. He was sometimes seen to cry and he did so when he resigned as Prime Minister. By some accounts, the King lent him his handkerchief.

Prosperity Robinson

He must have liked this one. It was accorded to him when the country's economic position improved and people became more prosperous while he was Chancellor of the Exchequer.

Goody Goderich

William Cobbett called him this because of his lack of force of character and the name stuck.[3]

The Duke of Phussandbussle

Goderich went about his business with a great deal of fuss and bustle, and in 1813, some of his companions dubbed him The Duke of Phussandbussle. One of them left a letter on his desk addressed in this manner. Goderich, as was his way, accepted the nickname in good part and started referring to himself as the Grand Duke.[4]

A Difficult Wife

Many, but by no means all Prime Ministers have drawn strength from the understanding and support of their spouse. Goderich was one that did not. She was generally unhappy and at times her behaviour almost amounted to madness. She constantly demanded a great deal of his time and attention, and her husband generally gave it to her. The diarist Charles Greville wrote:

... in the midst of all the squabbles which preceded the break up of his administration Goderich went whining to the King and said 'Your Majesty don't know what vexation I have at home with my wife's ill health'. The King telling the story said 'G.d ... the fellow, what did he bother me about his wife for? I didn't want to hear all his stories about her health'.[5]

Apparently her health and attitude improved in later years.

A misunderstanding in Court

Goderich once sat next to Lord Lyndhurst as two lawyers presented a case in court. Goderich whispered to him, 'I don't know how the case may be decided; but, in my opinion, Mr Hart has so completely answered Mr Bell that he has not a leg to stand on.'

Lyndhurst whispered back, 'I cannot agree with you, for ... they are both on the same side.'[6]

The Corn Laws

The Corn Laws imposed restrictions and tariffs on imported grain. They favoured landowners and farmers and disadvantaged the poor who had to pay more for food; they were enormously resented and caused much discontent. In 1815, it fell to Goderich to present to the Commons the Bill that introduced them. This triggered riots in which his house and its contents were badly damaged, and in which one person was killed. In 1841, serving in the government of Sir Robert Peel, he was given the task of reforming the Laws. They were repealed in 1846 and then Goderich resigned and retired. He claimed to have been against the principle of the laws that he had introduced.

A link to 1964

The son of Viscount Goderich served in the same government as Sir Winston Churchill, who retired from the House of Commons in 1964. The 1st Marquess of Ripon was born in 10 Downing Street on 24 October 1827. He served in every Liberal cabinet from 1861 to 1908, when he retired at the age of eighty. From 1905 to 1908, he was Leader of the House of Lords in the cabinet of Sir Henry Campbell-Bannerman. Sir Winston was Under Secretary for the Colonies in the same government.

21

Arthur Wellesley

DUKE OF WELLINGTON

1828–30; 1834

Arthur Wellesley, Duke of Wellington (1769–1852), portrait by Sir Thomas Lawrence (1769–1830). *English Heritage Images*

THE DUKE OF Wellington is the only Prime Minister most famous for what he or she did outside politics. He was a great soldier and a great man, but not a great Prime Minister. He was born in Dublin in 1869. His father was the Earl of Mornington, an Irish peer. Arthur's original name was Arthur Wesley, but in 1798, he started signing himself Arthur Wellesley. He was made Viscount Wellesley in 1809 and progressed through the ranks of the peerage, becoming the Duke of Wellington in 1814.

His first military campaign was in the Netherlands, but he made his name over eight years fighting in India. Following this, he was elected to the Commons in 1806 and was soon appointed Chief Secretary for Ireland. This position had to be resigned in 1808 because he was required to lead his country's campaign against Napoleonic France in Spain and Portugal. It was a long, hard, and ultimately successful five-year slog. Wellington, hampered by inferior resources, was brilliant. In 1815, Napoleon escaped from Elba and Wellington rushed back from the Congress of Vienna to lead the consequent military campaign. On 18 June 1815, his triumph at Waterloo ended the Napoleonic Wars and resulted in Napoleon's final exile on St Helena. It was his final and greatest victory.

Wellington joined Lord Liverpool's cabinet in 1819 as Master-General of Ordnance. In the turbulent times that followed, he generally advocated repressive measures and he became a leading member of the ultra-wing of the badly divided Tory Party. He strongly opposed Catholic emancipation. He had very profound differences with Canning and Goderich and did not serve in either of their brief administrations.

Following the Goderich shambles, the King needed a decisive Prime Minister and sent for Wellington. This was a man who believed in firm, autocratic government and was determined to provide it. He gave the orders and demanded that his cabinet colleagues follow them. It was a good way of winning the Battle of Waterloo, but not such a good way of running a government. To show his firm intentions, he symbolically rode 'Copenhagen' to Downing Street when he took up his appointment as Prime Minister. This was the splendid, but now elderly horse that had served him so well at Waterloo. Following his first cabinet meeting as Prime Minister, he said: 'An extraordinary affair. I gave them their orders and they wanted to stay and discuss them'.

Throughout his military and political career, Wellington felt a very pronounced obligation of duty. He did not want to be Prime Minister, but he took the job to serve his country and his king. Throughout his political career, he put the interests of his country first and the interests of his party and himself second.

Wellington's two years and ten months as Prime Minister were not happy and not a success. They were dominated by two very different issues. The long-smouldering issue of Catholic emancipation came to a head, and he bowed to the inevitable and forced the measure through. This was despite his personal opposition, the opposition of a significant part of his party, and the outrage of George IV who said that it violated his coronation oath.

The other divisive issue was parliamentary reform. Wellington was vehemently opposed and would not bow to the inevitable on this. Not only was he opposed to particular reforms, he was opposed to any reform at all. He wanted to keep intact the absurd arrangement whereby one man at Old Sarum could effectively choose two MPs. He had ratted on Catholic emancipation and he would not rat on this. It led to his loss of office.

Wellington's career, influence, and status were most certainly not at an end. He served twenty-six days as the interim Prime Minister in 1834 and was Leader of the House of Lords in Sir Robert Peel's second government. He was Commander in Chief of the Army until the day he died. His many other positions included Lord Lieutenant of Hampshire, Constable of the Tower of London, Lord Warden of the Cinque Ports, Elder brother of Trinity House, and Chancellor of Oxford University. In the words of the title of the second volume of Elizabeth Longford's biography, he truly was a 'Pillar of State'.

A Delayed and Unhappy Marriage

At a time when his position and prospects were not apparent, Wellington fell in love with Kitty Pakenham, the daughter of Lord Longford. The convention of the time required the marriage to have the permission of the head of Kitty's family, which, as her father had recently died, was her brother. This was Tom, who was younger than Wellington, and he felt that his sister could do better. So he said no. Wellington accepted the decision, but told Kitty that when his situation in life had improved, he would ask her again.

On his return from India eleven years later, he proposed for a second time. He did so by letter and there had been no contact in the meantime. Kitty was anxious that he should meet her and should not be bound by his promise if his feelings had changed. However, Wellington was a man who knew his duty and thought that this was not necessary. Not surprisingly, brother Tom did not object to the marriage this time.

When, just before the wedding, they did meet, Wellington was disappointed. He turned to his brother and whispered, 'She's turned ugly by jove.'[1] Kitty's looks had faded badly and she had become introspective. She later suffered with very poor eyesight and it did not help that she was irresponsible with money. She tried hard to please him but did not succeed. It was very sad. Wellington forged friendships with other women and conducted a number of affairs. They did, however, draw closer during Kitty's last illness. She died in 1831. Wellington lived until 1852.

Intimate Relations with Napoleon's Mistresses

While ambassador in Paris in 1814, Wellington definitely enjoyed intimate relations with one of Napoleon's mistresses and probably with a second. Josephine Weimer was walking through a park when Wellington stopped his carriage and offered her a lift. Was Wellington a better lover then Napoleon? According to the lady, Wellington was '*de beaucoup le plus fort*'.[2]

A cartoon of the Duke of Wellington trying to stem the tide of demand for parliamentary reform, published *c.* 1830. *Alan Sutton Collection*

Giuseppina Grassini was an Italian opera singer and she denied an affair with him, but it was probably true. He kept a portrait of her in his room, which was indicative, but on the other hand, it was next to a portrait of Pope Pius VII.[3] Portraits in rooms are not conclusive evidence of the existence of sexual relations.

Lady Frances Wedderburn-Webster

Lady Frances Wedderburn-Webster was the wife of one of Wellington's officers and he became friendly with her when his army was stationed in Brussels prior to the Battle of Waterloo. The two were seen to go into a hollow in a Brussels park together, and Wellington was talking to her at the Duchess of Richmond's ball when news arrived that Napoleon had crossed the frontier from France at Charleroi. On the morning of the battle, Wellington rose at 3 a.m. and wrote numerous letters, one to Lady Frances advising her to leave Brussels and go to Antwerp. On the evening of the great victory, he wrote to her again, this time to tell her that it was safe to be in Brussels. Wellington subsequently denied that there had been any impropriety.

No Submission to Blackmail

Harriette Wilson was a courtesan who had Wellington among her long list of prominent clients. In later life, she fell on hard times and decided to publish her memoirs in order to raise some money. Just before publication, her agent wrote to Wellington and other prominent clients asking for money in order to ensure that their names were not mentioned. It is widely, but mistakenly believed that Wellington wrote 'Publish and be damned' on the letter and posted it back. This is not true, but it is true that he indignantly refused to pay. Harriette did publish and Wellington featured with considerable details. However, the book contained a number of obvious untruths. The public generally sympathised with Wellington.

Angela Burdett-Coutts

Angela Burdett-Coutts was a fabulously wealthy heiress and philanthropist, and she enjoyed a long and chaste friendship with Wellington. They exchanged more than 800 letters. At the age of thirty-three, she proposed marriage to him. He was seventy-eight at the time, and he turned her down in the most charming way possible. Angela must have felt an attraction for men with a very different age from her own. At the age of sixty-seven, she married her twenty-nine-year-old secretary.

A Very Poor Shot

Wellington enjoyed shooting, but he was a notoriously poor shot. At one shooting party, Lady Shelley advised her daughter to stand behind him—he winged a dog, a gamekeeper, and an old lady doing her washing. Lady Shelley told her, 'This ought to be the proudest moment of your life. You have the distinction of being shot by the great Duke of Wellington.'

Wellington's Watch

Sir Thomas Lawrence painted a famous picture of Wellington standing on a battlefield at Waterloo, and it depicted him holding a watch. He complained that it made him look as though he was anxiously waiting for the arrival of the Prussians, so it was painted out and a telescope substituted.

The King's Delusion

Wellington could be tactful, even though he was not noted for it, and at times, he was exceedingly untactful. This was never more needed than when dealing with George IV. One of the King's many ridiculous delusions was that, disguised as General Bock, he had personally led a great charge at the Battle of Salamanca. He would assert this as a fact and bawl 'Was that not so?' across the dinner table to Wellington. He invariably replied, 'I have often heard your majesty say so.'

The Cato Street Conspiracy

The Cato Street Conspiracy was a plot to assassinate the whole cabinet, including Wellington, for whom the conspirators had a special hatred. They intended to do it during a dinner to be held at the Lord President's Grosvenor Square mansion on 23 February 1820. Fortunately, the plotters were very inept and the details of the plan were disclosed by an informer. Wellington characteristically proposed that they should attend the dinner but that each cabinet member should take a brace of pistols. They would then join servants and the police in detaining the assassins, while soldiers would surround the mansion then burst in. This brave, but foolhardy idea was rejected by his cabinet colleagues and the fourteen conspirators were detained by other means. Five ringleaders were convicted of treason and hanged in public. They were not without supporters and a sympathetic crowd attacked the hangman.

God Save the Queen

Princess Caroline had been separated from the Prince Regent for a long time, and during the separation had lived a dissolute and immoral life, though not as dissolute and immoral as the life of her husband. On the Prince's accession to the throne (as George IV), she returned to Britain to claim her place as Queen. The King would have none of it and persuaded his ministers to introduce a Bill to deprive her of all her prerogatives and dissolve the marriage. On 5 July 1820, a Bill was duly introduced, and although Wellington had a very low opinion of his King, as a loyal monarchist, he gave it his support. The mob sided with the Queen, not because they approved of her, but because they disapproved of the King and his ministers. Shortly afterwards, Wellington was surrounded by a gang of road menders who demanded that he say 'God Save the Queen'. 'Well gentlemen,' he replied, 'since you will have it, God Save the Queen—and may all your wives be like her.'

This is a good story, but accounts differ about who said the words. They are often attributed to Wellington, but claims are also made for Lord Anglesey and others.

An Apology from a French Officer

Towards the very end of the Peninsular Campaign, Wellington, accompanied by just two officers, rode forward to reconnoitre. He was fired upon by a French sentry, but the shot missed. There was an informal understanding that pickets did not fire upon one another and a French officer came forward to deliver an apology. Wellington, who spoke good French, had a conversation with him before riding off. Had the French officer acted differently and had Wellington been killed or captured, the later Battle of Waterloo might have had a different outcome.

The Duel

Duelling was illegal and indeed amounted to murder or attempted murder. Nevertheless, at 7.45 a.m. on Sunday 21 March 1829, at Battersea Fields, Wellington fought a duel with the 9th Earl of Winchelsea. Wellington, who was Prime Minister at the time, was a notoriously bad shot, aged fifty-nine, and, of course, a courageous man. Both men lived to tell the tale. The cause was Wellington's offence at Winchelsea's remarks on his policy of Catholic emancipation, including the words 'an insidious design for the infringement of our liberties and the introduction of Popery into every department of the State'. Wellington's response was to demand 'that satisfaction ... which a gentlemen has a right to require, and which a gentleman never refuses to give'.

The Secretary at War, Sir Henry Hardinge, was Wellington's second and Lord Falmouth acted for Winchelsea. However, neither was able to load the pistols, Hardinge because he only had one arm and Falmouth because he was shaking too badly. After the ground had been paced out, Wellington objected to the Earl's position and called out, 'Don't stick him up so near the ditch. If I hit him, he will tumble in.' At the order to fire, Winchelsea kept his hand firmly by his side. Seeing this, Wellington, who had intended to aim at his legs, deliberately shot wide. Winchelsea then fired into the air and his second read out a prepared statement that was rejected by Wellington because it did not amount to an apology. After a suitable amendment had been made, Wellington bowed, touched his hat, said, 'Good morning my Lords,' and rode away. Wellington received a lot of criticism, but his popularity, which was low at the time, rose as a result.

Huskisson

William Huskisson was Colonial Secretary and a leading member of Wellington's cabinet. His relationship with the Prime Minister was not an easy one, and he had previously come close to resignation. Matters came to a head when Huskisson failed to vote with the government over a bill to absorb a rotten borough into another constituency. Following this, he submitted his resignation to Wellington. This was in accordance with convention, but it was not done in the hope or expectation that it would be accepted. However, Wellington thought differently and did accept the resignation. Horrified friends and associates of the Colonial Secretary sent one of their number to explain that Wellington had misunderstood and there had been a mistake. The Duke responded by saying, 'There is no mistake, there can be no mistake, there shall be no mistake,' and he then went for a walk in case another envoy or Huskisson himself arrived. Huskisson was an able man and his loss weakened the government, especially as other members of the cabinet felt obliged to resign too.

The tale has a tragic and poignant ending. In September 1830, Wellington made his first train trip as a passenger on the inaugural run of the Liverpool to Manchester railway, and when the train stopped to take on water, he encountered Huskisson. The two men shook hands, but very unfortunately, Huskisson stepped on to the track and was knocked down and killed by Stephenson's *Rocket*, which was travelling in the other direction. Wellington was very upset and only continued his journey when told that there might be a riot in Manchester if he failed to appear.

A cartoon of the Duke of Wellington, pipe in mouth rake in one hand and his army uniform in the other; Robert Peel is pointing to the threatening mob. The 'reign coming on' was the accession of William IV, 26 June 1830, who succeeded his elder brother George IV. Cartoon published *c*. 1830. *Alan Sutton Collection*

A Favour Repaid

George Hudson, the Conservative MP and so-called Railway King, advised Wellington's two sisters to sell their large holdings in a railway company that he believed would shortly collapse. They did so and saved a great deal of money when the collapse duly happened. A grateful Wellington asked Hudson if there was anything that he could do to repay the favour. Hudson replied that his daughter was at an expensive private school and was being victimised because of her humble origins. Wellington visited her at the school, brought flowers, and took her out to tea.[4]

Interim Prime Minister

In 1834, when the Tories returned to power, Wellington declined the position of Prime Minister and Peel was chosen instead. Peel was in Italy and Wellington took the position until his return twenty-six days later. He took most of the ministries himself and rode from building to building to sign papers. Crowds followed him from place to place.

Queen Victoria's Grief

Wellington's wish to be buried at Walmer was disregarded and instead he was interred near Nelson in St Paul's Cathedral. It was the greatest funeral that London had ever seen and Queen Victoria' grief was palpable. She had been given a lock of his hair to have enclosed in a gold bracelet and she had been the first visitor at his lying in state. However, her distress had been so great that she had been unable to approach the coffin. Estimates of crowd numbers, then as now, tend to be exaggerated and unreliable, but some estimates of the crowd lining the funeral route put it at 1½ million. If this remarkable figure was correct, it amounted to 8 per cent of the total population of England and Wales.

22

Charles

2nd EARL GREY

1830–34

To students of parliamentary democracy mention of Earl Grey will evoke mention of the Great Reform Act and a short, reforming ministry. To millions of others, the name will probably evoke mention of Earl Grey tea. Both the students and the tea connoisseurs will probably think that he was a great man.

Charles, 2nd Earl Grey (1764–1845), portrait by an unknown artist in the style of Sir Thomas Lawrence, *c.* 1828. *National Portrait Gallery*

Grey came from and loved Northumberland, England's most northerly county and the one furthest from the capital. Born in 1764, he was the second but first surviving son of a distinguished general who had been elevated to the peerage. Charles was educated at Eton and Trinity College, Cambridge, then elected to the Commons for a Northumberland constituency at the tender age of twenty-two. He moved to the House of Lords in 1807.

On arrival at Westminster, he rapidly made a name for himself and became recognised as a very good speaker. He was a leading Whig and supporter of Charles James Fox, and his democratic instincts ensured his consistent and at times unpopular support for Catholic emancipation and parliamentary reform.

Grey almost did what Ramsay Macdonald and Tony Blair would do later, namely become Prime Minister without having held any previous government office. He reached the age of sixty-six before becoming PM, and his only period of office was thirteen months in Lord Grenville's ministry of all the talents, initially as First Lord of the Admiralty and then as Secretary of State for Foreign Affairs. Grenville's ministry ended because Grey and others refused to promise the King that they would not raise the issue of Catholic emancipation.

Following the death of Fox in 1806, Grey took on the leadership of the Whigs, and he did this in opposition for no less than twenty-four years. His very long period out of government, both before and after 1806–07, was partly due to the dominance of the Tory Party and partly due to his views on Catholic emancipation, parliamentary reform, and other matters.

The 1832 Reform Act has justifiably become known as the Great Reform Act. The franchise was extended, parliamentary seats were redistributed, the rotten boroughs were eliminated, and voting qualifications were made more uniform. It was a formidable achievement.

Grey had to contend with a Tory opposition that had an overwhelming majority in the House of Lords. He also had to contend with William IV, who was generally supportive but at times ambivalent. He secured the King's promise that he would, if absolutely necessary, create enough new peers to override the Tory majority in the Lords. He managed his own party, whose members wanted reform but had different views on the changes that they wanted. It was all done with the country in an uproar. During the worst of the disturbances, around 400 people died in Bristol. This happened after the second Reform Bill was rejected by the House of Lords.

The Reform Act was not the only achievement of Grey's government. There was a notable factory act and slavery was abolished throughout the British Empire. However, the new Poor Law was a mistake. He left office due to cabinet disagreements over Irish issues.

Earl Grey Tea

The facts are not absolutely clear, but it is believed that a Chinese diplomat presented Grey with a box of the bergamot-oil-flavoured tea as a gift. It went so well with the limey water at his house at Howick that he asked a tea merchant to produce further supplies for him. The rest, as they say, is history.

A Terrifying Experience

At the age of just six, Grey was despatched on a four-day journey to a school in Marylebone, London. Shortly after arrival, he fell ill and was sent to convalesce with a nurse who lived in nearby Tyburn. While in her care, she took him to watch some public executions. In those days, hanging meant slow strangulation, not the quick death that was the consequence of a sharp drop. Not surprisingly, he was terrified and was still suffering nightmares more than fifty years later.[1]

An Affair with Georgiana, Duchess of Devonshire and an Illegitimate Child

Georgiana was a noted beauty and leader of fashion. She had married the cold, unemotional, and adulterous, but very rich and powerful 5th Duke of Devonshire on her seventeenth birthday. This was the woman with whom the unmarried Charles Grey commenced an affair. At the time, he was in his mid-twenties and she was seven years older. The affair resulted in pregnancy. The Duke ordered Georgiana to give birth in France, then give the child away. To compel her acquiescence, he told her that if she did not do so, he would ensure that she would never see her much-loved other three children again. The law at the time allowed married men, and not just rich and powerful ones, to do this.

Georgiana did give birth in France and the child was given to Charles Grey's parents, who brought her up as though she was Charles's sister. The situation affected Georgiana badly, but Charles much less so. Shortly afterwards, he married Mary Ponsonby.

Bad Relations with Two Kings

Grey's views were often unwelcome to George III and George IV, which was one of the reasons that he was so long out of office. His sometimes injudicious remarks did not help. He said of Lady Hertford—mistress of George IV when he was Prince of Wales—that she was 'an unseen and pestilent influence that lurked behind the throne'.[2]

A Cabinet of Aristocrats

When Grey became Prime Minister, all thirteen members of his cabinet (including himself) held hereditary titles.

Marriage, Children, and Life at Howick

Grey married Mary Ponsonby when he was thirty and she was eighteen. After a stillbirth in 1796, the couple had no fewer than fifteen surviving children. The first was born on 7 April 1797 and the last on 15 February 1819, when Mary was just short of her forty-fourth birthday. So she gave birth fifteen times in less than twenty-two years. The strain of almost continual pregnancy and childbirth did not prevent her living to the age of eighty-five.

Grey loved his family and he loved family life at Howick, his estate on the Northumberland coast north of Newcastle. His children were all educated at home. He took every opportunity to spend time at Howick, and his colleagues at Westminster sometimes felt that he went there too soon and came back too late. When his term as Prime Minister finished, he departed for Howick in a very happy frame of mind.

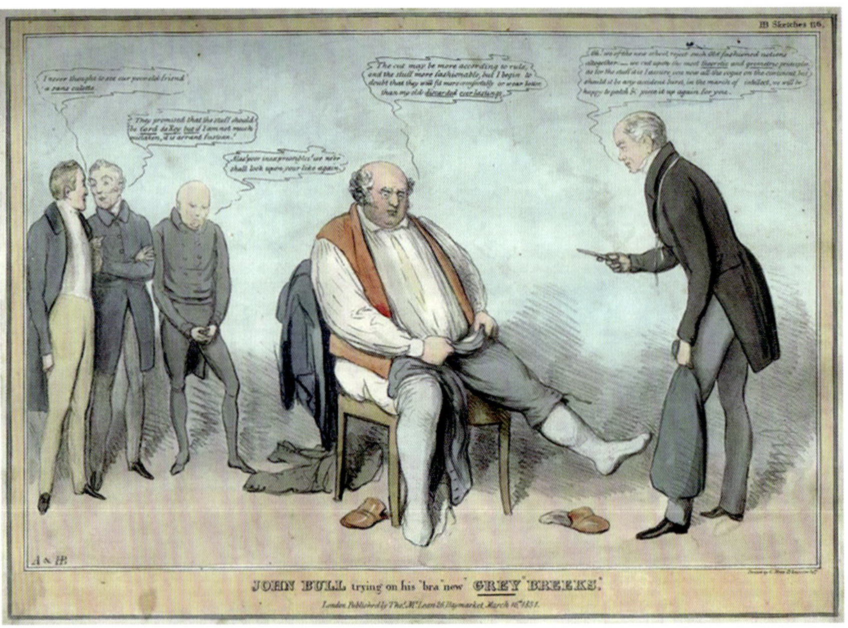

John Bull trying on his 'bra' new' Grey Breeks, a cartoon by John Doyle, published 26 March 1831.

23

William Lamb

2ND VISCOUNT MELBOURNE

1834; 1835–41

WILLIAM LAMB, BORN in 1779 into an aristocratic Whig family, was the second son of the 1st Viscount Melbourne and his wife Elizabeth. He became heir to his father's title on the death of his older brother in 1805, and became Lord Melbourne in 1828 on the death of his father. He was elected to the Commons in 1806 and remained a backbench Whig MP until 1827. He is not generally recognised as an above average Prime Minister and is quite often regarded as a below average one, but he rendered a very significant service to his monarch and the country. On the accession of Victoria at the age of eighteen, he gave her enormous and valuable support and guidance.

William Lamb, Viscount Melbourne (1779–1845), portrait by Sir Edwin Henry Landseer (1802–1873). *National Portrait Gallery*

Victoria had lost her father when just eight months old and had had a very sheltered upbringing, so much so that she slept in her mother's bedroom until the day in 1837 that she became Queen at the age of eighteen. She needed help, guidance, friendship, and instruction about her role and duties. Prime Minister Melbourne was on hand to provide all of these things. For more than two years, he spent many hours of many days in her company and writing to her.

So close was the relationship that some thought that it was improper and that a romance had developed. The Queen was even scurrilously referred to as Mrs Melbourne. There was in fact no impropriety. Melbourne was forty years older than Victoria and fondly looked on her as he might a favourite niece. It was friendship and mutual respect, but nothing more.

Lord Melbourne was a cultured man with a friendly disposition, which partly accounted for his rise in politics. He did not display strongly held convictions and was a man willing to compromise. He was a non-radical Whig, but at times could well have been a liberal Tory. Indeed, his first government appointment was Chief Secretary for Ireland in 1827–28, in the short-lived Tory governments of Canning and Goderich.

Melbourne served as Home Secretary under Earl Grey. He did not personally approve of parliamentary reform, but he knew that it was essential and gave it his reluctant support. He was a success in the job, dealing firmly with unrest in the country. Examples were his support for the transportation of the Tolpuddle martyrs and the way that he handled the Swing Riots by agricultural workers. Despite this, he wisely resisted the clamour for more extreme laws and measures.

Melbourne succeeded Grey because he was acceptable to the King and because he was best placed to hold together the different Whig factions. Lord Durham said: 'Melbourne is the only man to be Prime Minister because he is the only one of whom none of us would be jealous'.[1] His acceptability to William IV only lasted a few months because the King found the Whig reforms unpalatable. He dismissed Melbourne and turned to Peel, this being the last time that a monarch tried to impose a government that did not have a majority in parliament.

It did not last long. Peel's disappointing performance in a general election saw Melbourne back in office after just five months, and he served for a further six years. There were Poor Law reforms, local government reforms, and other measures. However, there were financial difficulties, and the government ran out of steam and became fractious. The end came when it lost a confidence motion and did badly in the ensuing general election.

Doubtful Parentage

William Lamb's mother and father enjoyed what we now call an open marriage—at least his mother did. There was adultery by both parents and William's biological father may have been Lord Egremont with whom his mother was conducting an affair at the relevant time. His brother George was possibly fathered by the Prince of Wales.

A Turbulent Marriage

In 1805, Melbourne married Caroline Ponsonby, who on marriage became Lady Caroline Lamb. She was spoiled, very highly strung, and caused him no end of trouble. Her behaviour was at times bizarre and scandalous. Her most notorious affair was with Lord Byron, during which she coined the famous phrase 'mad, bad and dangerous to know'. Following Byron's breaking off the affair, she penned a scandalous novel. It contained thinly veiled caricatures of Byron, herself, and several prominent people. It was a sensation and led to her being ostracised. Throughout their marriage, Melbourne was tolerant and supportive, and he always had feelings for her. They separated in 1825 and she died three years later at the age of forty-two. This was six years before Melbourne became Prime Minister.

A Handicapped Son

Melbourne and Caroline's first child died shortly after birth and their second, a boy, was mentally handicapped. They did not send him away but looked after him themselves. He died eight years after his mother at the age of twenty-nine.

Two Suits for Damages

Two aggrieved husbands brought civil suits for damages against Melbourne, alleging seduction of their wives. In both cases, the evidence was very weak and the actions failed. However, it should be noted that Melbourne left one of the women an annuity in his will.[2]

Beatings

One of the suits for damages was brought by the Irish peer Lord Branden. Melbourne's biographer, Philip Ziegler, noted that thirty-six out of the forty letters between Melbourne and Lady Branden contained references to beatings.[3]

Disrespect for Honours

Melbourne had little regard for honours, whether for himself or others. He turned down the garter for himself four times, saying on one of the occasions: 'The garter: what would be the use of my taking it? I cannot bribe myself'.[4] Told that a marquis wanted another honour, he said: 'Confound it, does he want a garter for his other leg?'[5] One wishes that some more recent Prime Ministers had displayed similar principles.

An Unhealthy Lifestyle

The future Prime Minister Lord Palmerston was Melbourne's brother-in-law. Palmerston once said that Melbourne ate too much and took no exercise.[6]

Some Wise and Unwise Words to Queen Victoria

When the Queen wanted to make Albert King Consort, he stated: 'For God's sake, let's have no more of it, Ma'am. If you once get the English people into the way of making Kings, you'll get them into the way of unmaking them'.[7]

The Queen told Melbourne that one of the things that she liked most about Albert was the way that he paid no attention to other women. 'No, that sort of thing is apt to come later,' Melbourne replied.[8] The Queen was not pleased.

Burial Place

Lord Melbourne is one of two Prime Ministers buried at St Etheldreda's church next to Hatfield. The other is Lord Salisbury.

24

Sir Robert Peel

2nd BARONET

1834–35; 1841–46

Sir Robert Peel was born in 1788 and his background was different from that of previous Prime Ministers. His father, Robert Peel, 1st Baronet, was an MP who owned one of the largest of the Lancashire cotton mills. The mill owners do not have a good reputation, but by the standards of the time, he was one of the better ones and he promoted legislation to benefit factory workers. The second Sir Robert was, to use a modern term, new money, and after the death of his father in 1830, he had a lot of it.

Sir Robert Peel, 2nd Baronet (1788–1850), portrait by Henry William Pickersgill (1782–1875). *National Portrait Gallery*

Peel as we will now call him was educated at Harrow and Christ Church, Oxford, where he obtained a double first in classics and mathematics. Before his twenty-second birthday, his father's money and influence secured his election as an MP. This was for the constituency of Cashel, Tipperary, a rotten borough with only twenty-four electors. It was immediately clear that he was destined for great things. His maiden speech was so outstanding that the Speaker described it as the best first speech since William Pitt.

Peel was Chief Secretary for Ireland from 1812 to 1818, and while holding this position, he acquired the nickname 'Orange Peel'. It was a reference to the Protestant Orange Order and because of his opposition to more rights for Catholics.

He is remembered as an outstanding Home Secretary, holding the position from January 1822 to April 1827 and from January 1828 to November 1830. His many humane reforms included reducing by a hundred the number of offences that carried the death penalty, and in 1829, he was the founder of London's Metropolitan Police. In his honour, the early officers became known as bobbies and peelers. In the opinion of Harold Wilson, he was undoubtedly the greatest reforming Home Secretary of all time.[1]

While Home Secretary for the second time, he did what was necessary and, with Wellington, secured Catholic emancipation. This volte-face infuriated many of his supporters and laid the foundation of a reputation of a man sometimes willing to desert his principles.

Peel's first spell as Prime Minister lasted less than four months, and following a disappointing general election result, he resigned in April 1835. During the campaign, his statement to the electors of Tamworth became known as the 'Tamworth Manifesto'. It was a break with the past and one of the foundations of the modern Conservative Party. It pledged acceptance of the 1832 Reform Act, the reform of abuses, and directed the Tory Party in a new direction.

Peel's second government started in 1841 and lasted five years. He became Prime Minister at a time of economic recession, which made things difficult, and he reintroduced income tax, which has remained with us to this day. It was a reforming administration, the most notable measure being the Factory Act 1844. This restricted the number of hours that women and children could work in factories and imposed basic safety requirements. His father would have been proud.

The latter part of his second ministry was blighted (an apt word) by the Irish potato famine. For this and other reasons, he came to the conclusion that the Corn Laws would have to be repealed. These levied tariffs on imported grain and kept the price of food artificially high. They benefited the land owners at the expense of the consumers, including the very poor. Supporters of the laws contended that they gave landowners an incentive to increase production. Peel's actions split what we will still call the Tory Party. His bitter critics said that it was another reversal of policy, following Catholic emancipation and other retreats. Due to the support of the Whigs, he succeeded in getting the laws repealed, but two-thirds of the Tories voted against him. He resigned a few days later.

Sir Robert died tragically at the early age of sixty-two. He was thrown from his horse, which then stumbled on him. In the view of many historians and commentators, he ranks highly in the list of Prime Ministers. This is my opinion too.

Wife and Family

In 1820, Sir Robert married Julia, the youngest and very attractive daughter of General Sir John Floyd, 1st Baronet. The couple enjoyed a happy marriage, which resulted in seven children—five boys and two girls. Four of the boys achieved considerable distinction. Three of them became MPs and one of them served as Chief Secretary for Ireland in the government of Lord Palmerston. A second became Speaker of the House of Commons and a third was a railway commissioner as well as an MP. A fourth son, Sir William Peel, became a naval captain and was awarded the Victoria Cross during the Crimean War.

A Somewhat Cold Manner

Peel sometimes displayed a cold and aloof manner to the world. It often did not reflect his true feelings and he sometimes apologised for it.[2] Queen Victoria found her relationship with him difficult, and the Duke of Wellington once said: 'How are we to get on? I have no small talk and Peel has no manners'.[3] Disraeli cruelly remarked: 'The right honourable gentleman is reminiscent of a poker. The only difference is that a poker gives off the occasional signs of warmth'.

A Tragic Murder

In January 1843, a twenty-nine-year-old Scot called Daniel M'Naghten (sometimes called McNaughtan) shot and killed Peel's private secretary, Edward Drummond. M'Naghten was suffering paranoid delusions and he thought that Drummond was Robert Peel. He pulled the trigger because he believed that he was being persecuted by the Tories and followed by their spies. M'Naghten was found not guilty on the grounds of insanity and spent the rest of his life in Bethlem and Broadmoor hospitals. Queen Victoria did not approve of the jury's verdict. Peel himself, though very sad, took it all stoically and did not alter his behaviour. The rules used for deciding McNaghten's sanity passed into legal history as the 'McNaghten Rules'.

Degraded Honours

Peel's attitude to honours reflected the views of his predecessor, Lord Melbourne. He said: 'It seems to me that the distinction of the Peerage, and every other distinction, has been degraded by the profuse and incautious use which has been made of them'.[4]

The Bedchamber Crisis

In May 1839, Melbourne, following a bad parliamentary vote, decided to resign. Wellington declined Victoria's invitation to form a government and she then reluctantly turned to Peel. He accepted the invitation, but only on the understanding that she would replace some of her ladies in waiting. They were Whig supporters, and some of them were the wives and daughters of Whig politicians. Victoria, not yet twenty, was distraught and refused. She did not want to lose the trusted Melbourne and she did not want to lose her friends the ladies. Peel was adamant and refused to serve. Melbourne, wrongly believing that Peel had demanded the replacement of all the ladies and not just some of them, agreed to carry on. There was a principle at stake, but it was all rather silly. It was two more years before Peel became Prime Minister for the second time.

Dealing with a Perfidious Disraeli

Disraeli was at his worst in the debate on the repeal of the Corn Laws. Leading the charge against Peel, he acted without principle. He almost certainly did not believe that the Corn Laws should be retained and he did nothing to reinstate them when he was in a position to do so. Peel challenged him by asking, 'why then had he been ready, as I think he was, to unite his fortunes with mine in office?' Disraeli insisted that he had never solicited office. Peel almost certainly had in his pocket Disraeli's letter doing just that, but he did not use it.[5] Why not? We will never know, but perhaps he was too much of a gentleman to use a private letter.

25

Lord John Russell

1st EARL RUSSELL

1846–52; 1865–66

Born in 1792, Lord John Russell became an MP in 1813. He was the third son of the 6th Duke of Bedford, which meant that he came from one of the grandest and richest of the great Whig families. Despite this, he did not have much money. As the son of a duke, he had the courtesy title of Lord, but sat in the House of Commons. In 1861, he was created Earl Russell and moved to the House of Lords. From 1846 to 1852, he was the last Whig Prime Minister. Then, thirteen years later, in 1865, he became the first Liberal Prime Minister, though only for eight months.

Lord John Russell, 1st Earl Russell (1792–1878), portrait by Sir Francis Grant (1803–1878). *National Portrait Gallery*

In the middle years of the nineteenth century, Russell was a leading Whig and Liberal statesman. As well as being twice Prime Minister, he was Leader of the Commons, Leader of the Opposition, Paymaster of the Forces, Home Secretary, Colonial Secretary, Minister without Portfolio, Lord President of the Council, and twice Foreign Secretary. It is a substantial record.

Russell's name will forever be linked with the cause of parliamentary reform. Serving under Earl Grey, he introduced two unsuccessful reform bills and then the one that became the great 1832 Reform Act.

Russell consistently favoured liberal measures. He was always a strong supporter of free trade and backed Peel's move to repeal the Corn Laws. He believed in Catholic emancipation and religious freedom, and as Home Secretary, he greatly reduced the number of offences that could result in the death penalty. As Prime Minister, he presided over the Factory Act 1847, which reduced to ten hours the working day in factories.

On the debit side, his government made a poor showing in dealing with the devastating Irish potato famine. A big problem was his long-running rivalry with Lord Palmerston, which at times amounted to a feud. Russell sacked him in 1851, then soon afterwards, Palmerston engineered a no-confidence motion that ended Russell's first government. However, in the end, they made up their differences and Russell served as Foreign Secretary in Palmerston's second government. Following Palmerston's death in office, Russell succeeded him as Prime Minister.

Looking back from the twenty-first century, it is likely that most of us will identify with Russell's principles and objectives, and that most of us will admire the constant way that he pursued them. We would probably be inclined to say that he was a good or even a very good Prime Minister. However, many historians and commentators take a different view. The problem was his character and leadership style. He was rather shy and not naturally sociable. Queen Victoria once called him 'Peevish Johnny' because of his grumbling, pettiness, and lack of tact.[1] He did not give his government colleagues enough leadership, and firmness was missing when firmness was required. His principles were sound, but with a different approach, he could have achieved much more.

Health and Appearance

Russell was born after a seven-month pregnancy. He never enjoyed good health, and this was the reason that he was withdrawn from school and educated at home. Despite this, he was Prime Minister at seventy-three and lived to be almost eighty-six. He was less than 5 feet 5 inches tall, which made him the shortest Prime Minister, and he weighed just 8 stone. His head seemed just very slightly too large for his body.

Wives and Children

Russell's proposals of marriage were rejected by several women and he was a bachelor until the age of forty-two. His bride was a widow fifteen years younger than him, but she died after just three years, leaving him two children and a number of step-children. At the age of forty-eight, he married once more, this time to a woman twenty-four years his junior. The couple had four children, the second of which was born while he was Prime Minister. It was not until Tony Blair that another serving Prime Minister had a child in office. After the death of both his oldest son and his daughter-in-law, the then elderly Russell and his second wife took over care of their children.

Queen Victoria disapproved of many people and Russell's second wife was one of them. The antipathy was mutual. On 16 October 1853, Victoria wrote in her journal: 'The quiet passing off of the last cabinet was mainly owing to her not having come up to town with Lord John'.[2] It seems an unlikely judgment.

The Memory of a Famous Grandson

The famous grandson was Bertrand Russell. He was many things, including a logician, mathematician, pacifist, and philosopher. He won the Nobel Prize for Literature in 1950 and was a leading member of the Campaign for Nuclear Disarmament. At the age of four, and following the death of his mother and father, he was taken in by Lord John and his younger wife. The former Prime Minister died two years later, but he fondly remembered him as a kindly old man in a wheelchair.

A Very Misleading Nickname

Speaking in Parliament in 1837, Russell ruled out further Parliamentary reform, which led to him acquiring the nickname 'Finality Jack'.[3] Never was a nickname more misleading. Starting shortly afterwards, he campaigned for more reform for the rest of his political career. The failure of his government's Reform Bill in 1866 led to his resignation as Prime Minister and retirement.

Rotten Boroughs

In 1813, Russell's father, the 6th Duke of Bedford, used his influence and money to have him elected as an MP for the rotten borough of Tavistock. There were only thirty electors and Russell was underage and abroad at the time. He was a member for the borough when he introduced the first Reform Bill to parliament and, of course, one of the Bill's main measures was the abolition of rotten boroughs. His position was ironic and embarrassing.

Lord John Russell, 1861. A portrait photograph for a *carte de visite* by John Jabez Edwin Mayal (1813–1901). *National Portrait Gallery*

A Conversation with Napoleon

In December 1814, the then twenty-two-year-old Russell paid a visit to Napoleon, who was then in exile on the Mediterranean island of Elba. The two had a ninety-minute conversation, during which, according to George Malcolm Thomson, Napoleon relieved himself in the corner of the room.[4] Napoleon was not a gentleman.

Inspiration for a Twentieth-Century Pop Song

When he was created 1st Earl, Russell chose for his motto '*Che sara sara*', which translates as 'What will be will be'. With a slightly different spelling, this was the title of a 1956 popular song. It went to number one in the UK singles chart and became Doris Day's signature tune.

The Admiration of Charles Dickens

Charles Dickens was an admirer of Lord John Russell, and he dedicated his book *A Tale of Two Cities* to him. He wrote 'in remembrance of many public services and private kindnesses'.

Queen Victoria's Displeasure

It is widely believed that Queen Victoria's three least favourite Prime Ministers were all Liberals, and that in descending order of opprobrium, they were Gladstone, Palmerston, and Russell. She once referred to Palmerston and Russell as 'those two dreadful old men'.

Mr Gladstone's Assessment

After reading Russell's biography in 1889, Gladstone remarked that it took two volumes. He went on to say that 'Palmerston's occupies five, but Lord John's place in history is five times as great'.[5]

26

Edward Geoffrey Stanley

14th EARL OF DERBY

1852; 1858–59; 1866–68

Born in 1799, Stanley came from one of the long-established great Whig families, and his title came with a substantial landed estate at Knowsley in Lancashire. He was elected as a Whig MP for a rotten borough in 1822, and he became 14th Earl on the death of his father in 1851. He had, however, already gone to the House of Lords in 1844 with a different title.

Edward George Geoffrey Smith-Stanley, 14th Earl of Derby (1799–1869), portrait by Henry Perronet Briggs (1791/1793–1844). *Bury Art Museum*

Derby was one of only four Prime Ministers to serve three or more separate periods in the office. The others were Lord Salisbury, Stanley Baldwin, and William Gladstone. However, his three terms were all short and totalled just three years and 280 days. The first two of them were as the head of minority governments. He led the Conservative Party for twenty-two years, all but for his brief periods as Prime Minister as leader of the opposition. It must have been very dispiriting. No leader of any party has done the job for longer.

His early career included spells as Chief Secretary for Ireland in 1830–33 and Secretary of State for War and the Colonies in 1833–34. In the first of these positions, he established an Irish board of national education and gave children of all religious denominations the opportunity to attend government-funded schools. In the second, he oversaw the abolition of slavery in the British Empire.

Derby was a first-class speaker and his reputation at this point was very high. In 1834, Lord Melbourne told the young Disraeli 'Stanley will be the next Prime Minister, you will see'.[1] Although he was a Whig at this time, his party loyalties were flexible. He had served under Canning, a Tory, but not Wellington. Later, from 1841 to 1845, he served under Peel. The break with Peel was over the repeal of the Corn Laws. Together with Disraeli and some others, he split away with the protectionists. As already recounted, he then led the Conservative Party for the rest of his time in politics.

His last spell as Prime Minister is mostly remembered for the second reform act. This was passed in 1867 and almost doubled the size of the electorate. Disraeli was a very powerful figure in all of Derby's administrations and he played the principal role in the passage of the act. Nevertheless, Derby supported him and presided over the government that achieved it. He succeeded where others had failed and deserves credit for it.

The Earl of Derby by an unknown photographer, *c.* 1855.

During his last period in office, Derby suffered failing health, and in particular from gout, which had plagued him for a long time. He retired on medical grounds and died less than two years later.

Two Weeks in Prison

I am only aware of one Prime Minister who spent time in prison, though some might say that one or two others should have done. During his Grand Tour of Europe, Derby spent two weeks in a Neapolitan gaol. It was because he had knocked down an officer who had used violent language.[2]

The Who? Who? Ministry

When Derby formed his first ministry, he only had a very limited number of experienced men from which to choose. His cabinet contained just three ministers who had already been privy counsellors. When the list of cabinet ministers was read to the House of Lords, the Duke of Wellington, who was eighty-two and very deaf, repeatedly called out 'Who? Who?' Derby's first administration became known as the Who? Who? Ministry.

The Scholar

Derby was educated at Eton College and Christ Church, Oxford, and like many of his class (including a number of Prime Ministers), he enjoyed a classical education. The word 'enjoy' is apposite because he translated the whole of the Iliad into blank verse. One suspects that no modern Prime Ministers would have done that for fun in their spare time. Enoch Powell was never Prime Minister, but he might well have been an exception.

Horses

The Epsom Derby, possibly the world's most famous horse race, was named after the 14th Earl's grandfather, so it is not surprising that he had a passion for racing. He was a steward of the Jockey Club and invested much money and time in breeding horses. He did not, however, succeed in breeding the winner of the race that carried his name.

A Worthy Benefactor

Derby had a philanthropic side to his character and was generous to his employees. At Knowsley, he paid a local doctor £300 a year to look after his cottagers and they received the same medical attention as himself.[3] He headed the Lancashire Relief Association and provided large sums to help Lancashire cotton workers who had lost their jobs due to the disruption caused by the American Civil War.

Last Words

His last words were sad. Asked how he was, he replied, 'Bored to utter distraction.'

Disraeli's Tribute

When unveiling Derby's statue in Parliament Square, Disraeli said: 'He abolished slavery, he educated Ireland, he reformed parliament'. Disraeli was not noted for his modesty, but he did not add that he himself had taken the leading part in securing parliamentary reform. He also did not mention that the abolition of slavery and the education of Ireland had been achieved when Derby was a Whig serving a Whig Prime Minister.

A Punch cartoon from August 1867 portraying the Reform Bill as a leap in the dark.

27

George Hamilton-Gordon

4TH EARL OF ABERDEEN

1852–55

HAMILTON-GORDON'S FATHER DIED in a riding accident when he was seven, and his mother died when he was eleven. He was educated at Harrow and St John's College, Cambridge, and he succeeded to the title at the age of seventeen on the death of his grandfather. His parliamentary career was entirely in the House of Lords. Harrow has educated seven Prime Ministers, and four of them were at the school at the same time; they were Aberdeen, Goderich, Peel, and Palmerston.

George Hamilton-Gordon, 4th Earl of Aberdeen (1784–1860), a portrait by John Partridge (d. 1872) *c.* 1847. *National Portrait Gallery*

For a year, starting in 1813 and at the age of twenty-nine, Aberdeen was his country's ambassador to Austria, a very important job at the time. He held other cabinet positions, but foreign affairs was his main interest and he was Foreign Secretary for both Wellington and Peel. In the latter instance, he pursued good relations with France and the term '*entente cordiale*' came into use. In all his cabinet positions, he was regarded as principled, competent, and industrious, but perhaps rather dull.

He started as a Tory and served Wellington as such, then he served Peel as a Tory/Conservative. After the Conservative split over the Corn Laws, he went with Peel and became a Peelite, and after Peel's untimely death, he became the leader of this group. In December 1852, he became Prime Minister as head of a coalition of Peelites and Whigs, which had the support of some others. The Peelites were in the minority, but they provided the Prime Minister.

Aberdeen's ministry was defined by his country's entry into the Crimean War and his prosecution of it. On both counts, his performance was very poor. He did not want Britain to be involved, but his cabinet (Palmerston in particular) and much of the country did. He vacillated and weakly allowed Britain to be drawn into the conflict. If he had fought hard for his beliefs, he just might have succeeded. On the other hand, if Britain's warnings had been more credible, Russia might have backed off. He took a middle course and should probably have resigned.

In the early months, the conduct of the war was a disaster and Aberdeen got the blame. He did do very badly, but it should not be forgotten that Britain had not fought a significant war since 1815. Successive governments and Prime Ministers had let the Army get into a poor state. In January 1855, he lost what amounted[2] to a confidence vote in the House of Commons. He resigned and never held office again. During the next five years, he was melancholy and his health declined badly. He died in 1860 at the age of seventy-six.

Aberdeen's cabinet contained several able men with strong views and strong characters, notably Palmerston, Russell, and Gladstone. This could be said to be good, but they needed firm management and direction. Aberdeen did not provide it and his ministry is regarded as a failure. Had there not been a war, the verdict might have been different.

A Happy, but Brief First Marriage

At the age of twenty-one, Aberdeen married Lady Catherine Hamilton and the couple had three girls and a boy, who died shortly after birth. It was a very happy union, but with a sad end and a sad aftermath. After six years of marriage, his wife died of tuberculosis. He wore mourning clothes for the rest of his life, something that must have been hard for his second wife. All three of his daughters died of tuberculosis in their teens. Aberdeen was a devoted father and he spent a lot of time on their upbringing and nursing. It was admirable and not the way that most fathers behaved at the time.

Second Marriage

After four years as a widower, Aberdeen married the widow of his first wife's brother. It was to a considerable extent a marriage of convenience: he wanted a son and he wanted a stepmother for his daughters. This second union resulted in five more children—four boys and a girl. The couple were happy at first but drifted apart. Among other things, his wife was prone to complain when she felt unwell and this irritated him. Four years after his marriage, he wrote to her: 'I hope you feel comfortable today as I do not like the thought of your being low and nervous, especially as you have no good reason'.[1]

His second wife died in 1833, like her predecessor and stepchildren of tuberculosis. At the age of forty-nine, he had lost both parents, a brother, two wives, and four children. No wonder he was prone to melancholy.

The Battle of Leipzig

As envoy to Austria in 1813, Aberdeen witnessed the Battle of Leipzig in the company and entourage of Napoleon's son-in-law Francis I, Emperor of Austria, whose army was one of those fighting the French led by Napoleon. The terrible battle lasted three days and around 100,000 soldiers were killed, wounded, or missing. Napoleon's defeat led to his first exile a few months later. Aberdeen was greatly affected and it influenced his anti-war behaviour throughout the rest of his career. Later, his brother was killed at Waterloo, and this gave him another reason to hate war.

Ancient Artefacts

Aberdeen was a noted archaeologist and he brought many ancient artefacts from Greece to Britain. A particularly fine one, the so-called 'foot of Hercules' was subsequently lost, but many are in the British Museum.[2] This was controversial then and it is controversial now. The poet Lord Byron, Aberdeen's cousin, was one of those who furiously objected.

His Final Judgment on Himself

Shortly before he died, Aberdeen uncharacteristically refused to rebuild a parish church. After his death, it was found that he had written out the same biblical text on several scraps of paper.[3] It was from Chronicles and read as follows:

> And David said to Solomon, My son, as for me, it was in my mind to build an house unto the name of the Lord, my God: but the word of the Lord came to me saying: Thou has shed blood abundantly, and hast made great war; thou shalt not build an house unto my name, because thou hast shed much blood upon the earth in my sight.

Was this Aberdeen's judgment on himself because of the Crimean War. It seems possible, but we will never know.

George Hamilton Gordon, 4th Earl of Aberdeen reluctantly took Britain into Crimean War. A John Tenniel *Punch* cartoon of February 1854 shows him unable to restrain the British lion from chasing after the Russian bear.

28

Henry John Temple

3RD VISCOUNT PALMERSTON

1855–58; 1859–65

LORD PALMERSTON'S TITLE was Irish, which did not allow him to sit in the House of Lords. He became an MP in 1807 at the age of twenty-two, and with a couple of very short breaks, he remained one until he died two days short of his eighty-first birthday. He served as a minister for forty-six years, nearly sixteen of them as Foreign Secretary and nearly ten of them as Prime Minister.

He became Prime Minister for the first time at the age of seventy, which makes him the oldest person to take the position for the first time. He was the second oldest person to be Prime Minister, behind Gladstone and ahead of Churchill, and he was the last Prime Minister to die in office, which he did three months after increasing his majority at a general election.

Henry John Temple, 3rd Viscount Palmerston (1784–1865), a portrait by John Partridge (d. 1872) *c.* 1845. *National Portrait Gallery*

Palmerston was made a junior minister shortly after becoming an MP, and six months later, Spencer Perceval asked him to be Chancellor of the Exchequer. He declined and instead took the more junior position of Secretary at War. The appointment lasted nineteen years, only the last one of them as a cabinet position.

He was Britain's most famous Foreign Secretary and some would say that he was the greatest of them all. His three terms were between 1830 and 1851, and at a time when Britain's power and influence were very considerable indeed. The power was wielded, generally successfully, in pursuit of his country's interests. His attitude to foreign countries was usually liberal, but Britain's interests very clearly came first. The policies are sometimes described as 'gunboat diplomacy', but the gunboats did not often fire. He worked for a balance of power in Europe, again often successfully. This was all controversial, then and now, but had the approval of most of the British people. His time as Foreign Secretary ended due to his autocratic manner. He annoyed Queen Victoria and Prince Albert and had to resign.

He took the position of Home Secretary in Aberdeen's government and is considered to have been a success in that role. The fall of Aberdeen over the dismal prosecution of the Crimean War is told in the last chapter. The country demanded Palmerston as the man for the job. The Queen did not like him and did not want him, but after failing to find anyone else able to form a majority government, she did her constitutional duty and made the appointment. Palmerston did indeed win the war, though it might be more accurate to say that he was in office when it was won. He was forced out in 1858, but returned in triumph after sixteen months. He increased his party's majority in the July 1865 general election and died on 18 October 1865.

Lord Palmerston started his career as a Tory, became a Whig, and is generally recognised as the first Liberal Prime Minister. He had great energy, worked long and hard, and drove his clerks to do the same, which sometimes made him unpopular with them. He was liked by the public and approached the job with gusto. Harold Wilson ends his assessment of him with the words 'Palmerston wanted to see Britain top nation and keep her there. Not all Prime Minsters enjoy the job; few enjoyed it more than Palmerston'.[1] Not many would disagree.

An Attempted Assassination

In 1818, an ex-Army officer fired a shot at Palmerston, who at the time was Secretary at War. The would-be assassin was of unsound mind and nursing a grievance about his Army pension. Fortunately, the shot only inflicted a minor injury. Palmerston personally paid for his assailant's legal defence, and after he had been sent to a mental institution, he ensured that he was well looked after.

The Schleswig-Holstein Question

The constitutional relationship of the Duchies of Schleswig and Holstein with Demark and Prussia was exceedingly complicated, and it was the cause of a war between the two countries in 1848–51. There was a second war in 1864 between Denmark on the one side and Prussia and Austria on the other. Palmerston said: 'The Schleswig-Holstein question is so complicated only three men in Europe have ever understood it. One is Prince Albert who is dead. The second was a German professor who became mad. I am the third and I have forgotten all about it'.

Pride in his Country

A Frenchman said to Palmerston: 'If I were not a Frenchman, I should wish to be an Englishman'. Palmerston replied: 'If I were not an Englishman, I should wish to be an Englishman'.[2]

Tribute from his Fag

At Harrow School, Admiral Sir Augustus Clifford was fag to Palmerston, Viscount Althorp, and Viscount Duncannon. He later said that Palmerston was by far the most merciful of the three.

Palmer the Poisoner

The following is a splendid story and quite widely believed. It is, however, not true. Like many apochryphal stories, it is believed because of the character of the subject.

> William Palmer from Rugeley poisoned up to twelve people and was one of the most notorious of English murderers. His public execution in front of 30,000 people took place on 14 June 1856. His fame brought opprobrium on the town of Rugeley and the citizens sent a delegation to the Prime Minister to request that the name of the town be changed. The Prime Minister, Lord Palmerston, agreed, but only on condition that the town be named after himself.

Don Pacifico

Lord Palmerston, a studio portrait photograph by Pierre Louis Pierson (1822–1913), *c.* 1865.

Pacifico was a Gibraltarian Jew and therefore entitled to British protection. In 1847, his house in Athens was vandalised by an anti-Jewish mob. The police did not intervene and his inflated claim for compensation was rejected by the Greek Government. Palmerston, the Foreign Secretary, despatched a squadron of the Royal Navy to blockade the Port of Piraeus, and after eight weeks, the Greek Government capitulated and paid the compensation.

In defeating a censure motion in the House of Commons, Palmerston made a speech lasting almost five hours. It is regarded as the greatest of his many great speeches.

The speech is particularly noted for the peroration '*Civis romanus sum*', which translates as 'I am a Roman citizen', which indicated that all Roman citizens were entitled to the full protection of Rome. Similarly, Gibraltarian Jews were entitled to the full protection of the United Kingdom.

The 1851 Resignation

In the middle of the nineteenth century, the monarch had much more power than was the case later. Queen Victoria expected to see and at least be consulted on despatches made by her Foreign Secretary. Palmerston did not always comply and the quarrel came to a head in 1851.

Napoleon III staged a *coup d'état* in France. Palmerston, without consulting the Queen or his cabinet colleagues, told the French ambassador that he approved. Victoria and the Prince Consort were furious. They objected in principle and they were not thrilled at the prospect of a republican who was Napoleon Bonaparte's nephew having unrestricted power in France. They demanded that he be removed and Prime Minster Russell asked for his resignation. Palmerston duly complied. As was so often the case, the country supported Palmerston, and his resignation weakened Russell's government. He was soon back in the cabinet as Home Secretary.

Liaisons, Mistress, and Marriage

Palmerston enjoyed (an apt word) many sexual liaisons throughout his life, including a number with high-born and well-placed society hostesses. One of these was Lady Cowper, the sister of Lord Melbourne. She became his mistress, and then on the death of her husband, his wife. At the time of the marriage, he was fifty-five and she was fifty-two. By all accounts, they were very happy together, both before and after the marriage. According to George Thomson, they were reasonably faithful to one another.[3] Emily had five children, all born while she was married to Lord Cowper. It is widely believed that Palmerston was the father of her youngest child.

Missing the Soup

Both Lord and Lady Palmerston were notoriously unpunctual. They would frequently keep people waiting and routinely arrive late. Queen Victoria was just one of the many eminent people to be inconvenienced. There was a saying that the Palmerstons always missed the soup, and there was much truth in it.

Ladies-in-Waiting

In 1839, late at night and while staying at Windsor Castle, Palmerston entered the bedroom of one of the Queen's ladies-in-waiting. She made a tremendous fuss and accounts of the incident varied from inappropriate behaviour up to attempted rape. The Queen heard of it and she was most definitely not amused. It was one of the reasons for her long-standing dislike of him. Palmerston contended that he had entered the room by mistake and that he had intended to visit a different lady who he had reason to believe would welcome his visit.

Cited in a Divorce Petition

At the age of seventy-eight, Palmerston was cited as co-respondent in a divorce case. In what may have been attempted blackmail, the husband, who was a radical journalist, demanded damages of £20,000. The case was dismissed. Disraeli said that it was a pity that news of the case had got out and that Palmerston would now sweep the country. The lady in question was a Mrs Kane, which prompted the contemporary joke, 'She was Kane, but was he able?'

Last Words

It is generally accepted that Palmerston died in bed while working and that his last words were 'that's article 98, now go on to the next'. An alternative and pleasing belief is that he said, 'Die my dear doctor? Why that's the last thing I shall do.' It is nice to think this, but it is probably not true.

'The New Years' Gift'. Sir Colin Campbell 'offers' a tamed India to Palmerston at the end of the Mutiny: 'Well upon my word, eh! I'm really extremely obliged to you, but eh! How about keeping the brute?' Published in *Punch*, 2 January 1858.

29

Benjamin Disraeli

EARL OF BEACONSFIELD

1868; 1874–80

A. J. P. Taylor wittily and perceptively commenced his essay on Disraeli with the words 'You may know the story of the man who saw a giraffe and said "There ain't no such animal."'[1] Disraeli was a one-off. It was almost inconceivable that he could ever become Prime Minister, but he did.

Benjamin Disraeli, Earl of Beaconsfield (1804–1881), a portrait by Sir John Everett Millais (1829–1896), 1881. *National Portrait Gallery*

His Jewish origin is a good place to start. Britain was more tolerant than many countries, but it was nevertheless a considerable handicap. His father abandoned his Jewish faith and had Benjamin baptised into the Church of England when he was twelve. Nevertheless, he had a Jewish name and his appearance was typical of many Jews. There was no mistaking his origins and he was periodically taunted because of it. He was very capable of delivering a devastating response. Daniel O'Connell insulted him in the House of Commons and his Jewishness was part of the abuse. He replied: 'Yes I am a Jew and when the ancestors of the right honourable gentleman were brutal savages on an unknown island, mine were priests in the temple of Solomon'.

Disraeli did not attend a leading public school and he did not attend a university; apart from Wellington, he was the only Prime Minister before Lloyd George not to do so. Instead, and at the age of sixteen, he was articled to a firm of solicitors. The law proved to be not to his liking and he abandoned it after two years.

At twenty-two, he started speculating on the stock exchange and did so very unwisely. He borrowed and lost a great deal of money, and was not able to pay it all back until he was well into his forties. This was probably the main reason for a nervous breakdown that lasted four years. He came out of it after an extensive tour in southern Europe and the Middle East.

Restored to health, he turned his attention and curious genius to politics, and resolved to become an MP. Characteristically, he was not too fussed about what he needed to do to achieve this. Before being elected, he fought and lost four elections, three of them as a radical and one as a Conservative. Finally, in 1837, he was one of the two Conservatives returned for the borough of Maidstone. The other was Wyndham Lewis, who helped finance his election campaign.

Portrait photograph of Benjamin Disraeli by W. & D. Downey, *c.* 1878.

He was in opposition until 1841, then much to his chagrin, he was not offered a position in the Conservative Government of Sir Robert Peel. This was no doubt a factor in his sometimes critical attitude towards his leader. It culminated in the split over Peel's successful attempt in 1846 to abolish the Corn Laws. Peel lost office and Disraeli marched off into opposition with Lord Derby, Lord Bentinck, and some others.

He was now firmly established as one of the leading Conservatives in the Commons (many would say the leading Conservative in the Commons), but it was not until 1868 that he became Prime Minister for the first time. In the intervening twenty-two years, he was Chancellor of the Exchequer three times under Lord Derby, but his periods in office lasted less than four years. His first budget was a disaster.

Even though Derby was Prime Minister, the 1867 Reform Act was a personal triumph for Disraeli, and he was very briefly Prime Minister when the sick Lord Derby retired. Afterwards, he had to settle down to more than five more years in opposition.

By February 1874, Gladstone and the Liberal Government had run out of steam and Disraeli's Conservatives convincingly won the general election. It was late in life, but at the age of nearly seventy, he had finally achieved both position and power.

His six-year government is remembered for reforming legislation at home, especially in its early years. In 1876, Disraeli, in poor health and feeling his age, went to the House of Lords as Lord Beaconsfield. Thereafter, his attention, with considerable success, was mainly devoted to foreign affairs. He had a notable triumph at the Congress of Berlin in 1878. However, as is often the way, things finally went wrong. Wars in Afghanistan and South Africa went badly and Gladstone returned to Downing Street after the 1880 General Election. Disraeli remained as Leader of the Opposition until his death in 1881.

Quotes

Disraeli ranks highly in the ranks of quotable Prime Ministers. The following are four examples.

In response to an MP who had said that he would either die by hanging or by some vile disease: 'That depends Sir, upon whether I embrace your principles or your mistress'.

On Sir Robert Peel: 'The Right Honourable Gentleman's smile is like the silver fittings on a coffin'.

When dying, on being told that Queen Victoria wished to see him: 'No it is better not. She would only ask me to take a message to Albert'.

Some good advice: 'Never complain and never explain'.

Maiden Speech

There is a House of Commons convention that a maiden speech is listened to with respect. The courtesy was not extended to Disraeli. He was shouted down and forced to resume his seat. His last words before doing so were, 'Though I sit down now, the time will come when you will hear me.' He was right, they did.

Henrietta Sykes

In his early thirties, Disraeli had an affair with Henrietta Sykes, the wife of Sir Francis Sykes. At the same time, Sir Francis Sykes had become the lover of Disraeli's former mistress. Henrietta was a demanding woman and was also intimate with Lord Lyndhurst, who was having a favourable influence on Disraeli's career.[2] She then started another affair, this time with a painter. At this point, Disraeli terminated the relationship.[3] It was all very complicated.

Marriage

In 1839, Disraeli married Mary Wyndham Lewis. She was twelve years older than him and the widow of his running mate at the recent election. He had warm feelings for her, but her money, which he needed, was a factor. However, it developed into a love match. In 1868, the Queen at his request made her a viscountess in her own right. Mary died in 1872 and her husband was devastated.

An Extravagant Style of Dressing

Disraeli, especially in his younger years, was given to an extravagant style of dressing. The following is an account of his attire: 'green velvet trousers, a canary coloured waistcoat, low shoes, silver buckles, lace at his wrists, and his hair in ringlets'.[4]

Words on Becoming Prime Minister

Disraeli's words on assuming the highest office are revealing. In 1868, after a lifetime of striving, he jubilantly said: 'I have climbed to the top of the greasy pole'. In 1874, in poor health and conscious of the passing years, he said: 'Power, power at last, but it has come too late'.

Mrs Brydges Williams

Mrs Brydges Williams was an elderly widow without children, and like Disraeli, she was a Christian of Jewish descent. In 1851, she wrote to him to ask if he would agree to be a beneficiary of her estate. Not surprisingly, he did agree. A genuine friendship developed, and they corresponded very frequently and exchanged presents. Disraeli and his wife visited her. Mrs Brydges Williams died in 1863 and left him £30,000. She was buried in the churchyard at Hughenden, close to the tomb that would later be occupied by Lord Beaconsfield (Disraeli) and his wife.

Two cartoons by Sir John Tenniel (1820–1914). *Punch*

Relationship with the Queen

Disraeli was undoubtedly Victoria's favourite Prime Minister. He spent a lot of time and effort cultivating the relationship and it paid off. Flattery was part of his technique and he described it as 'laying it on with a trowel'.[5] Beneficial as it was to him, there was a benefit to the nation too. He was a big factor in persuading the 'Widow of Windsor' to come out of her seemingly perpetual mourning and seclusion after the death of the Prince Consort. So fond of him did the Queen become that she sent him bunches of primroses, and in 1880, a valentine.

A Benefit not Forgotten

In the 1840s, Disraeli received political support from Lord George Bentinck, and he had received financial support from him and the Bentinck family.

In 1880, Disraeli asked the then-head of the Bentinck family to visit him at Hughenden. This was the twenty-two-year-old Duke of Portland, who was serving in the Coldstream Guards. The young man was understandably nervous. Disraeli came down for dinner in the blue riband of the garter. The two of them, plus Disraeli's secretary, ate the meal in almost total silence.

When the meal was over, Disraeli, who was in the last year of his life, rose and said: 'My Lord Duke I come from a race that never forgets an injury, nor forgets a benefit'.[6]

The Novels and Other Writing

Between 1826 and 1880, Disraeli published fifteen novels, and there were also works of non-fiction and poetry. Opinion is divided about the merits of the novels. He extensively used them to get over his political ideas, and the characters in them could often be seen to be based on political contemporaries.

He received a £10,000 advance for *Endymion*, his last novel finished in 1880. At the time, this was the largest advance ever paid for such a work.[7] At the time of his death, a further novel was unfinished. The central character in it was a thinly disguised, rather priggish Mr Gladstone.

Rivalry with Gladstone

Gladstone had served in Peel's cabinet and remained loyal to him after the 1846 split. This was the beginning of the great political rivalry that would last until Disraeli's death thirty-five years later. It is often exaggerated but their differences were personal as well as political. In fact, they amounted to strong dislike. Gladstone thought that Disraeli was a charlatan, and Disraeli thought that Gladstone was a sermonising prig. Disraeli expressed himself on the subject with the greater wit. He once said: 'The difference between a misfortune and a calamity is this: If Gladstone fell into the Thames, it would be a misfortune. But if someone dragged him out again, that would be a calamity'.

Mr Punch presents lunch. The Marquess of Hartington, leader of the Liberals in the House of Commons (1875–1880), says 'here's a pretty lunch'. The Earl of Granville (with beard), Foreign Secretary 1880–1885, says 'indigestible I'm afraid, but we must make the most of it'. Behind him stands Gladstone, and behind Gladstone stands Disraeli depicted as a coloured lady. Published 29 May 1880. *Punch*

30

William Ewart Gladstone

1868–74; 1880–85; 1886; 1892–94

WHEN ROY JENKINS wrote his great biography of Churchill, he thought that his subject just pipped Gladstone as the country's greatest Prime Minister.[1] There is room for different views, but it is almost universally agreed that Gladstone was a remarkable man and one of the greatest Prime Ministers. He has at least two unique achievements. He resigned for the last time at the age of eighty-four years and sixty-three days, which makes him the oldest Prime Minister. Additionally, he is the only one to have served four non-consecutive terms.

William Ewart Gladstone (1809–1898), a portrait by Franz von Lenbach (1836–1904), 1886. *Art in Parliament*

The great man was born in Liverpool on 29 December 1809. His parents were of Scottish descent and his father was a very wealthy slave owning merchant. William's education was at Eton and Christ Church College, Oxford, where he obtained a double first in classics and mathematics. He was President of the Oxford Union and was extremely religious, specifically Anglican, as he was for the rest of his life. He had the reputation of being rather priggish and sanctimonious. This too lasted. Disraeli certainly thought so; he once said that Gladstone did not have a single redeeming vice.

At the age of just twenty-two, he became an MP for Newark. This was a rotten borough, and his success was due to the Duke of Newcastle who controlled it. Roy Jenkins says that there had been the distribution of far more money on Gladstone's behalf than he was aware of or subsequently approved.[2]

It is sometimes said that most politicians move to the right during their careers. The future Grand Old Man of Liberalism did the opposite. He started as a reactionary Tory, and at Oxford, he opposed the extension of the franchise. In his early days in Parliament, he opposed factory legislation and the abolition of slavery. In 1884, his government extended the franchise.

His first cabinet post was in 1843, when Sir Robert Peel made him President of the Board of Trade, and in his brief occupancy, he did very well indeed. His achievements included the Joint Stock Companies Act and railway legislation, both in 1844. However, not long afterwards, he resigned because of an increase in the amount of a government grant to a Roman Catholic seminary in Ireland. This offended his religious principles and did not conform to the views that he had expressed in a religious book. The row was a storm in a teacup and his resignation was rather silly. In the great split over the repeal of the Corn Laws, he followed Peel into opposition.

Gladstone enjoyed four terms as Prime Minister and two terms as Chancellor of the Exchequer. In addition, he was, unwisely, for a time Chancellor in one of his own administrations. Disraeli had three much shorter terms as Chancellor and they were often in bitter opposition. Gladstone is remembered as one of the great chancellors. Had he never been Prime Minister, this alone would have secured his place in history.

One of the most remembered things about his time at 10 Downing Street is his long, passionate, and unsuccessful attempt to secure home rule for Ireland. Another is the Third Reform Act of 1884; this increased the size of the electorate from around 3 million men to slightly more than 5 million men. About 60 per cent of men then had the vote, but there were still no votes for women.[3]

Three Proposals, an Extraordinary Letter, and a Very Happy Marriage

Gladstone had two proposals of marriage rejected before he was accepted by Catherine Glynne. It was an extremely happy marriage that lasted from 1839 until his death in 1898. They had eight children, the youngest of whom was a future Home Secretary. Before proposing to his future wife, he wrote an exceedingly opaque letter of affection to her. It included the following sentence, which contains 142 words:

> I seek much in a wife in gifts better than those of our human pride, and am also sensible that she can find little in me: sensible that, were you to treat this note as the offspring of utter presumption, I must not be surprised: sensible that the lot I invite you to share, even if it be not attended, as I trust it is not, with peculiar disadvantages of an outward kind, is one, I do not say unequal in your deserts, for that were saying little, but liable at the best to changes and perplexities and pains which, for myself, I contemplate without apprehension, but to which it is perhaps selfishness in the main with the sense of my too real unworthiness, which would make me contribute to explore another—and that other![4]

The Cow that Died for Ireland

At a time of bitter recriminations over Gladstone's attempt to secure Home Rule for Ireland, he was attacked by a mad cow. The cow was shot and Gladstone, who was eighty-two at the time, was shaken but unhurt. The next day, an enormous wreath was delivered to his home. The inscription on the card read: 'To the memory of the patriotic cow which sacrificed its life in the attempt to save Ireland from Home Rule'.[5]

Fallen Women

For half a century, Gladstone, with the knowledge and support of his wife, tried to help and redeem prostitutes. His motives are still a matter of debate, and it may be significant that his work was exclusively with attractive women in the prosperous West End of London. He did not assist the desperate harlots of the East End.

He would frequently leave home late at night and walk the streets. He would meet prostitutes, talk to them, direct them to places of safety and help, and sometimes take them home. There, with his wife, he would provide food, talk further, and pray with them. Inevitably, his failures greatly outnumbered his successes, but he did genuinely help some women.

Yet was Christian charity his only motive? In his favour was the fact that he was completely open about what he was doing, and if his wife ever had any doubts, she never expressed them. On one occasion, a young man saw him talking to a prostitute and tried to blackmail him. Gladstone reported him to the police and the blackmailer was sentenced to a year's hard labour.

It is almost certain that Gladstone got some sort of sexual thrill from his activities. He kept a diary and recorded some of his encounters in it. At times, he would insert a drawing of a whip or scourge to indicate that he had punished himself for his thoughts or actions. On one occasion, he wrote that a particular girl was 'half a lovely young woman, beautiful beyond measure'.[6] He wrote the entry in Italian, a common practice when he had disturbing thoughts.

Close to the end of his life, he told his son, the Reverend Stephen Gladstone, that he had 'not been guilty of the act which is known as that of infidelity to the marriage bed'.[7] We should, I think, believe him. There is much evidence that he was highly sexually charged, and that he struggled with it for all his adult life. He got a vicarious thrill from what he did, but it was no more than that. What is more, he did genuinely give help.

An informal photograph of Gladstone by Elliott & Fry, *c.* 1887.

Posthumous Vindication

The great man's reputation was posthumously vindicated in 1928. A Captain Peter Wright had published a book that contained scurrilous accusations about William Gladstone's activities with prostitutes. Herbert Gladstone, his son, responded with a violent denunciation of the author. Wright sued Herbert Gladstone and lost. The jury, with the judge's permission, added a rider that the evidence had 'completely vindicated the high moral character of the late Mr W. E. Gladstone'.[8]

Queen Victoria

Gladstone served his Queen devotedly, but she was a trial to him and took a great deal of his time and attention. For example, during his term as Prime Minister in 1880–85, he wrote to her 1,107 times. This excluded communications on honours and the formation of the government. She sent him 207 letters and 170 telegrams.[9] He was her least favourite Prime Minister. One of her complaints was as follows: 'He speaks to me as if I was a public meeting'.

General Gordon

General Gordon was a very popular, larger-than-life, muscular Christian, perpetually optimistic junior general. He was capable of insubordination and a very unwise choice to lead a military expedition with strictly limited objectives. A self-proclaimed Mahdi or Messiah had slaughtered an Egyptian Army led by an English commander. In 1884, a British force under Gordon was despatched to clear up the mess and conduct the withdrawal. His orders were badly expressed and badly communicated. Regardless of this, Gordon disregarded them and led an advance. Fifty-four days after leaving England, he was besieged in Khartoum, and remained in this state for a further 310 days.

Although Gordon insisted that he did not need rescuing, there was a public clamour for a rescue force to be despatched without delay. In line with public opinion, the Queen several times communicated

A chromolithograph cartoon depicting Gladstone, possibly dressed as a Greek marathon runner, passing an 'Altar of Peace'. The dogs are labelled 'Assassin, Ribbon Man, Desperado, Secret Society, [and] Fenian'. Michael Davitt and Charles S. Parnell, with leash labelled 'Land League' struggle to hold onto the dogs; Davitt has stumbled over John Dillon, all three are lying on the ground. Published in *Puck*, New York, 17 May 1882. Created by Joseph Ferdinand Keppler (1838–1894). *Library of Congress*

her strong wish that this be done. However, Gladstone and the cabinet were justifiably very cross and prevaricated. When the eventual rescue force reached Khartoum, it found that Gordon had been killed two days previously.

The people were furious and so was the Queen. In disregard of normal practice, she sent Gladstone an unencrypted telegram of rebuke. It was done in this way with the intention of insulting him and the telegram was handed to him at Carnforth Railway Station by the Station Master. Victoria's ungrammatical rebuke included: 'These news from Khartoum are frightful and to think that all this might have been prevented and many lives saved by earlier action is too fearful'.[10] Gladstone's more grammatical response included:

> Mr Gladstone does not presume to estimate the means of judgement possessed by Your Majesty, but so far as his information and recollection at the moment go, he is not altogether able to follow the conclusion which Your Majesty has been pleased to announce.[11]

Carnforth Station's other claim to fame is that the film *Brief Encounter* was shot there. It was one of the lowest points of Gladstone's career.

Nicknames

As befitting an elder statesman, Gladstone acquired a number of nicknames. Public affection and respect was indicated by 'The People's William'. Another was 'Grand Old Man', often shortened to 'G.O.M'. After the General Gordon debacle, the order of the letters was sometimes reversed to 'M.O.G'. This was intended to indicate 'Murderer of Gordon'. An unfriendly interpretation of 'G.O.M' was 'God's Only Mistake'.

The Last Goodbye

Gladstone resigned as Prime Minister for the fourth and last time on 2 March 1894. At his final cabinet meeting the previous day, his colleagues paid tributes to him and several of them were overcome with emotion and resorted to tears. Gladstone was dry eyed and unmoved. He later dubbed it 'the blubbering cabinet'.

His resignation was courteously received by the Queen. She thanked him for his service, but did not ask for his advice on his successor. She appointed Lord Rosebery. According to Roy Jenkins, he would have advised Earl Spencer.[12]

State Funeral

Gladstone was a great man and a great Prime Minister, so it was fitting that he had a great state funeral at Westminster Abbey. Among Prime Ministers, only the funerals of Wellington and Churchill bear comparison. The ten pallbearers included two future monarchs (The Prince of Wales and the Duke of York) and three Prime Ministers (Salisbury, Rosebery, and Balfour).

The Prince of Wales had never shared his mother's low opinion of Gladstone. The Queen telegraphed him to ask what precedent he planned to follow and what advice he had taken. The Prince replied that he had taken no advice and knew of no precedent.[13]

William Gladstone is kicked out of power.

31

Robert Arthur Talbot Gascoyne-Cecil

3rd MARQUIS OF SALISBURY

1885; 1886–92; 1895–1902

Robert Arthur Talbot Gascoyne-Cecil, 3rd Marquess of Salisbury (1830–1903), portrait by George Frederic Watts (1817–1904). *National Portrait Gallery*

SALISBURY WAS THE last Prime Minister to sit in the House of Lords. He was a descendant of Lord Burghley, who served Elizabeth I, and he came from a grand and long-established Conservative family. It would have been reasonable to assume that as he approached manhood, his political prospects were very bright. Glittering success did ensue, but there was much trial and tribulation first.

He had few friends as a child and was badly bullied at both his schools. As a result, he left Eton at the age of fifteen. He went to Christ Church, Oxford, and was clearly very bright, but due to poor health, he only obtained an honorary fourth-class degree in mathematics. Following this, he was advised that travel would be good for him and he travelled for two years, primarily in South Africa, Australia, and New Zealand. This gave him practical first-hand knowledge of the colonies, something that many of his contemporaries lacked. During his travels, he decided that he did not much care for the Boers.

Later, he was estranged from his father and elder brother, and his father for a while cut off his income. As a result, he wrote very extensively for money, and he continued writing for many years. He became heir to the title on the death of his older brother, and he succeeded to it at the age of thirty-six on the death of his father.

Salisbury became an MP at the age of twenty-three in 1853, and in the next thirteen years, he was unopposed in his Stamford constituency. He was Secretary of State for India for eight months starting in 1866, but resigned because he could not stomach the Derby–Disraeli Reform Act. He held the same position under Disraeli for four years starting in 1874. He was then Foreign Secretary for the last two years of his administration. During this time, he played a part in Disraeli's triumph at the Congress of Berlin.

Salisbury's three terms as Prime Minister lasted for nearly fourteen years, which was longer than the sum of Gladstone's four terms. For nearly all this time, he acted as his own Foreign Secretary. He was extremely skilled and knowledgeable about foreign affairs and they were his passion. Unlike Gladstone, he was an imperialist, and during his terms in power, Britain acquired Kenya, Uganda, Nigeria, and

Rhodesia. The capital of the last of these was named after him. It was before his time in power, but he supported the south in the American Civil War.

He was most definitely a conservative—with both a capital and a lowercase 'c'. He was worried about the march of democracy and resigned over the issue. He instinctively disliked much change and often had a pessimistic outlook. He generally feared the worst. It is a negative assessment, but he was a very clever man with rock-solid principles. He had much success.

Religion

It is probably true to say that Salisbury and his contemporary Gladstone were Britain's two most religious Prime Ministers, and this was a guiding factor in their work and policies. It did not lead them to the same conclusions, though. Salisbury started every day by praying in church, and like Gladstone, his church was the Church of England. His Christian conscience made him oppose allowing Jews to sit in Parliament, and it made him oppose the abolition of religious tests for entry to universities.

The Commendation of Two Prime Ministers

Disraeli and Salisbury did not always see eye to eye, but Disraeli paid him a massive compliment. Speaking to Salisbury's daughter, he said: 'Your father is the only man of real courage that it has been my lot to work with'.[1]

Harold Wilson asked Clem Attlee, then in old age: 'Yourself excluded, and politics apart, who of all the Prime Ministers Britain has had since you became old enough to take an interest do you consider the best, as Prime Minister?' Attlee replied that it was Salisbury.[2]

A chromolithograph cartoon 'The pig has the pull'. Parnell (the pig) carrying a shillelagh labelled 'Obstruction', walking down a road with leashes attached to a nose ring on the Marquess of Salisbury and on the former Prime Minister Gladstone, who is crawling on his hands and knees. Published in *Puck*, New York, 9 December 1885. Created by Bernhard Gillam (1856–1896). Uncanny similarity to 2017. *Library of Congress*

A chromolithograph cartoon 'Misery loves company'. Nicholas II, the Marquess of Salisbury and Meiji, Emperor of Japan try to give the Emperor of China 'ultimatum' pills, while the sultan of Turkey looks on: 'Allah be praised!—Now that they've got another "sick man", maybe they'll let up on me a little!' Published in *Puck*, New York, 6 November 1895. Created by Louis, Dalrymple (1866–1905). *Library of Congress*

Relations with the Queen

Victoria had problems with three of the last four Liberal Prime Ministers of her reign, namely Russell, Palmerston, and Gladstone. Rosebery was the exception. She got on well with the Conservatives—Derby, Disraeli (especially), and Salisbury. In contrast with her normal practice, she allowed Salisbury to sit down in her presence because he was 'bad on his legs'. When they were both on holiday in France, she would sometimes without warning drive over to his house for tea.[3]

Bullied at School

Salisbury was bullied very badly at both his prep school and at Eton. At the age of fifteen, he finally persuaded his father to take him away. Despite this, he sent his four sons to the school. He delivered the first two there himself, but the memories of his experience were so upsetting that he left it to his wife to deliver the other two.[4]

Marriage

Salisbury's father strongly opposed his marriage. The unhappy son put his case in the following words:

> Your objections to my marriage rested mainly on the 'privations' it would entail. 'Privation' means the loss of something I enjoy now. If the privation in question is the want of food, warmth, clothing, I am not prepared to face it. But I cannot lose anything else I now enjoy, for the simple reason that I do not enjoy anything. Amusements I have *none*.... The persons who will cut me because I marry Miss Alderson are precisely the persons of whose society I am so anxious to be quit.[5]

The subsequent marriage ceremony was not attended by his father or elder brother, but the family was subsequently reconciled. Like his contemporaries Palmerston, Gladstone, Disraeli. and Rosebery, Salisbury was blessed with a happy marriage. The couple had eight children.

Modern Inventions and a Fatality

Salisbury took a keen interest in modern inventions and the uses to which they could be put. This explains why his residence at Hatfield was one of the very first to be served by electricity and the telephone. Electricity was something of a varied blessing. The wires kept overheating and it was sometimes necessary to put out small fires. Sadly, Hatfield was the site of one of the first fatalities caused by electricity, some say the first death of all. A servant picked up a live wire that was laying in wet grass. He died as a consequence.

Robert Arthur Talbot Gascoyne-Cecil, a Spy cartoon from *Vanity Fair*.

32

Archibald Philip Primrose

5TH EARL OF ROSEBERY

1894–95

LORD ROSEBERY, BORN in 1847, was rich before his marriage and extremely rich after it. Like Gladstone and Salisbury, he was educated at Eton and Christ Church, Oxford. His father died before his grandfather, so he inherited the title at the age of twenty-one, which meant that for his entire adult life, he served in the House of Lords. He never fought an election and he never experienced the rough and tumble of the House of Commons.

He was twice Foreign Secretary under Gladstone, but is not remembered as being particularly successful. In the second of the two periods, relations with France were poor because of clashing colonial aspirations in Africa. He was Prime Minister for just sixteen months starting in March 1894. He was troubled and ineffectual and has to be regarded as one of the more disappointing holders of the office.

Archibald Phillip Primrose, 5th Earl of Rosebery (1847–1929), a lithograph published in Germany, 1902, in *Weltrundschau zu Reclams Universum.*

Rosebery was in many ways a brilliant man and with a very wide range of interests outside politics. Furthermore, he was a very good speaker. Nevertheless, his character and approach were handicaps, Churchill's appraisal included the following:

> He was often palpably out of touch with his environment; perhaps that is no censure upon him. It must however be emphasised that physically he did not stand the stresses well. In times of crisis and responsibility his active, fertile mind and imagination preyed upon him. He was bereft of sleep. He magnified trifles. He failed to separate the awkward incidents of the hour from the long swing of events, which he so clearly understood. Toughness when nothing particular was happening was not the form of fortitude in which he excelled.[1]

Despite this, there were compensations. It is said that at Oxford, he told a friend that his three ambitions were to marry an heiress, win the Derby, and become Prime Minister. He denied having said it, but he probably did. Be that as it may, he had accomplished all three aims by the age of forty-seven.

In his middle to late twenties, he was courted by both Gladstone and Disraeli. Gladstone won and he joined the Grand Old Man in the Liberals. He came to prominence and earned Gladstone's gratitude when he sponsored and organised his barnstorming and successful Midlothian Campaign of 1879–80.

With the personal handicaps described by Churchill, he had a tough time as Prime Minister. The Unionist-dominated House of Lords hampered and blocked his government's legislation. An especially difficult problem was his relationship with Sir William Harcourt. Rosebery was on the right of the party and Harcourt on the left. Harcourt who was the leader in the House of Commons thought that he should have been Prime Minister and constantly undermined him.

Although resignation was probably not necessary, his troubled government threw in its hand after losing a parliamentary committee vote. The Unionists won the consequent general election with a large majority. After a year, he resigned as leader of the opposition and retired from national politics. He was still aged under fifty.

'Little Bo Peep', the Earl of Rosebery caricatured by Spy in *Vanity Fair* 14 March 1901.

Marriage to an Heiress

Rosebery had a substantial fortune of his own, and he married for love rather than money when he wed Hannah, the only child of Baron Meyer Amschel de Rothschild. She was a remarkable woman, devoted to him and a great help to his political career. Sadly, she died in 1890, having given him four children. This happened four years before he became Prime Minister and he was never quite the same man.

Horses

Rosebery purchased a racehorse while an undergraduate at Oxford. This was not allowed and he was told to sell it or leave. He kept the horse and left the university. Horses were a lifelong passion and one of his many interests outside politics. He won several of the classic races, including the Derby in 1894, 1895, and 1905. The first two of the wins were during his sixteen-month term as Prime Minister.

Insomnia

Rosebery suffered from insomnia for much of his life, and it was at its worst when he was Prime Minister. He took to driving round London in the night and it is reported that he once went nine nights without sleep.

The Commonwealth

It was Rosebery who coined the term 'Commonwealth of Nations'. Speaking in Australia in 1883, he said: 'There is no need for any nation, however great, leaving the Empire, because the Empire is a Commonwealth of Nations'.[2]

Entente Cordiale

The *entente cordiale* was a series of agreements and understandings made in 1904 between Britain and France. It brought the two countries into something close to an alliance that was potentially hostile to Kaiser Wilhelm II's Germany. It was regarded as a triumph at the time and to a large extent it still is.

A chromolithograph cartoon of John Bull standing in the House of Lords, and at his feet Rosebery. Caption: John Bull: 'Rosebery says he can be mended, but I guess he'd better be ended!' Published in *Puck*, New York, 12 December 1894. Created by F. Opper and Frederick Burr. *Library of Congress*

Rosebery, nearly twenty years out of office, saw it differently. In public, he warned that it was far more likely to lead to war than peace. In private, he said: 'Straight to war'.[3] Could it be that he was right?

The Fading of the Light

After his resignation in 1896, Rosebery sought no office in national politics, though he made his views known from time to time. He had many interests, and in 1889, he became the first chairman of the newly formed London County Council, an office that he held with distinction.

His life took a sad turn for the worse in 1917 when his son was killed on active service in Palestine. Then, in October 1918, he suffered a stroke. He recovered his faculties, but his hearing, movement, and sight were impaired. By the end of his life, he was almost totally blind. His last eleven years were very difficult.

His estate was probated at £1,500,122 3*s* 6*d*. In accordance with his prior request, the Eton Boating Song was played on the gramophone as he passed into the next world. What a way to go.

33

Arthur James Balfour

1902–05

Arthur James Balfour (1848–1930), a studio photograph by George Grantham Bain. *Library of Congress*

ARTHUR BALFOUR, BORN in 1848, came from a very wealthy Scottish family. His mother was the sister of the 3rd Marquess of Salisbury, which made him the nephew of his predecessor as Prime Minister. His godfather was Arthur Wellesley, Duke of Wellington, and he was named after him. The future Prime Minister was only seven when his father died and he inherited a very large sum of money on his twenty-first birthday.

He habitually approached life with an air of detachment and in a languid manner. Ramsay MacDonald said that he saw a great deal of life from afar.[1] He conserved his energy and frequently got up very late, at noon even, something that he had in common with Churchill. However, it is sometimes overlooked that he had often worked before rising. He seemed to float through and above the fray. It was almost certainly meant ironically, but he said that 'nothing matters very much and very few things matter at all'. Common sense tells us that there must have been much more to him—there was. He was capable of being decisive and ruthless, though often he was neither.

Balfour's career was very long and it continued for more than a score of years after he ceased to be Prime Minister. At the age of seventy-nine, he was Lord President of the Council in the government of Stanley Baldwin. He became an MP at the age of twenty-six and joined his uncle's cabinet as Secretary for Scotland in 1886. Then, after a few months, he was given the much more demanding job of Chief Secretary for Ireland. With Lord Salisbury in the Lords, he led his party in the Commons from 1891 and was Leader of the House from 1895 to 1902.

Towards the end of his time as Prime Minister, Lord Salisbury's health was failing. Balfour acted almost as co-Prime Minister, and he was the obvious person to take over from his uncle. His period in office is remembered for his party's split over tariff reform, and the train crash of his resignation and the party's landslide defeat at the 1906 General Election. It was an unhappy time and he was not a success.

He continued as party leader until 1911 and, with Lord Lansdowne, was ruthlessly obstructive in using the House of Lords to block legislation that they did not like. Lloyd George called the Upper House 'Mr

Balfour's poodle'. It culminated in the 1911 Parliament Act that curtailed the veto powers of the House of Lords.

His return to office came in May 1915. In the special circumstances of the First World War, Asquith formed a coalition government and Balfour succeeded Churchill as First Lord of the Admiralty. He backed Lloyd George in his December 1916 coup and was rewarded with the post of Foreign Secretary. He held this position until after the Versailles Peace Conference in 1919, then remained in Lloyd George's cabinet until he lost office in 1922.

Caricature of Balfour, the caption read 'Dialectics'. Published in *Vanity Fair*, 27 January 1910.

Nicknames

Early in his career, he acquired the nickname 'Miss Nancy Balfour' and somewhat later 'Pretty Fanny'. The latter of these two nicknames stuck. My attempts to discover the origin of them have failed. A study of his photograph may or may not convince you that he was pretty, but I speculate that it had something to do with his somewhat delicate manner.

Another nickname was 'Bloody Balfour', and there is no doubt where this came from. His appointment as Chief Secretary for Ireland in 1887 was greeted with incredulity and the belief that he was not tough enough to do the job. The perception was misplaced. Ireland was in turmoil and he performed his duties ruthlessly. The nationalist element of the island did not like it, but the unionists did, and so did his party.

Bob's Your Uncle

The origin of the phrase is believed to be the appointment of Arthur Balfour by his uncle Lord Salisbury (whose first name was Robert) to the position of Chief Secretary for Ireland. Much of the public thought that it was nepotism and that Balfour would not be up to the job.

Before his Time

Balfour was well before his time in warning of the consequences of mankind polluting the environment. In 1895, he wrote: 'The energies of our system will decay, the glory of the sun will be dimmed, and the earth, tideless and inert, will no longer tolerate the race which has for a moment disturbed its solitude. Man will go down into the pit and all his thoughts will perish'.[2]

The Women in his Life

Balfour is one of the four Prime Ministers never to have married. In 1875, he was very close to May Lyttleton, and perhaps unofficially engaged to her. When she died of typhoid, he was terribly upset and asked that a ring that had belonged to his mother be put in her coffin.[3] Each year afterwards, he tried to spend the anniversary of her death in the company of her twin sister and her husband. After Mary's death, he enjoyed the friendship of many women, but never let things develop into anything more.

A cartoon of 1903. Joseph Chamberlain tries to lead Balfour into deep water with free trade and German *Zollverein.Westminster Gazette*

A close friendship was with Margot Tennant, a very outgoing socialite who later became the second wife of Herbert Asquith, the future Liberal Prime Minister. She would have liked to marry him, but he said, not to her: 'No that is not so. I rather thought of having a career of my own'.[4]

The Balfour Declaration

The Balfour Declaration was a letter written by Arthur Balfour, on behalf of the cabinet, to Walter Rothschild, 2nd Baron Rothschild. It was intended for transmission to the Zionist Federation of Great Britain and Ireland. It included: 'His majesty's government view with favour the establishment of a national home for the Jewish people, and will use their best endeavours to facilitate the achievement of this object'. The letter was hugely influential and a step towards the setting up of the state of Israel in 1948.

34

Sir Henry Campbell-Bannerman

1905–08

Sir Henry Campbell-Bannerman (1836–1908), portrait by James Guthrie (1859–1930). *The Stirling Smith Art Gallery & Museum*

SIR HENRY CAMPBELL-BANNERMAN was sixty-nine when he took office, which makes him the oldest person to become Prime Minister for the first time since Palmerston in 1855. He is the only person to have been Father of the House while a serving Prime Minister. He only held the position of Prime Minister for two years and four months, and his term was marred by his bad health and by the bad health and death of his wife. He was a pleasant man and was generally liked and respected by his colleagues and opponents. He tended to lead in a restrained and competent manner.

He was Scottish and favoured home rule for both Scotland and Ireland, though his vision of home rule was some way short of independence. Like nearly all Liberals, but only some Conservatives, he was very firmly in favour of free trade and against so-called tariff reform. After leaving university, he joined his family's prosperous business and was soon made a partner. In 1868, at the age of thirty-one, he was elected MP for Stirling Burghs, and then represented the constituency until his death nearly forty years later.

He briefly served in Gladstone's cabinet as Chief Secretary for Ireland, then he was, again briefly, twice Secretary for War, once for Gladstone and once for Rosebery. In 1899, he became leader of the opposition and the Boer War gave him an early problem. His party was split between the imperialists, who supported or at least accepted the war, and the remainder, led by Lloyd George, who opposed it. Campbell-Bannerman leaned towards the anti-war side, but skilfully worked to keep his party together. Towards the end of the war, he castigated the government for setting up so-called concentration camps.

After 1905, his government operated at an enormous disadvantage because the Tory-dominated House of Lords blocked and hampered its legislation. Balfour said: 'The great Unionist Party should still control, whether in power or opposition, the destinies of this great empire'.[1] Nevertheless, the government set about a programme of social reform. Abroad, the Transvaal and the Orange River Colony were given self-government.

Campbell-Bannerman is one of the lesser known Prime Ministers and is often underrated. In late 1999, *The Guardian* newspaper published a league table of the nineteen twentieth-century Prime Ministers.[2] The

A postcard of Campbell-Bannerman published shortly after his death.

rankings were based on the views of politicians, historians, and political journalists. It has to be a matter of opinion, but Campbell-Bannerman was ranked ninth. Churchill was first and Eden was nineteenth.

His Name

For the first thirty-five years of his life he was Henry Campbell. Then his uncle died and left him a considerable sum of money and a life interest in an estate in Kent. This was on condition that he added Bannerman to his name. He very reluctantly made the change. Ten years later, he wrote to Lord Spencer:

> I see you are already tired as I have long been, of writing my horrid long name. I am always best pleased to be called Campbell tout court, and most of my old friends do so.... An alternative is C.B.[3]

An Animated Discussion

In 1905, an illustrated paper published a photograph of Campbell-Bannerman in an animated discussion with the King. The paper's caption was 'Is it peace or war?' Campbell-Bannerman later said that they had been discussing whether halibut was better served baked or boiled.[4]

His Tory Family

The Liberal Prime Minister came from a family of Tories. His father was Lord Provost of Glasgow from 1840 to 1843 and he stood unsuccessfully as a Tory in two general elections. His brother was a Tory MP from 1880 to 1906.

Some Wisdom about Bed

Campbell-Bannerman once said: 'Personally I am an immense believer in bed, in constantly keeping horizontal: the heart and everything else goes slower and the whole system is refreshed'.[5] What a wise man he was.

A Happy Marriage with a Sad End

Campbell-Bannerman was one of the Prime Ministers blessed with a very happy marriage. Sadly, his wife became very ill and she was probably suffering from diabetes, which made her extremely fat. Insulin was not then available. It was terrible for her husband, and for her too of course. Despite his responsibilities as Prime Minister, he nursed her and gave her a great deal of his time. She died in August 1906 and he was devastated. They had no children.

Death in Downing Street

Campbell-Bannerman suffered at least two heart attacks in 1907, which was the year after his wife died. His own health deteriorated and he resigned on 3 April 1908. He was a dying man and because of this, he did not move out of 10 Downing Street and he passed away nineteen days later at the age of seventy-one. He remains the only Prime Minister or former Prime Minister to die in 10 Downing Street.

A contemporary cartoon. In 1906 Campbell-Bannerman's government granted the Boer states, the Transvaal and the Orange River Colony, self-government within the British Empire. This led to the Union of South Africa in 1910.

35

Herbert Henry Asquith

1908–16

Asquith was Prime Minister for eight years and eight months, which is the longest uninterrupted spell between Lord Liverpool, whose term started in 1812, and Margaret Thatcher, whose term started in 1979. How does he rank? Most commentators say that from April 1908 to August 1914, he was good or even exceptional. The same commentators mostly say that from then until he lost office in December 1916, he was poor or very poor. It was of course the war that made the difference.

Henry Herbert Asquith 1st Earl of Oxford and Asquith (1852–1928), portrait by James Guthrie (1859–1930). *National Galleries of Scotland, Scottish National Portrait Gallery*

This gifted man did not have an easy start in life. He was born in Yorkshire in 1852 and his father died when he was seven. His mother was an invalid, so he stayed with an uncle until he went to a boarding school. Following this, he stayed in lodgings in London and went to a day school. University and a career as a barrister followed. He became an MP in 1886, and from 1892 to 1895, he served as Home Secretary in the cabinets of Gladstone and Rosebery. When the Liberals returned to power in 1905, he was Chancellor or the Exchequer and introduced three budgets.

As Prime Minister, Asquith inherited Campbell-Bannerman's landslide majority and set about one of the country's great programmes of social reform. Although there was no nationalisation and it was not a socialist government, it is sometimes compared with Attlee's 1945 administration. It included the introduction of state pensions and Lloyd George's 1909 budget, which introduced land taxes and redistributive income taxes.

Asquith had to face enormous difficulties. The House of Lords rejection of the 1909 budget provoked a constitutional crisis. Following two general elections in 1910, and the King's promise to create new peers if necessary, the 1911 Parliament Act restricted the powers of the Upper House. The government faced industrial unrest and had to deal with militant suffragettes. There was also the long-running problem with Ireland, which by 1914 was in a state approaching civil war.

The First World War required a dynamic inspirational leader and Asquith was not the man to provide it. His relaxed approach had worked well, but something different was needed. In May 1915, a coalition

A studio photograph of Asquith after he had stood down as Prime Minister. *Library of Congress*

government was formed with him at the head. This helped, but he was still under pressure. A devastating blow was the death of his brilliant son, killed fighting in France in September 1916, and another son lost a leg later in the war. His premiership came to an end in December 1916. Sections of the press campaigned against him and he was deserted by leading Conservative coalition colleagues. The dynamic and ambitious Lloyd George was ready, willing, and able to step in and take over.

Asquith did not retire. The Liberal Party split and most of its MPs remained loyal to him. He continued as leader of the opposition, but lost his seat in the 1918 General Election. He came back at a by-election, but he and his party were in a big decline. He lost again in 1924 and then went to the House of Lords. He resigned the Liberal Leadership in 1926 and died in 1928.

Squiffy

Asquith was a man who liked a drink, sometimes quite a lot of them, and as the years went by, he liked more and more. People noticed and it was one of the reasons that his wartime leadership came under pressure. It was also the reason for his nickname 'Squiffy'. In 1911, Churchill said to his wife: 'On Thursday night the PM was very bad: and I squirmed with embarrassment. He could hardly speak: and many people noticed his condition'.[1] On the other hand, Bonar Law, the future conservative Prime Minister, once said: 'Asquith, when drunk, can make a better speech than any of the rest of us when sober'.[2]

A Harrowing Schoolboy Experience

When walking to school one morning, he came across the corpses of five murderers hanging outside Newgate gaol. Half an hour earlier, they had been publicly executed and their bodies were on display for inspection.[3]

The Suffragettes

During the lead up to the First World War, Asquith was the head of a government that would not give votes to women, and as a consequence, he was a particular target for the suffragettes. Sometimes it was demonstrations and inconvenience, but at other times it was worse. A woman threw a hatchet through the window of a railway carriage that he was sharing with the Irish leader John Redmond. It missed him, but hit Redmond. A group of women jumped on the running boards of his car and hit him with dog whips. On another occasion, a group of women tried to rip his clothes off. He was helped by the intervention of his daughter, Violet. The intimidation did not work. It just made him more convinced that the perpetrators were not ready for the vote.

A younger Herbert Henry Asquith. A Spy cartoon from *Vanity Fair*, 1 August 1891.

Kissing Hands in Biarritz

There was no doubt that the King would ask Asquith to succeed Campbell-Bannerman. In fact, he told him so before departing on a six-week holiday in Biarritz. When the close-to-death Campbell-Bannerman finally resigned, Asquith took the boat train and went there to kiss hands. He travelled alone, something that would not happen now.[4]

The Two Mrs Asquiths

In 1877, Asquith married Helen Melland, and by all accounts, including his own, it was a very happy marriage. They had five children together. Helen was of a friendly, placid disposition, with interests that were mainly domestic. Tragically, she died of typhoid in 1891.

In 1894, he married Margot Tennant and this too seems to have been a happy union. He was forty-one and she was fifteen years younger. Margot was very different from Helen, so much so that people wondered how he could be happy with two such very different women. Margot knew everyone that mattered. She had been close to Arthur Balfour and there had even been a rumour of an impending engagement. She was an extrovert ball of energy and not afraid to express her often controversial views. After her husband was deposed, she had a particular loathing for Lloyd George. Gladstone once sent her an invitation in the form of a rather good four-verse poem that he had written. The first verse was as follows:

When Parliament ceases and comes the recess,
And we seek in the country rest after distress,
As a rule upon visitors place an embargo,
But make an exception in favour of Margot.[5]

Margot became stepmother to five children and the couple had two more. She also had three miscarriages, and after the last one, she decided that there would be no more. Asked if she took precautionary measures, she replied: 'Oh no, Henry always withdraws in time. Such a noble man!'[6] To use a modern expression—too much information.

Venetia Stanley

Asquith had a wide circle of women friends and enjoyed spending time with them. The friendships were platonic and his wife, Margot, appeared not to mind. The friendship with Venetia Stanley, however, while almost certainly platonic, was of a different order.

Venetia was twenty-nine years younger than him and they met because she was a close friend of his daughter, Violet. This was in 1910, and after a while, they started writing to each other. From 1912, the volume of the correspondence increased until it became a flood. Furthermore, he took to taking her for drives in his chauffeur-driven car. In August 1914, the month that war was declared, he sent her twenty six letters, and in the first three months of 1915, it was a total of 151 letters. Many of them were lengthy and some were written during cabinet meetings. His letters to her survived and some are valuable historic records of events and his thinking. Her letters to him did not survive and were presumably destroyed.

During all this, Venetia was being courted by Edwin Montagu, who had been pursuing her for some time, and in May 1915, she agreed to marry him. Asquith was considerably upset.

Politics seemed more fun in 1909. A satirical cartoon by Edward Tennyson Reed (1860–1933) published in *Punch*, 1909. Back row (left to right) Richard Haldane, Winston Churchill, David Lloyd George, H. H. Asquith and John Morley. Front Row: Reginald McKenna, the Marquess of Crewe and Augustine Birrell. The caption reads: 'Awful Scene of Gloom and Dejection, When the Ministry Heard of the Lords' Decision to Refer the Budget to the Country'.

36

David Lloyd George

1916–1922

IT MUST HAVE seemed extremely unlikely that the young David Lloyd George would ever become Prime Minister. None of his predecessors in that office came from a working-class background. He did, and his mother was widowed when he was just one year old. Her brother, a very religious shoemaker, played a large part in his upbringing. David grew up in the tiny village of Llanystumdwy, near Criccieth, in a remote part of north-west Wales. He became a supreme master of spoken English, but he was Welsh, very Welsh, and English was his second language.

David Lloyd George (1863–1945), a portrait by Christopher Williams (1873–1934). *National Library of Wales*

Lloyd George was a political genius and a great war leader. He also achieved a great deal in peacetime. He is frequently and justifiably ranked among the very highest of Britain's leaders, but his character was slippery and many say that he was lacking in principles. He was ruthless in pursuing his aims and ruthless in pursuit of his career.

In 1890, at the age of twenty-seven, he won a by-election and entered Parliament as the Liberal member for Carnarvon Boroughs, a constituency that he would represent without interruption for the next fifty-four years. He earned a name for himself in Parliament, but really came to national prominence when he led opposition to the controversial Second Boer War, which started in 1899.

When the Liberals returned to power in 1905, Campbell-Bannerman made Lloyd George President of the Board of Trade, and when in 1908 Asquith stepped up to be Prime Minister, he made him Chancellor of the Exchequer. In the years leading up to the First World War, Lloyd George, with others, laid the foundations of the welfare state. The highlights were the 1911 National Insurance Act and his controversial 1909 budget. Although it did ultimately go through, the budget was at first rejected by the House of Lords. This led to a constitutional crisis and the limiting of the powers of the Upper House.

The First World War started in August 1914, and in May 1915, Prime Minister Asquith formed a coalition government. Lloyd George was made Minister of Munitions. He performed with great energy and success, so when Lord Kitchener perished at sea in the following year, he was the obvious choice to replace him as Secretary of State for War.

Dissatisfaction with Asquith came to a head in late 1916, and following a lot of plotting, Lloyd George replaced him as Prime Minister in December of that year. It was a coalition government with the Conservatives, but only a minority of the Liberals. Most commentators praise him for swiftly taking control, shaking things up, and pursuing the war to a successful conclusion.

David Lloyd George, a studio photograph by George Grantham Bain (1865–1944). *Library of Congress*

At the general election held in December 1918, Lloyd George claimed to be the man that won the war, and he promised to provide a land fit for heroes. His coalition won by a landslide, but he was a Liberal leading a government dominated by Conservatives. The next four years presented him with massive problems. He led Britain's delegation to the Versailles Peace Conference. Afterwards, he said: 'I did as well as might be expected, seated as I was between Jesus Christ and Napoleon Bonaparte'. He was referring to President Wilson of the United States and Prime Minister Clemenceau of France. He handled the bitterness and civil strife that led to the establishment of the Irish Free State.

Coalitions inevitably come to an end, at least British ones do, and towards the end of 1922, most of his unhappy Conservative colleagues withdrew their support. The astonished Prime Minister expected a quick return to power, but he was mistaken. He was fifty-nine and never held office again.

He did not fold his tent and steal away into the night. He carried on leading his faction of the Liberals. The distressed party reunited and he then led it until 1931. It then split three ways and the Lloyd George-led faction held only four seats after the 1931 election. Most of his faction was related to him. How the mighty are fallen.

David Lloyd George became Earl Lloyd George of Dwyfor on 12 February 1945. He died the following month at the age of eighty-two.

Margaret Owen

David married Margaret Owen when he was twenty-five. It was a difficult courtship because her family were Methodists and his were Baptists. That mattered a lot at that time and in that place. In fact, for a while, her parents forbade her to see him and his mother did not attend the wedding. Despite all his subsequent womanising, she remained as fond of him as he was to her. A major problem was that she thought that she was marrying a local solicitor who might one day be an MP, and she was unwilling to spend much time away from her home in Wales. He bitterly resented this and always put his career first. He once wrote to her:

> Be candid with yourself. Drop that infernal Methodism which is the curse of your bitter nature and reflect whether you have not rather neglected your husband. I have more than once gone without breakfast, I have scores of times come home in the dead of night to a cold, dark and comfortless flat without a soul to greet me.[1]

She was a good mother to their five children and she worked hard for him in his constituency, which he frequently neglected. Although there were resentment and rows, she became reconciled, perhaps because

CUSTOMER: (Mr Lloyd George) 'Good day, ma'am! I am afraid I have come with rather a large order. I want an army corps of forty thousand Welshmen for the front'. DAME WALES: 'Certainly, sir. Indeed, look you, I shall no trouble whatever in executing the order. When shall I send them, sir?' Lloyd George took the lead in the movement to raise, in Wales, an Army Corps, of 40,000 men for service at the front. *Western Mail*, 30 September 1914. *University of Cardiff*

she had to be, to his ways with other women. She did eventually spend much more time in London and she became a substantial public figure in her own right. She died in 1941. Their affection never faded.

The Goat

Goats are said to be very promiscuous and that is the reason for his acquisition of this particular nick-name. He had numerous short-term affairs with women. During the early days of the First World War, Lord Kitchener is said to have remarked that he tried to avoid sharing military secrets with the cabinet because they all told their wives. The exception was Lloyd George, who would tell someone else's wife.

In 1909, *The People* newspaper implied that Lloyd George had had an affair with a married woman. Unless rebutted, this would have been disastrous for his career and he sued for libel. He denied it on oath, almost certainly committing perjury, and the newspaper apologised and paid damages of £1,000. His angry and dreadfully upset wife was persuaded to accompany him to court and support him as he did so. The money was given to charity.[2]

Frances Stevenson

In 1911, twenty-three-year-old Frances Stevenson was engaged by Lloyd George to coach his daughter, Megan, before she went to boarding school. Within two years, he had installed her as both his secretary and mistress. Right from the start, he made it clear to her that he would never leave his wife and she

On 4 September 1936, nearly 14 years after he had been prime minister, Lloyd George visited Adolf Hitler at the Berghof, Obersalzburg. This was lack of judgement on his part, although well-intentioned, for which he faced considerable criticism. He quickly realised his mistake and by 1938 his distaste for Neville Chamberlain led him to disavow Chamberlain's appeasement policies.
Alan Sutton Collection

accepted this. She was infatuated with him and, incidentally, she was a very good secretary. They quarrelled occasionally, and in 1928, she had a child. Lloyd George was probably the father. Lloyd George effectively had two wives, which suited him well. Margaret did not like it, but put up with it. Lloyd George's relationship with Frances lasted for the rest of his life.

In October 1943, after the death of Margaret Lloyd George, the couple married. In February 1945, he was made an Earl. So the mistress became the Countess Lloyd-George of Dwyfor.

A Welsh Enclave

The London home of David and Margaret Lloyd George was a Welsh enclave in the capital. The couple talked to each other in Welsh, and the staff were Welsh speakers recruited from the Principality. Even builders and painters came up to the house from Wales.[3]

A Close Shave in Birmingham

In the early days of the Boer War, Lloyd George toured the country making anti-war speeches. He got an extremely hostile reception in Birmingham, home city of the Colonial Secretary Joseph Chamberlain. The hall was stormed by ruffians who hated him and his anti-war policies. In front of 7,000 people, he started to speak, but he did not finish. He was smuggled out of the hall disguised as a policeman. At least forty people were injured, and a policeman and a rioter were killed.[4]

Margot Asquith's Opinion

Lloyd George's charm did not work on the wife of the Prime Minister that he had ousted in 1916. She reportedly said that he could not see a belt without hitting below it. When his war memoirs were published, she said that she had known that he had won the war, but she had not known that he had done it single handed.

Four Vicious Quotations

Lloyd George could employ vicious wit with devastating effect. Here are four examples.

On the House of Lords: 'A body of five hundred men chosen at random from amongst the unemployed'.[5]

On Herbert Samuel (who was Jewish and who led the Liberal Party from 1931 to 1935): 'When they circumcised Herbert Samuel they threw away the wrong bit'.[6]

On Field Marshall Lord Haig: 'He was brilliant to the top of his army boots'.[7]

On attempting to negotiate with the Irish leader Eamon de Valera: 'Like trying to pick up mercury with a fork'.[8]

Sale of Honours

Lloyd George was by no means the only Prime Minister to be involved in a cash for honours scandal, but he was by far the most blatant. He was a man with a problem and the sale of honours was his solution. After the 1918 General Election, he led a coalition government dominated by the Conservatives. Naturally, the Conservative party's money was for the benefit of the Conservatives, and following the Liberal Party split, the Liberal's money was under the control of the faction led by Asquith. The sale of honours was to finance his political fund, and with his Chief Whip and press agent, he appointed a chancer named Maundy Gregory to do the dirty work. The price list was £10,000 for a knighthood, £30,000 for a hereditary baronetcy, and £50,000 or more for a peerage.[9] A lot were sold.

The scandals were numerous and the King was outraged. Among the worst was Sir John Drughorn, who had been convicted of trading with the enemy. The scandal culminated with a proposed peerage for the eighty-two-year-old South African businessman Sir Joseph Robinson, who had been fined half a million pounds for defrauding the shareholders of his mining companies.[10] The King and others felt insulted and Sir Joseph was persuaded to decline the peerage. Sir Joseph, who was very deaf, at first thought that more money was being asked and reached for his cheque book.[11]

Lloyd George was forced to concede a debate in Parliament. The scandal did him no good at all and it has besmirched his reputation, but at the time, he managed to prevent much of the mud sticking to him.

37

Andrew Bonar Law

1922–23

Bonar Law was born in the colony of New Brunswick in 1858, which was nine years before the formation of the Canadian Federation. He was of Ulster Scots and Scottish descent, and his father was a minister of the Free Church of Scotland. His mother died when he was only two and her sister came out from Scotland to look after the family. When Bonar was twelve, his father remarried and his aunt returned to Scotland. Bonar went with her because it was felt that he would have better opportunities there.

Andrew Bonar Law (1858–1923), photographed in his office at 24 Onslow Gardens, South Kensington, London, 20 October 1922. *Alan Sutton Collection*

He left school at sixteen and started work as a clerk in the small merchant bank owned by his future wife's family. Then, in 1885, with help of an inheritance and a family loan, he became effectively the managing partner in a firm of iron merchants. He had great business talent, did well, and earned a lot of money.

Bonar Law entered Parliament as a Conservative in 1900. He was forty-two, which was a late age for a future Prime Minister, not though so late as Neville Chamberlain who was forty-nine when he became an MP. Bonar Law's rise was swift. Within two years, he was a junior minister, and after his party's 1906 election defeat, he was in the shadow cabinet. In 1911, he became party leader, still in opposition. In this position, he was an opponent of home rule for Ireland, and an implacable opponent of forcing Ulster to leave the United Kingdom. His opposition went as far as associating with people who were willing to use force to protect the status of Ulster.

In May 1915, he joined Asquith's wartime coalition in the relatively junior position of Colonial Secretary. During the coalition's crisis in December 1916, the King asked him to form a government. He declined and gave his support to the energetic and charismatic Lloyd George. Following this, he was Chancellor of the Exchequer in the Lloyd George-led coalition and he held this position until shortly after the war. It is generally recognised that he did a good job. Then, primarily due to ill health, he stepped down to the less demanding position of Lord Privy Seal. At the same time, he gave up his positions as Leader of the House of Commons and Leader of the Conservative Party.

John Bull: 'Aren't you taking off rather more than usual?' Bonar the barber: 'Yes sir; the military cut, you know.' John Bull: 'Right O!' A *Punch* cartoon by Leonard Raven-Hill, (1867–1942), published 1 May 1918.

Bonar Law was a tough businessman, a tough politician, and a tough man. He had played a part in the overthrow of Asquith and he played a part in the overthrow of Lloyd George in 1922. Some leading Conservatives stayed loyal to Lloyd George and this was one of the reasons that Bonar Law came out of semi-retirement and became Prime Minister.

Bonar Law's time in 10 Downing Street was tragically short. At just 209 days, his tenure has been the shortest since Viscount Goderich managed 144 days in 1827–28. Peel and Derby had shorter terms, but they each served more than once. He developed terminal throat cancer and became unable to speak in Parliament. He resigned in May 1923 and died a few months later.

Bonar Law had very firm principles and was generally liked on both sides of the House of Commons. He was also a relatively modest man. Speaking of his rise to power, he said: 'If I am a great man, then a good many of the great men of history are frauds'.[1]

His Name

Bonar Law's mother wanted to name him after Robert Murray M'Cheyne, a preacher who she admired, but did not do so because his older brother was called Robert. Instead, she named him after the Reverend Andrew Bonar. The curious reason was that Bonar was the biographer of the admired M'Cheyne. Bonar was his forename. His friends and family called him Bonar, pronounced to rhyme with honour. Everyone else generally called him Bonar Law.

Family Tragedies

Bonar Law's first family tragedy was the death of his mother when he was only two. Another was the death of his wife when he was only fifty. They had been happily married for eighteen years and the couple had six children. He did not remarry and his sister came from Canada to look after his house. Then two of his three sons were killed fighting in the First World War. Both deaths were in 1917 when he was Chancellor of the Exchequer. One son was posted missing in action and a false report said that he was a prisoner. It was months before the truth was known. The other son trained as a pilot and was killed within a week of joining his squadron.[2]

A Game of Chess at Windsor Castle

Bonar Law started playing chess as a schoolboy and the game was a lifelong hobby. In his later years, he became very good and played mainly with professionals. In April 1921, he and his daughter stayed a weekend at Windsor Castle and an arrangement was made for him to play a game with Sir Walter Parratt. Before the game, Bonar Law whispered that his opponent looked rather old. He was in fact eighty.

After an hour's play, Parratt said that it was checkmate. Bonar Law responded by saying that this was not so because there were seven different moves available to him. Parratt then explained how he could respond to each of them and that whatever he did, checkmate would inevitably follow. Bonar Law studied the board for twenty minutes then agreed that this was indeed the case. Later, he told the King that the game had been very interesting.[3]

An Apology in Advance

At the State Opening of Parliament in February 1912, Bonar Law apologised to the Prime Minister in advance of his forthcoming speech. He said: 'I am afraid I shall have to show myself very vicious, Mr Asquith, this session. I hope you will understand'.

Asquith's Comment After his Funeral

Bonar Law was buried at Westminster Abbey. Asquith, the former Prime Minister, remarked: 'It is fitting that we have buried the Unknown Prime Minister by the side of the Unknown Soldier'.[4]

38

Stanley Baldwin

1923–24; 1924–29; 1935–37

Stanley Baldwin 1920, photograph by Walter Stoneman (1876–1958). *Library of Congress*

STANLEY BALDWIN WAS born in 1867. His wealthy father owned a large and prosperous iron and steel works and was, for a time, Chairman of the Great Western Railway Company. In addition, for his last sixteen years, he was a Conservative MP. Stanley, his only child, worked in the business and took over his father's seat in the Commons when he died in 1908. He was forty-one at the time. He is one of only three Prime Ministers to serve three non-consecutive terms (the others were Lord Derby and Lord Salisbury) and he is the only Prime Minister to have served under three monarchs (George V, Edward VIII, and George VI).

He joined Lloyd George's coalition cabinet as President of the Board of Trade, but he became increasingly unhappy with the Prime Minister's behaviour, particularly the sale of honours. For this reason, he played a leading role, perhaps the leading role, in the decision of most Conservatives to leave the coalition and bring down Lloyd George's government. Following this, he served as Bonar Law's Chancellor of the Exchequer in his brief premiership, then superseded him as Prime Minister in 1923.

He was leader of the Conservative Party for the next fourteen years, and during that time, he was Prime Minister for a total of seven years and eighty-two days. In addition, he was the effective number two in Ramsay MacDonald's National Government from August 1931 to June 1935. He enjoyed good relations with MacDonald and took over from him when he retired.

Baldwin was a successful politician who managed his party very well. He did not initiate many measures, but effectively managed his colleagues. He exuded charm and projected an image of a trustworthy country gentleman. He needed quite a lot of rest and holidays, and made sure that he had them. Possibly, or even probably, he let things drift too much. His triumphs included facing down the general strike. Like Churchill, he had a lot of sympathy for the miners, but could not accept the constitutional outrage of a general strike. He is also generally admired for the way that he handled the abdication crisis in 1936.

The biggest blot on his record is the failure to face up to the looming threat of the dictators and institute a significant rearmament programme. What he did was too little too late. In Baldwin's defence, it has

Stanley Baldwin receives the freedom of Bewdley, 8 August 1925. Baldwin stands with Joseph Oakes, ex-Mayor of Bewdley with the presentation clay pipes and various articles produced in the town. Photograph by Underwood & Underwood, New York. *Library of Congress*

been said that both the Labour and Liberal parties were totally opposed to rearmament, and so were most of the people. A significant weapons programme may well have led to his government's replacement by one that wanted no rearmament at all. It seems a weak argument, but it is a point worth considering.

Enoch Powell memorably wrote: 'All political lives, unless they are cut off in midstream at a happy juncture, end in failure, because that is the nature of politics and human affairs'.[1] Baldwin is perhaps one of the exceptions. He retired on a date of his choosing, immediately following the coronation of George VI and moved to the House of Lords. He was popular and respected. However, his reputation plummeted with the imminence and then the reality of war. In recent years, it has recovered somewhat, but only somewhat.

A Local Belief Honoured

On the day of his birth in Bewdley, Stanley was taken to the top of the house and held high. It was a local belief that babies shown in this way would do well in the world. He did do well, so perhaps there was some justification for the conviction.[2]

A Thrashing at School

While at Harrow, Baldwin sent a pornographic composition to his cousin at Eton. When it was discovered, Stanley's headmaster administered a thrashing. When he later went to Trinity College, Cambridge, he was dismayed to find that his old headmaster had been made Master of Trinity. He subsequently sent his son to Eton.[3]

Tears of the King and his Prime Minister

At the culmination of the abdication crisis, Baldwin said to Edward VIII: 'Well sir, whatever happens my missus and I wish you happiness from the depths of our souls'. The King was moved and so was Baldwin. They both began to cry.[4]

Father and Son

Stanley Baldwin's son, Oliver Baldwin, was a Labour MP from 1929 to 1931, and again from 1945 to 1947. During the first period, father and son represented opposing parties and faced each other across the floor of the House of Commons. When Stanley died in 1947, Oliver inherited his title and became 2nd Earl of Bewdley.

Stanley Baldwin and James Ramsay MacDonald at a Press Conference at the Foreign Office, 26 August 1931. Photograph by Erich Salomon (1886–1944). National Gallery of Victoria, Melbourne

Encounter on a Train

While Prime Minister in the 1920s and while travelling alone on a train, a fellow passenger said to him: 'You are Baldwin aren't you?' When told that he was, the man said: 'Weren't you at Harrow in 84?' Again the answer was affirmative. The man's next question was 'So tell me Baldwin, what are you doing these days?'[5] It is inconceivable that a Prime Minister would now travel alone on a train.

From Stanley Baldwin to Stanley Baldwin

Shortly after becoming Prime Minister for the second time, Baldwin received a letter from a ten-year-old Canadian boy called Stanley Baldwin. He wrote back as follows:

> Dear namesake, I am glad you wrote to me and don't ever forget that you have got a name worth taking care of when you grow up. I will try and not let it down so long as I bear it and you do the same after my work is finished. Good luck to you.[6]

Reducing the National Debt

In 1919, *The Times* published a letter from F. S. T. The writer said that he had bought £120,000 War Loan for cancellation, and that this was about a fifth of his fortune. He was doing this 'as a thank-offering in the firm conviction that never again shall we have such a chance of giving our country that kind of help' and he went on to ask others to consider doing the same.[7] It was only four years later that it became known that F. S. T. stood for Financial Secretary to the Treasury, and at that time, Stanley Baldwin had held the position.

Above left: Baldwin election poster. *Conservative Party Archive Trust*

Above right: A cartoon from *Punch* 1936, by Bernard Partridge (1861–1945).

Power without Responsibility

In 1930, Lord Rothermere and Lord Beaverbrook conducted a vitriolic and unfair press campaign to have Baldwin removed from the leadership of the Conservative Party. In a magnificent speech too long to quote here, he defended himself very effectively. One sentence has justifiably become very famous: 'What the proprietorship of these papers is aiming at is power, and power without responsibility—the prerogative of the harlot throughout the ages'.

His Iron Gates

On Baldwin's retirement, some ornamental iron gates were presented to him by the Worcester Conservative Association. In 1941, iron gates were being requisitioned for scrap to help the war effort, but owners could appeal on the grounds that they were of artistic or historic merit. Baldwin's gates were requisitioned and he appealed. Following this, an architect appointed to assess the gates advised that they should be exempt. However, the Ministry of Supply overruled this and ordered that apart from the gates at the main entrance, they should be taken. At the time, the Minister of Supply was his old enemy, Lord Beaverbrook.

39

James Ramsay MacDonald

1924; 1929–35

BORN IN 1866, MacDonald was the first Labour Prime Minister, and he ranks with Keir Hardie and Arthur Henderson as one of the main founders of the Labour Party. Lloyd George claimed to be the lowliest born Prime Minister to date, but MacDonald's origins were more humble still. The illegitimate son of a housemaid and a farmworker, he was born and raised in Lossiemouth, which is on the south side of the Moray Firth in Scotland. Money and material comforts were in very short supply.

James Ramsay MacDonald, a photograph of *c.* 1910 to 1915. *Library of Congress*

After a variety of jobs and work in the Labour movement, he was elected to Parliament in 1906 and became party leader (technically Chairman of the Labour MPs) in 1911. Although not a pacifist, he opposed Britain's participation in the First World War, which in the jingoistic attitudes of the time made him extremely unpopular, and as a result, he lost his seat in the 1918 election. However, he returned to Parliament in 1922, and two years later, he was Prime Minister. This was in a minority Labour Government put in with the support of the Liberal Party. He was his own Foreign Secretary and had some success in ameliorating the harshness of the reparations imposed on Germany by the Treaty of Versailles. He was replaced as Prime Minister by Baldwin after just nine months.

Following the 1929 election, MacDonald returned as Prime Minister, once more in a minority Labour Government, and before long, he had to deal with the start of the Great Depression. This was enormously difficult for him because it made it almost impossible to deliver what he and his supporters wanted.

The 1931 financial crisis led to the end of the Labour Government. Most of MacDonald's cabinet, to say nothing of his party, were unwilling to stomach the cuts and orthodox financial policy that he and his Chancellor thought were essential. Consequently, he offered his resignation to the King. He was expecting to be replaced by Baldwin, but to his surprise, he was asked to lead a National Government. MacDonald continued in office, joined by the Conservatives and the National Liberals. Only two members of his cabinet stayed with him. All three of them were expelled from the Labour Party and to Labour he became the 'Lost Leader'. Large parts of the Labour movement still refer to him in this way.

James Ramsay MacDonald, portrait, 1911, by Solomon Joseph Solomon (1860–1927). *National Portrait Gallery*

MacDonald's presence at the head of the government was thought to be essential, but his health, mental faculties, and performance progressively declined. In fact, from 1933, he was at times an embarrassment. Like Churchill twenty years later, he went on too long. The role of Baldwin became progressively more important and the exhausted Prime Minister resigned in 1935. George V told him: 'You have been the Prime Minister that I have liked the best'.[1] Perhaps the King was just being kind, but if he meant it, he was placing MacDonald ahead of Asquith, Lloyd George (not surprisingly), Bonar Law, and Baldwin.

Did he do well? From humble beginnings, he was a leading figure in a new political party, and within thirty years, he was Prime Minister. A modern parallel would be Nigel Farage being Prime Minister of a UKIP government in 2025. When he formed the National Government, he did what he thought was right, what the King thought was right, and what much of the British people thought was right. On the other hand, in 1931, he was expelled from his party. In his 1954 autobiography, *As it happened*, Clement Attlee said that what he did was 'the greatest betrayal in the political history of the country'.

An Exchange of Letters

Ramsay married Margaret Gladstone (no relation to the Liberal Prime Minister) in London in 1896. She was comfortably off and from a middle-class family. His wife shared his socialist views and worked hard with him. Before the wedding, Margaret wrote a beautiful letter to her future mother-in-law in Lossiemouth. It included the remarkable question: 'There is one thing that I should be very glad if you would tell me, and that is by what name I am to call your son. I only know him as Mr MacDonald and really don't know what Christian name he uses'.[2] Did she really not know? It seems so. The reply answers the question and is a charming letter. It reveals the limitations of her future mother-in-law's education.[3]

The couple had six children. Sadly, Margaret died of blood poisoning fifteen years after the wedding. Ramsay was devastated and her death put a cloud over the rest of his life.

Messages from Beyond the Grave

MacDonald believed that, via a medium, he received messages from his dead wife. He sometimes replied to them.[4]

An American cartoon showing John Bull in appreciation of a Labour Prime Minister.
Library of Congress

Three Memorable MacDonald Quotes

They pushed the nomination down my throat behind my back.[5]

We hear war called murder. It is not: it is suicide.

The Observer
4 May 1930

Tomorrow every duchess in London will want to kiss me.

After forming the National Government
1931

Winston Churchill's Harsh Judgement

Speaking in the House of Commons on 17 February 1931, Churchill said the following:

> I remember when I was a child, being taken to the celebrated Barnum's circus which contained an exhibition of freaks and monstrosities. The exhibit on the programme that I most desired to see was the one described as 'The Boneless Wonder'. My parents judged that the spectacle would be too revolting and demoralising for my youthful eyes. I have waited fifty years to see the Boneless Wonder—sitting on the Treasury Bench.

The Kindness of Mrs Baldwin

In January 1924, twenty-year-old Ishbel MacDonald, Ramsay's daughter, received a note from Mrs Lucy Baldwin inviting her to visit 10 Downing Street. Mrs Baldwin greeted her warmly and said that her husband would shortly lose a vote of confidence and that Ishbel's father would soon be Prime Minister. She presumed that as her mother had died, Ishbel would be in charge of the house. Lucy Baldwin showed her

A cartoon by Herbert Johnson. It shows 'British fire-eaters' and 'American fire-eaters' in heated argument, and another scene showing Herbert Hoover and Ramsay MacDonald in rational discussion at the London Naval Conference of 1930. *Library of Congress*

round and gave her some practical advice. She said with a chuckle: 'First Labour government in history. Rather exciting! The boat trains to the continent are already jammed with people stampeding abroad'.[6]

Poverty in 10 Downing Street

In 1924, MacDonald's appointment to the position of Prime Minister resulted in financial problems for him. The Board of Works supported the government part of 10 Downing Street, but the Prime Minister had to pay for the private apartments. MacDonald, who had little money, had to provide furniture and things such as crockery and linen, and he had to pay servants and for heating part of the house.

Some friends in Lossiemouth sent their daughters to work in Downing Street, and in order to save on heating, the family ate in the official banqueting rooms. For a while, MacDonald used public transport, and to save the bus fares, his two youngest daughters walked to and from their school in Camden.

Lady Londonderry

During his later years, MacDonald enjoyed close friendships with a number of high-born women. The most notable and enduring of them was with the Marchioness of Londonderry, a leading Tory hostess. The friendships, and this one in particular, upset some of his colleagues and former colleagues. It was a class issue. They did not mind him being close to a woman, but they objected to him being close to a rich, married, upper-class, aristocratic Tory one. The friendship was genuine and deep, and it amounted to a platonic love affair.

They met at a Buckingham Palace dinner in 1924. He was a lonely widower and she was feeling neglected by her husband. He would often call on her at Londonderry House, and they would write affectionate letters and poems to each other. MacDonald's detractors said that it was one indication of many that he had 'gone native' and abandoned his working class and socialist roots.

Final Session in Ramsay MacDonald's hotel room, during the during the reparations conference in Lausanne, June 1932. To MacDonald's right is Alexis Leger the French poet-diplomat (more commonly known by his pseudonym of Saint-John Perse). To Leger's right is The French Prime Minister Edouard Herriot. To the left of the photo, with cigar in left hand and looking over his right shoulder is Franz von Papen (1879–1969), German Chancellor 1 June 1932–17 November 1932, who inadvertently let Hitler into power. Photograph by Erich Salomon (1886–1944).

In April 1933 Ramsay MacDonald visited Washington at the invitation of Franklin Delaney Roosevelt. On 22 April he had luncheon at the White House. During the visit, Roosevelt's pet Alsatian dog, Major, disgraced himself. His attack on the ministerial trousers was so vigorous that MacDonald's trousers were nearly ripped off, and a replacement pair had to be found so that he could decently exit the presidential residence. Although no official complaint was lodged, this was extremely embarrassing for Roosevelt. After all, here was a dog whose breed originated in Germany. The press did not miss the symbolic significance of this, and Major was banished to FDR's mansion in Hyde Park. *Library of Congress*

40

Arthur Neville Chamberlain

1937–40

Mention of Neville Chamberlain's name inevitably results in thoughts of appeasement and Munich. In these matters—very big matters—the verdict of history has not been kind.

Neville Chamberlain (1869–1940), portrait by Sir William Orpen (1878–1931), 1929. *Sothebys*

Born in 1869, he was educated at Rugby, then at Mason's College (later Birmingham University). He was a rather solitary child and young man. After leaving college, he was apprenticed to a firm of accountants, then he went into business. First there was a failed venture in the Bahamas, but then he was very much a business success. He made money and showed himself to be hard working and a very good administrator. These traits remained evident through his subsequent political career.

Following in his father's footsteps, he engaged in public service and in local politics. In 1915, this culminated in his appointment as Lord Mayor of Birmingham. He was forty-six at the time.

In December 1916, following a ten-minute discussion with Lloyd George, he abandoned his second term as Lord Mayor of Birmingham and accepted the position of Director General of National Service. It was difficult because he was outside Parliament and he was not given the authority to do the job properly, so after a few months, he resigned. With a great deal of justification, he blamed Lloyd George, but the latter blamed him. There was bad feeling between them for the rest of Chamberlain's life. Lloyd George believed in phrenology and later wrote that he was put off by the shape of Chamberlain's head.[1]

Chamberlain became an MP in 1918 at the late age of nearly fifty. He was offered junior ministerial roles but he would not serve under Lloyd George. This self-imposed exclusion from office ended with the appointment of Bonar Law as Prime Minister. During the next fifteen months, he was progressively Postmaster General, Paymaster General, Minister of Health, and then Chancellor of the Exchequer. After the short-lived Labour Government, Baldwin asked him to again serve as Chancellor. However, he turned down this more prestigious role in favour of another nearly five years as Minister of Health. We may well think that this does him credit. He chose the job that he thought he could do best. Later in the National Government, he was Minister of Health for a few months, then Chancellor of the Exchequer for more than five years.

Neville Chamberlain with Adolf Hitler, at Hitler's home, the Berghof, Obersalzburg, near Berchtesgaden, 15 September 1938. 69-year-old Chamberlain had left Croydon at dawn, taken a seven-hour flight to Munich and after a short car journey had a three hour train journey to Berchtesgaden. From left to right: Neville Chamberlain, Adolf Hitler, Paul Schmidt (Hitler's interpreter) and Nevile Henderson, British Ambassador to Berlin. *Alan Sutton Collection*

Chamberlain accompanied by Sir Horace Wilson, left Heston Aerodrome early in the morning of 29 September 1938 and arrived at the Führerbau in Königsplatz, Munich, where a second meeting with Hitler commenced at 12:45 p.m. Chamberlain returned to Heston in triumph on 1 October, brandishing the declaration which he had signed with Hitler, saying 'Peace for our time'. *Alan Sutton Collection*

Prime Ministers are invariably judged on their performance in that office, and in his case, the judgment is harsh. However, in the view of Harold Wilson, Harold Macmillan, and many others, he was an exceptionally good Minister of Health.[2, 3] He also had some success as Chancellor. However, he must share with MacDonald and Baldwin the blame for not rearming quickly enough. He worked hard, had ideas, and was a good administrator. When Baldwin retired in 1937, he was the obvious choice to succeed him as Prime Minister.

Right from the start, Chamberlain decided to appease Hitler. He dominated his cabinet and his party, so he received general support. The most blatant example was his abandonment of Czechoslovakia and his three flights to see Hitler in Munich. As we know, Hitler did not keep his promises. Eventually, Chamberlain decided that enough was enough and the country went to war when Germany invaded Poland.

Chamberlain was not a good war leader and he knew it. Following the so-called Phoney War and the failed Norway campaign, he was forced to resign in favour of Churchill, who formed a coalition government. Chamberlain, who was still leader of the Conservative Party, retained considerable sympathy and served in Churchill's war cabinet. The two men got on surprisingly well, but it did not last long. Chamberlain developed bowel cancer and died in November 1940.

A Political Family

Neville Chamberlain came from a very prominent political family based in Birmingham. His father, Joseph Chamberlain, was a self-made businessman, who before he was forty had been Mayor of Birmingham three times. What is more, he had come to national prominence due to his progressive and successful policies. He acquired the nickname 'Radical Joe'. In Parliament, he became President of the Board of Trade, and he played a leading role in opposing Home Rule for Ireland and splitting the Liberal Party. Later, he became Secretary of State for the Colonies at the time of the Second Boer War, and then he split the Conservative Party over tariff reform.

Neville's half-brother was Sir Austen Chamberlain, six years his senior. Sir Austen held a number of cabinet posts including Foreign Secretary and Chancellor of the Exchequer (twice). He was, for a time, Leader of the Conservative MPs, but never Prime Minister. Neville's uncle Richard was also an MP.

An American cartoon by Lute Pease (1869–1963), 'What the cat brought in'. Subsequent events showed that Hitler completely repudiated Chamberlain's pieces of paper. *Library of Congress*

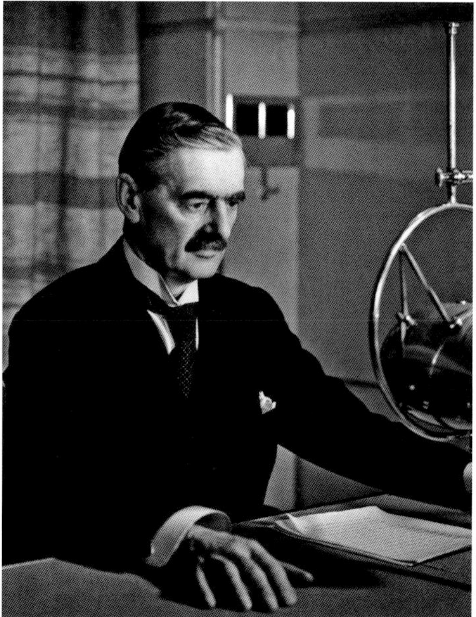

11:15 a.m., Sunday 3 September 1939: 'This morning the British Ambassador in Berlin handed the German Government a final Note stating that, unless we heard from them by 11 o'clock that they were prepared at once to withdraw their troops from Poland, a state of war would exist between us. I have to tell you now that no such undertaking has been received, and that consequently this country is at war with Germany'.

Sisal

In early 1891, the Chamberlain family fortune was in a poor state and Joseph decided on a speculative venture to try and improve the finances. The plan was to grow sisal in the Bahamas. Twenty-two-year-old Neville was put in charge of the venture. He found a 10,000-acre site on Andros Island and set about clearing it and planting the sisal. In the early days, he did physical work himself and he was the only white person at the location. At the peak, 800 labourers were employed.

The venture did not succeed. The sisal was not of the right quality, the bailing shed and its contents were destroyed in a fire, and the market price of sisal moved sharply downwards. Joseph Chamberlain lost £50,000, though his finances in other areas had improved. Twenty-seven-year-old Neville had been given an almost impossible task, but it was not a good start to adult life for the future Prime Minister.

A Lloyd George Jibe

From 1917, Chamberlain did not like Lloyd George and the feeling was mutual. Lloyd George had a witty and acid tongue and the following is one of his many jibes. It unfairly disparages Chamberlain's background in local government: 'Not a bad Lord Mayor of Birmingham in a lean year'.[4]

Flying

Chamberlain did not use an aeroplane until 1938 when he made his three flights to Germany to meet Hitler. He was sixty-nine at the time. Other Prime Ministers were more adventurous. MacDonald was piloted round the country in an open cockpit, and Churchill first flew in 1912 and was a regular flyer afterwards. In the early days, fatal crashes were common.

Munich

Czechoslovakia was a young state created by the Treaty of Versailles in 1919. Within its borders were Czechs, Slovaks, Hungarians, Poles, Ruthenians, and 3½ million ethnic Germans of the Sudetenland.

Winston Churchill with Chamberlain. Churchill succeeded Chamberlain, on 10 May 1940. Chamberlain died of cancer on 9 November 1940. After his funeral, Churchill spoke in the Commons: 'Whatever else history may or may not say about these terrible, tremendous years, we can be sure that Neville Chamberlain acted with perfect sincerity according to his lights and strove to the utmost of his capacity and authority, which were powerful, to save the world from the awful, devastating struggle in which we are now engaged ...'.

Hitler stirred up trouble and violence as a prelude to annexing the Sudetenland and the whole of the country later. France was committed by treaty to defend the country and the USSR had also agreed to do so provided that France acted first.

As Europe teetered on the brink of war, Chamberlain flew to Germany three times. Eventually, the Czechs were betrayed and a programme was agreed for Germany to take over part of the country. Hitler declared that this was his last territorial claim in Europe. On his return, Chamberlain was mobbed and his reception was ecstatic. From the window of 10 Downing Street, he declared that, like Disraeli in 1878, he had brought back from Germany 'peace with honour ... I believe that it is peace for our time'. The King and Queen unwisely allowed him to appear on the balcony of Buckingham Palace with them.

The mood of euphoria changed very quickly. In early 1939, Hitler seized the parts of the country that he had not already taken. Poland was next, and war came later that year.

The Funeral

Chamberlain died on 9 November 1940. He was cremated on 14 November and his remains were interred in Westminster Abbey next to those of Bonar Law. Churchill and other cabinet members acted as pall-bearers. Churchill shed tears as he often did. The funeral was a quiet one with details not released in advance. This was because most of the government gathered at a known time and place would be a tempting target for the Luftwaffe.

41

Sir Winston Leonard Spencer Churchill

1940–45; 1951–55

WINSTON CHURCHILL REGULARLY tops polls to establish Britain's greatest Prime Minister, and he regularly tops polls to establish Britain's greatest person. His interests went beyond politics and included painting, bricklaying, and writing. His great outpouring of books and articles resulted in the Nobel Prize for Literature. Some Prime Ministers have had few interests outside politics, and have not enjoyed a happy retirement. Margaret Thatcher comes to mind. This is not true of Churchill. He was a charismatic Prime Minister and had a memorable way with both the spoken and written word. It is not surprising that this is one of the longer chapters in this book.

Winston Leonard Spencer Churchill (1874–1965). Churchill with a Tommy-gun during an inspection near Hartlepool, 1940. Joseph Goebbels took delight with this photograph and used it many times in anti-British propaganda saying that it proved Churchill was a gangster.

Born in 1874, Churchill was educated at Harrow and then as a soldier at Sandhurst. He was often a rather curious cross between a soldier, a war correspondent, and a writer of military books, something sometimes resented by his senior officers. He reported on a war in Cuba and served on the north-west frontier of India. His exploits included taking part in the last cavalry charge made by the British Army. This was at Omdurman in the Sudan in 1898. He fought in and reported on the Second Boer War in South Africa, and while doing this, he was captured and then escaped. During the First World War, he served in a senior role on the Western Front. He was a great leader and did not show fear, perhaps because he did not feel it.

It is sometimes said that Churchill served in the parliaments of six monarchs, but this is not quite right. He was elected as a Conservative in the khaki election of October 1900. This was in the reign of Victoria, but he did not take his seat until after her death. He served in the parliaments of Edward VII, George V, Edward VIII, George VI, and Elizabeth II. In 1904, he changed parties and sat as a Liberal. This was because he supported free trade and disagreed with many Conservatives on tariffs.

He rapidly ascended the ministerial ladder and held a succession of cabinet positions. Then he was forced out of office in 1915 following the failure of the Dardenelles campaign in the First World War. However, he returned and held a further round of senior positions under Lloyd George. He was out of

'Go to it', a *Daily Express* cartoon on 8 June 1940 by Sidney Conrad Strube (1892–1956).

Parliament for two years starting in 1922, then came back as a Conservative. He was Chancellor of the Exchequer under Baldwin for nearly five years. During this time, he returned Britain to the gold standard, which many consider to have been a mistake.

Churchill's wilderness years started in 1929 and he was then out of office for ten years. During the 1930s, he repeatedly warned about Hitler, appeasement, and the need for rearmament, but his views did not find favour. He was right, though, as events proved. He returned to government as First Lord of the Admiralty on 3 September 1939, and he became Prime Minister in May 1940.

No Prime Minister has had a more troublesome initiation. A few days after his appointment, German forces swept through the Low Countries and forced France to surrender. Shortly afterwards, the British Army evacuated through Dunkirk. The country stood alone.

Churchill's genius triumphed in two ways. He ran the war well and he brilliantly rallied the country with his speeches and leadership. Britain, with its Allies, did eventually triumph, but the British people ejected him from office in the July 1945 General Election.

He returned and was again Prime Minister for three and a half years, starting in October 1951. He was still a great Prime Minister and a great man, but as is the case with many great men and women, he went on too long. A major stroke and other illnesses were covered up by his colleagues and the press. He resigned at the age of eighty and died at the age of ninety. On 30 January 1965, he was accorded a magnificent state funeral, the only non-royal one since William Gladstone in 1898.

His Memory

Winston was blessed with a remarkable memory. In his early days at Harrow, he won a prize open to the whole school by faultlessly reciting from memory 1,200 lines of Macaulay's *Lays of Ancient Rome*. Most of his early political speeches, some up to half an hour long, were meticulously prepared then memorised word for word.

His Mother

In perhaps his best book, *My Early Life*, Winston wrote of his mother: 'She shone for me like the Evening Star. I loved her dearly—but at a distance'. The evidence of letters supports this. She was a loving, but rather remote figure, and Winston was a boy who craved love and attention. She was widowed at the age of forty-one.

Winston's mother, Jenny, Lady Randolph Churchill, was American by birth. She accepted Lord Randolph's proposal on their third meeting and they married when she was twenty. Winston, a full-sized baby, was born in Blenheim Palace seven months and fifteen days after the wedding. The couple said that he was conceived on their wedding night, which might or might not have been true—Jenny had a fall that brought on the labour.

Jenny had affairs during her twenty-year marriage and considerably more of them afterwards. Many were with powerful and titled men—the Prince of Wales (later Edward VII) being one. She married three times, the last two marriages being with men much younger than herself. Her third husband was three years younger than Winston.

Nanny Everest

Elizabeth Everest tended Winston and later his brother, Jack. Winston's parents were rather neglectful of him and she was a big influence in his formative years. He was devoted to her. One of her services was to spot that he had been sadistically beaten by the headmaster at his first school. She reported this to his parents with the result that he was moved to another establishment. He once said that when he had a really intractable problem, he would ask himself what Nanny Everest would have done. He would then do it and it would generally turn out to be the right thing.

Winston was twenty when Nanny Everest died at the age of sixty-three. He contacted the archdeacon who had been her employer before his parents and they both attended her funeral. Churchill paid for her headstone and for many years paid an annual sum to a local florist for the upkeep of her grave.

A Long Letter to his Wife

Winston and his wife were often apart for lengthy periods and they wrote to each other very frequently. Winston ended one letter with the words, 'I am sorry that this is such a long letter. I did not have the time to write a short one'. This was not a joke. It reflects the fact that it takes longer to write something

'Hitler's Nightmare', a cartoon by 'Kem', Kimon Evan Marengo (1904–1988) in *Le Petit Parisien*, 6 April 1944. This was so popular it was reproduced in 126 different periodicals, but *Le Petit Parisien* ceased publication that year, possibly closed by the Nazi occupation authorities.

The Yalta conference, 4 to 11 February 1945. From left to right: Winston Spencer Churchill, Franklin D. Roosevelt and Joseph Stalin.

carefully crafted where every word counts. Throughout his life, Winston spent a great deal of time getting his speeches and writing exactly right. Longer and nearly right would not do.

An Invitation from George Bernard Shaw

In 1924, George Bernard Shaw sent him two complimentary tickets for the opening night of his play *Saint Joan*. His letter said: '[they are] for yourself and a friend, if you have one'. Churchill replied that he had a prior engagement but would come to the second night: 'if there is one'.

A Jibe at Old Etonians

During a speech in the House of Commons, Churchill used the Latin phrase '*primus inter pares*'. There were calls for a translation and he responded: 'Certainly I shall translate (pause)—for the benefit of any Old Etonians who may be present'.

An Encounter in a White House Bathroom

Japan attacked Pearl Harbor on 7 December 1941. Churchill's reaction was, 'We had won after all.'[1] Four days later, Germany declared war on the United States—surely one of Hitler's biggest blunders. Churchill immediately crossed the Atlantic and was for a while the guest of President Roosevelt in the White House. While there, Roosevelt entered a bathroom occupied by a naked Prime Minister. Churchill was not perturbed. His words to the visitor were, 'The Prime Minister of Great Britain has nothing to hide from the President of the United States.'

Painting

Everyone should have a hobby and Churchill's hobby was painting. He came to it relatively late and it gave him much pleasure for the rest of his life. In the opinion of many experts, his talent was sufficient for him to have earned his living in this way. He started during a grim period in 1915 after resigning as First Lord of the Admiralty. He painted mainly in oils and his subjects were mainly landscapes. He completed more than 500 canvases and continued painting well into his eighties.

The Books

Churchill wrote because he enjoyed writing and because he had something to say, but money was a major factor. He was hard up for most of his life and writing was his main source of income. He wrote for newspapers and magazines, but he is best known for his books. There was a novel and a short story, but he mainly wrote non-fiction.

There were fourteen non-fiction titles, but as some were in several volumes, there were thirty-two books in all. Many of them were long or very long. After the Second World War, Churchill said that he knew that history would be kind to him because he intended to write it. He did; his six-volume *The Second World War* comprised 1½ million words. The first volume was published in 1948 and the last in 1953 so it was all written when he was Leader of the Opposition or Prime Minister. The advances for the six volumes finally solved his seemingly perpetual money problems. His first book was published in 1898, and the last in 1958, when he was eighty-three.

In 1953, he was awarded the Nobel Prize for Literature for 'his mastery of historical and biographical description as well as for brilliant oratory in defending exalted human values'.

Two Examples of his Wit

Churchill is famed for his witticisms, sometimes to make a point and sometimes just to be funny. There are scores to choose from, but here are two:

During an election campaign, a prospective voter shouted, 'I'd sooner vote for the devil than I would you Mr Churchill.' The reply quickly came, 'I do understand sir, but as your friend is not a candidate I am going to ask for your support.'

During a lecture tour in the United States, Churchill asked his hostess for some breast of chicken. She complied but said that in the US, it was normal to refer to it as white meat. The next day, he sent the lady an orchid with a note suggesting that she might like to pin it to her white meat.

Support for a Maid at Chequers

A friend of my family worked at Chequers during the Second World War and she said that both Winston and his wife, Clementine, were loved by the staff. She told us the following:

> One Sunday morning, Clementine mentioned that she had not seen one of the young maids and asked if she was alright. She was told that the girl in question had walked over the fields in order to be confirmed at the local parish church. Clementine was very pleased and enquired if her friends and family would be there to support her. She was told that no one had been able to come and that she would be on her own. Clementine immediately fetched Winston and his guests. They all got into cars and drove to the church. So in the middle of the war, the young maid was confirmed with the support of the Prime Minister, his wife, and a number of other very important people.

A Remarkable Example of Modern Art

By the time of his eightieth birthday in November 1954, Churchill, still Prime Minister, was almost above politics. As a present to mark the occasion, many members of the House of Lords and nearly all

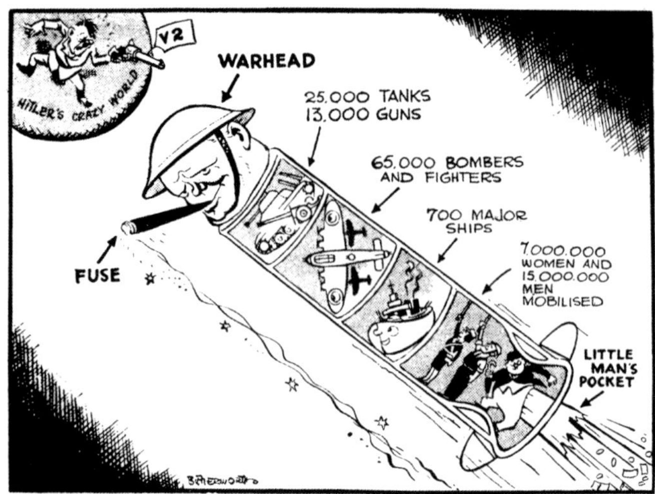

'And we mean V, too!' The cartoon response to the V1 and V2 attacks, a cartoon in the *Manchester Daily Despatch*, 29 November 1944 by George Butterworth (1905–1988).

the MPs commissioned and paid for a Graham Sutherland portrait. It was unveiled by Churchill in a ceremony at Westminster Hall.

When the great man removed the covering drape, shocked gasps were heard from all quarters. Sutherland had painted what he had seen or thought that he had seen. This was a very old man who had suffered strokes. The renowned bulldog spirit was there, but some observers thought that they could see a hint of senility. An on-form Churchill smiled, took a step back, and then said: 'I want to thank you for this remarkable example of modern art'. It was not meant as a compliment. The audience roared with laughter.

Churchill took the picture home and it was never seen again. He hated it and his wife, Clementine, hated it even more. It was put away and then burned on Clementine's instructions. One can see why they hated it, but it was, in its way, a fine picture.

An Unattractive Fiancée

Tom Driberg, the Labour MP, was homosexual and behaved outrageously for a very long time, often in public lavatories. His behaviour was illegal and exposure would have had devastating consequences. Almost everyone at Westminster knew, but he got away with it. To everyone's amazement, he was engaged to be married in 1951, and his fiancée was of exceptionally plain appearance. Churchill commented, 'Oh well, buggers can't be choosers'.[2]

42

Clement Richard Attlee

1945–51

BORN IN 1883, Clement Attlee was elected to Parliament in 1922. He became Deputy Leader of the Labour Party in 1931 and then Leader in 1935. He took his party into Winston Churchill's wartime coalition, and from February 1942, he was Deputy Prime Minister. Following Labour's landslide victory, he became Prime Minister and held the position for more than six years. His government gave independence to India, set up the National Health Service, nationalised key industries, and vastly expanded the welfare state, and what is more, it did it all quickly at a time of considerable economic difficulty. It transformed the country.

Clement Richard Attlee (1883–1967). The newly appointed Prime Minister Clement Attlee stands at the entrance to his residence shortly after his arrival in Berlin, Germany to attend the Potsdam Conference, 29 July 1945. *Harry S. Truman Library*

It was a formidable record and he was a formidable man. Regardless of one's view of his policies, it is right to acknowledge that he should be very close to the top of the list of Britain's most successful Prime Ministers, and he is almost invariably so regarded. Why then was he so underrated at the time? It was partly because of his modest, self-effacing manner. He worked behind the scenes—so unlike his predecessor and successor Winston Churchill. He was famously taciturn and would not use two words when one would do. It was rather humorously said that he would not use one word when none would do. Another reason was that he neglected presentation in favour of substance. He would have been the despair of our present-day spin doctors.

Attlee was the seventh of eight children of a prosperous London solicitor. He was educated at Haileybury, then University College, Oxford. He worked in a boys' club in East London and the experience shaped his socialist views. He was a lecturer at the London School of Economics.

Unlike one of his brothers, who was a conscientious objector, he volunteered and was commissioned at the start of the First World War. He served with distinction in Gallipoli, Mesopotamia, and on the Western Front. He was badly wounded, but served for the entire war and finished with the rank of major. Returning home to local politics, he was the Mayor of Stepney in 1919.

Attlee's contribution to Churchill's wartime coalition was considerable. He chaired the Lord President's Committee, which was responsible for domestic affairs, and was deputy chairman (to Churchill) of the

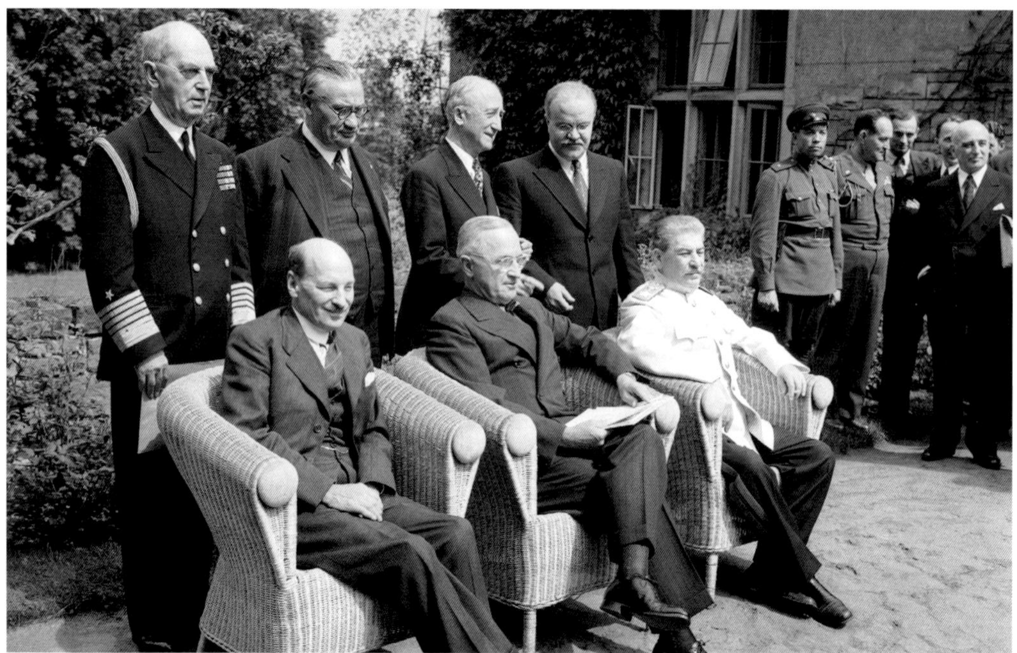

Clement Attlee with President Truman and Marshal Stalin at the Potsdam Conference in Berlin, 1 August 1945. A photograph by No. 5 Army Film & Photographic Unit.

War Cabinet and the Defence Committee. Insiders were aware of his crisp, administrative skills. He chaired the cabinet and ran the government during Churchill's frequent absences.

The achievements of the post-war Labour Government were many, but by 1950, it had run out of steam. Some of its leaders were old or ill (or both) and one or two were dead. The 1950 election gave Attlee a majority of just five, and Churchill returned to Downing Street in October 1951. Some of Attlee's authority in the Labour Party was gone, and during the early 1950s, the party descended into factional infighting. It did somewhat diminish the former Prime Minister's reputation. He retired at the age of seventy-two after losing the 1955 election.

Acknowledgment of his Shyness

Attlee was well aware of his shyness and of the problems it could cause. In 1945, he said to his junior ministers: 'One more thing: If I pass you in the corridor and don't acknowledge you, remember it's only because I'm shy'.[1]

A Brusque Dismissal

It is said that a Prime Minister needs to be a good butcher, meaning that he (or she) must know when to dismiss colleagues and be able to do it. Many Prime Ministers hated the need to do this. On one occasion, his conversation with an about to be sacked minister went as follows:

> I want your job
>
> But why Prime Minister?
>
> Afraid you're not up to it.[2]

Subjects of Conversation

Like John Major, Attlee loved cricket and it was one of the few subjects on which it was easy to talk to him. One of his ministers, George Strauss, once said that 'it was very difficult to have a relaxed discussion with him on any subject except bishops or cricket'.[3]

A Tribute to Himself

Modest as he was, Attlee penned a rather nice tribute to himself when he became a knight of the garter. It went as follows:

Few thought he was even a starter
There were many who thought themselves smarter
But he ended PM
CH and OM
An earl and a knight of the garter.[4]

His Poem to a Schoolgirl

Attlee loved children and he had a talent for writing light verse. Both were evident in his reply to a complaint sent to him in verse by Ann Glossop, a fifteen-year-old schoolgirl. Her verse was as follows:

Would you please explain, dear Clement,
Just why it has to be
That certificates of education
Are barred to such as me?
I've worked through thirteen papers
But my swot is all in vain,
Because at this time next year
I must do them all again.

Clement Attlee with his wife Violet.

Please have pity Clement,
And tell the others too.
Remove the silly age limit
It wasn't there for you.

The Prime Minister replied as follows:

I received with real pleasure
Your verses, my dear Ann.
Although I've not much leisure
I'll reply as best I can.

I've not the least idea why
They have this curious rule
Condemning you to sit and sigh
Another year at school.

You'll understand that my excuse
For lack of detailed knowledge
Is that school certs were not in use
When I attended college.

George Tomlinson is ill, but I
Have asked him to explain.
And when I get the reason why
I'll write to you again.[5]

George Tomlinson was the Minister of Education, who was ill at the time.

A Letter from his Godson

Every small boy should have a Hornby train set. I did and it gave me a lot of pleasure. Attlee received the following letter from his godson:

> Dear Godfather
>
> It's long past time that you started the Hornby factories going again. Shooly they should be started by now.[6]

In reply, the Prime Minister told him that the trains were being produced, and he enclosed a postal order so that one could be purchased.

A Challenge to a Duel

In 1935, an Italian Army captain called Fanelli challenged him to a duel. His reason was that he had taken offence about Attlee's remarks on the subject of the Italian invasion of Abyssinia. In reply, Attlee told him not to be so silly.[7]

A cartoon by John Fischetti (1916–1980), published in the USA in *Collier's Magazine*, July 1953. The cartoon urges the United States and Great Britain to renew their long-standing special relationship against the background of 'unpleasantness' occasioned by criticism of the United States by Attlee in May 1953. *Library of Congress*

The Absence of Scandal

Matthew Parris makes the point that John Belcher was 'the only minister in Clement Attlee's astonishingly clean post war government to resign after a scandal'.[8] It was a clean government and it was led by a clean Prime Minister. No hint of scandal attached to him at any time in his career. When he died in 1967, his estate was valued for probate purposes at £7,295. Even allowing for inflation, it was not a large sum.

His Delayed Retirement

After losing the 1951 election, Attlee continued to lead the Labour Party, which divided into left-wing and right-wing factions. Without power, his authority was diminished and it was not easy for him. After losing another election in 1955, he finally retired at the age of nearly seventy-three. It is widely believed that he delayed going to thwart the leadership ambitions of Herbert Morrison, who had in the past plotted against him to become Prime Minister. Attlee did not like him and the two men had political differences. If this was indeed his reason for the delay, it worked. Morrison was sixty-seven and seen as too old. It was Hugh Gaitskell who took over the leadership.

43

Sir Robert Anthony Eden

1955–57

BORN IN 1897, Eden was one of the nineteen Prime Ministers to be educated at Eton, and while there, he became very good at French and German, something very useful for his future career. His French was so good that he was able to converse in the language with Chou-En-lai, the Chinese Prime Minister.

He was the third of four successive Prime Ministers who fought in the First World War, following Churchill and Attlee and preceding Macmillan. He was awarded the Military Cross, and at the end of the conflict, he held the rank of brigade-major, the youngest in the British Army. He and his family were scarred by war. His older brother was killed in October 1914 and his younger brother, aged only sixteen, was killed at Jutland in 1916. His brother-in-law was wounded in the same year. Later, his son was killed in Burma in 1945.

Sir Anthony Eden (1897–1977), portrait by William Little. The artist William Little carried out commissions for the Ministry of Information during the Second World War. *The National Archives*

After the war, he graduated from Oxford with a double first in oriental languages, then it was politics, and at the age of twenty-six, he became an MP. Right from the beginning, he specialised in foreign affairs, and in 1931, he became Under-Secretary for Foreign Affairs in Ramsay MacDonald's National Government. Then he was Foreign Secretary from 1935 to 1938, during the Second World War and again in Churchill's post-war government. In all, he was Foreign Secretary for more than ten years.

In 1938, he resigned because he could not accept Chamberlain's policies towards Mussolini. He initially accepted appeasement but his views hardened. He opposed Chamberlain's Munich settlement and abstained in the House of Commons vote.

Eden was for many years the heir apparent to Churchill, but he had to wait a frustratingly long time. He was only Prime Minister for twenty-one months and things went badly wrong. He presided over the Suez calamity and is regarded as one of the least successful holders of the position. In his defence, it can be said that he was in pain, sleeping badly, and that his judgment was probably affected by prescribed drugs, but nevertheless, it was a humiliation for Britain and for him.

Eden equated Nasser with Hitler and wanted him stopped at all costs. He even went as far as to say that he wanted him killed. He eventually arranged with Israel and France that Israel would invade and then

Britain and France would issue ultimatums to Egypt and Israel, then move in to separate the two armies. In doing that, they would occupy and secure the Suez Canal zone. He miscalculated badly. Most of the world disapproved and the United States, which had not been informed, refused to help defeat a run on the pound. Although the military intervention was going well, the invasion had to be stopped before it was completed.

A cartoon by Edwin Marcus, published in the *New York Times* 5 April 1955, with a ghostly Churchill aiding Eden. *Library of Congress*

Immediately afterwards, Eden's health worsened and he was forced to take a holiday. When he returned, it was clear that he had lost the confidence of Parliament and that he had to resign. He was genuinely too ill to continue, but he would have had to have gone anyway.

Anthony Eden was good looking, always impeccably dressed, polite, suave, and charming. However, he was not good at delegating, and at times, he was very short tempered. These problems were manifest while he was Prime Minister, particularly during the Suez Crisis, and they were aggravated by his health problems. It is a shame that he is primarily remembered for his handling of the Suez Crisis. He was a decent man who, for a long time, gave great service to his country.

Precocious Political Knowledge

While still at school, Eden made a railway journey with his mother. As the journey progressed, he astonished her by naming the MPs through whose constituencies the train was passing. He also gave the size of their majorities.

George V's Witticism

Eden replaced Sir Samuel Hoare as Foreign Secretary in 1935 after the failure of the Hoare-Laval Pact. It is said that when Eden had his first audience with George V, the King remarked: 'No more coals to Newcastle, no more Hoares to Paris'.

The Anthony Eden Hat

Eden frequently wore a particular style of hat that became associated with his name. It was a homburg, similar to a trilby, but more rigid, with a single dent running down the centre of the crown.

Two Marriages and a Divorce

Eden married his first wife, Beatrice, in the year that he became an MP. She was eighteen at the time, so she became an exceptionally young political spouse. They had two sons, one of whom was killed in the Second World War. The marriage ended in divorce in 1950. At the time, divorce was frowned upon and relatively rare. Divorced people were not admitted to the Royal Enclosure at Ascot. He remarried in 1952. The *Church Times* commented that not many years previously, a Foreign Secretary would have had to resign rather than take a second wife while the first was still alive. It added:

Sir Anthony Eden with Her Majesty the Queen at a function in 1955.

> Mr Eden's action this week shows how far the climate of public opinion has changed for the worse ... the world is openly rejecting the law of Christ in this as in so much else.[1]

Edward Heath, the future Prime Minister, had been news editor of the *Church Times* from 1948 to 1949. Eden and the Duke of Grafton are the only two Prime Ministers to have been divorced.

Eden's second wife was Clarissa Spencer-Churchill, the niece of Sir Winston Churchill. She was twenty-three years younger than him. She was the niece of a Prime Minister and the wife of the next one. It was a happy marriage and it fell to her to look after him during his illnesses. At the time of writing, Clarissa is ninety-seven and still with us.

An Eccentric Father

Eden's father was eccentric and sometimes bad tempered. In his book *Another World*, Eden told of an occasion when rain was bearing down on hounds, huntsmen, and followers assembling outside his home. He continued:

> As my father came through the front hall to join them, his eye fell on a barometer hanging on the panelled wall. He walked up to it and tapped: it read 'Set Fair'. He tapped again: it still replied 'Set Fair'. He took it off the wall, walked through the front door to the top of the flight of steps and sent it clattering down before the assembled company saying 'Go see for yourself, you damned fool.'[2]

A Lie to the House of Commons

Telling a lie to the House of Commons is a very serious matter, as Mr Profumo found to his cost in 1963, but this is what Eden did on 20 December 1956. He said that 'there was not foreknowledge that Israel would attack'. This was only twenty days before he resigned, but the lie would inevitably have been discovered in time. Indeed, it was eventually discovered.

Ill Health

Eden's health was a major issue and he was dreadfully unfortunate. In April 1953, an operation to remove gallstones went wrong and his bile duct was damaged. This left him susceptible to recurrent infections, biliary obstruction, and liver failure. He had three further operations to try to alleviate the problems, and was in hospital in the United States when Churchill had a major stroke on 23 June 1953. In October 1956, during the Suez Crisis and with a temperature of 106 degrees Fahrenheit, he was admitted to hospital for a short stay. Things were different then and the public did not know.

Eden was prescribed Benzedrine, which is now associated with insomnia, restlessness, and mood swings. He was also prescribed Drinamyl (also known as purple hearts).These can impair judgment and make the patient lose contact with reality. It did probably affect the course of history.

No Regrets

Eden died in January 1977, twenty years after his resignation. He never apologised or expressed regrets for his role in the Suez Crisis. He particularly blamed the Americans for misleading him, then letting him down. He felt particularly strongly about the role of the Secretary of State John Foster Dulles.

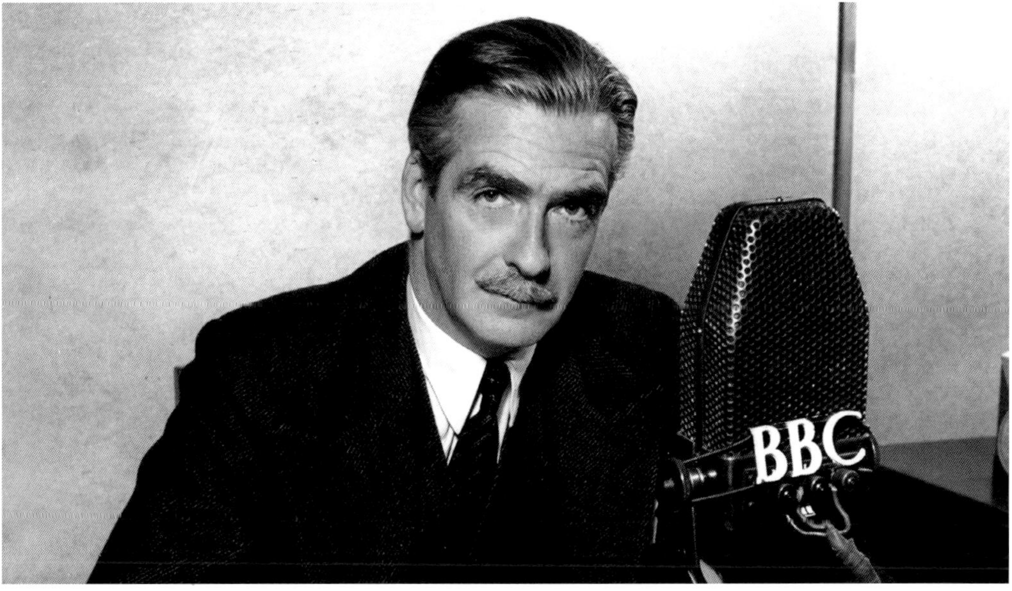

Eden at a BBC broadcast.

44

Maurice Harold Macmillan

1957–63

Born in 1894, Harold Macmillan, like Winston Churchill, had an American mother. He was educated at Eton, but missed the last year because of illness. Afterwards, he progressed to Balliol College, Oxford. His very successful studying only lasted two years and was ended by the onset of the First World War. He did not return to Oxford after the end of the hostilities.

Harold Macmillan (1894–1986), leaves No. 10 Downing Street to attend his first state opening of Parliament since becoming Prime Minister, 5 May 1957.

The call to arms did not find him lacking. He immediately volunteered and served in the Grenadier Guards. In 1915, he was twice wounded at Loos, and in 1916, he was severely wounded at the Somme. As a result, he spent the rest of the war in hospital. Then, after a spell in the family publishing business, he became the MP for Stockton-on-Tees in 1924. Apart from a two-year break in 1929–31, he represented the constituency until 1945. There was a short break in that year, then he represented Bromley until 1964.

Stockton-on-Tees was depressed in the 1930s and many of Macmillan's policies were shaped with a view to alleviating unemployment and hardship in the area. He was something of a rebel. He resigned the Conservative whip in protest at the lifting of sanctions on Italy, and he supported Churchill in opposing appeasement and the Munich settlement. In 1940, he was one of the Conservatives who voted against the Chamberlain government in the Norway debate that resulted in Churchill becoming Prime Minister.

Macmillan was forty-six before he obtained ministerial office in 1940. From then on, he held a number of wartime positions and his rise was swift. From 1942 to 1945, he was Minister Resident in the Mediterranean with cabinet rank. In this job, he got to know Eisenhower and de Gaulle, which was helpful in later years.

When Churchill returned to power in 1951, he made Macmillan Minister of Housing, and it fell to him to keep the government's rather rash promise to build 300,000 new houses a year. He did it and he achieved the target a year ahead of schedule. A spell as Minister of Defence followed, then it was eight months as Foreign Secretary. In December 1955, he was made Chancellor of the Exchequer and he did this job until he became Prime Minister in January 1957. He is particularly remembered for announcing

Selwyn Lloyd and Harold Macmillan are welcomed to Paris at Orly by Charles De Gaulle, 30 June 1958. De Gaulle proved inflexible and the meeting was unsuccessful. Britain was not to join the Common Market.

the introduction of premium bonds in his 1956 budget speech. Harold Wilson said that the government was reduced to organising a squalid raffle.

The Suez Crisis brought Macmillan to Downing Street, but it was not his finest hour. He was first in and first out. Right from the beginning, he wanted force used to recover the canal and topple Nasser. He misjudged the likely American and world reaction, and was wrongfooted by the run on sterling. Then, he was adamant that Britain had to withdraw. After Eden resigned, he was preferred to Butler as his successor.

Macmillan's first term as Prime Minister was successful and the Conservatives increased their majority at the 1959 election. The second term was beset with problems and he was increasingly seen as an Edwardian out of touch with the 1960s. He resigned in October 1963. Following the Profumo scandal, economic difficulties, and other problems, he was in political trouble, but a major cause was a prostate operation and fears for his future health. His many successes included big progress in disengagement from Britain's colonial role.

Scottish Heritage and the Family Publishing Business

Daniel and Alexander Macmillan, who were the sons of a crofter from the Isle of Arran, founded Macmillan Publishing in 1843. Harold was the grandson of Daniel. The publishing company was large and successful. Harold worked in it after the First World War and he was chairman from 1964 to 1974. Books were in his blood and he read widely. His extensive memoirs ran to six volumes.

The Cuckolded Prime Minister

In 1920, Macmillan married Lady Dorothy Cavendish, who was nineteen at the time. She was the daughter of the 9th Duke of Devonshire and a descendant of the 4th Duke of Devonshire, who was Britain's fifth Prime Minister. They do not come much more aristocratic than that, and it helped Macmillan's career. In 1929, Lady Dorothy started an affair with Robert Boothby, her husband's friend and a fellow Conservative MP. It lasted until her death in 1966. Boothby, who was involved in a number of scandals, was bisexual and had affairs with both men and women. Insiders knew all about it, but not the public. Divorce was unthinkable and Lady Dorothy continued to be a dutiful political wife. She had four children and it is suspected that the youngest, born in 1930, was fathered by Boothby.

In 1958, Macmillan made Boothby a life peer—an extraordinarily generous gesture. It probably pleased his wife, and Boothby too of course.

The Wounded Hero

At the Battle of Loos in 1915, Macmillan was shot in the hand and received a glancing bullet wound in the head. The wounds necessitated a stay in hospital in England. The wound to his hand affected his handwriting and left him with a rather limp handshake.

In September 1916, he was severely wounded while participating in the Somme offensive. He lay in a trench for ten hours, sometimes feigning death when Germans came close. He passed the time by reading Aeschylus in the original Greek. He happened to have a copy of the book in his tunic—as you do. The next two years were spent in hospital and he was left with a slight limp. His mother used her influence to have him transferred from a military hospital to a private one. It may have saved his life.

Harold Macmillan on the front cover of *Time* magazine in the USA, 19 October 1959 after winning the General Election.

Nikita Khrushchev converses with Harold Macmillan at the Soviet New York headquarters, 29 September 1960 following Macmillan's disarmament address to the United Nations. Earlier, he twice interrupted Macmillan's speech, pounding his desk with both fists and shouting interruptions to show his disapproval at the way UN forces had intervened in the former Belgian Congo. This was not the famous banging of the desk with his shoe; that happened on 12 October. *Library of Congress*

A Little Local Difficulty

In January 1958, the three Treasury ministers (Peter Thornycroft, Enoch Powell, and Nigel Birch) resigned. The issue was Macmillan's refusal to cut public expenditure in line with what they thought was necessary. Macmillan was about to visit a number of Commonwealth countries and he brushed off the resignations as 'a little local difficulty'. It did not damage him then, but with hindsight (and to be fair at the time too), it was clear that the three ministers were right.

Thornycroft and Powell rejoined the government in 1960. Birch remained an implacable enemy. At the time of the Profumo debate, he devastatingly quoted Browning's poem *The Lost Leader* including the words 'Never glad confident morning again'.

Gone North for the Grouse Shooting

Macmillan was installed as Chancellor of Oxford University in 1959. On one visit, he commented that there were few undergraduates around. On being reminded that it was August, he said, 'Ah yes, I suppose they have all gone north for the grouse shooting.'[1]

Translation Please

Macmillan was addressing a session of the United Nations when he was interrupted by the Russian leader, Nikita Kruschev, banging on a desk with his shoe. The unperturbed Macmillan paused and asked for a translation. It made Kruschev look foolish.[2]

Harold Macmillan with John F. Kennedy, 22 December 1961 at Hamilton, Bermuda. *John F. Kennedy Presidential Library & Museum*

The Night of the Long Knives

In the summer of 1962, the government was going through a bad patch and suffered a run of poor by-election results. Macmillan decided to make drastic changes to his cabinet and he replaced seven members, one-third of the total. Due to a leak by R. A. Butler, it was done in a rush. Macmillan wanted to bring in younger ministers, and the average age was reduced from fifty-nine to fifty. He also wanted to replace the Chancellor of the Exchequer, Selwyn Lloyd, with Reginald Maudling. Selwyn Lloyd had been resisting his plans for a more expansionist economic policy.

The reshuffle became known known as 'The Night of the Long Knives', and in the short term at least, it damaged Macmillan's credibility. It was pointed out that although the average age of the cabinet was reduced, he was sixty-eight and he was keeping his job. Harold Wilson (inaccurately) said that half the cabinet was being sacked, but it was the wrong half. Jeremy Thorpe said: 'greater love hath no man than this, than to lay down his friends for his life'.

Four Macmillan Quotes

When General de Gaulle vetoed Britain's entry to the Common Market: 'The French always betray you in the end'.[3]

On Mrs Thatcher's policy of privatisation: 'Like selling the family silver'.[4]

At a fete in Bedford: 'Let us be frank about it—most of our people have never had it so good'.[5]

To Harold Wilson, who had made claims about his childhood saying that he had no boots to go to school: 'If Mr Wilson did not have boots to go to school, that is because he was too big for them'.[6]

A Cabinet of Old Etonians

Macmillan's first government contained no fewer than thirty-five Old Etonians, of which seven were in the cabinet. It was an extraordinarily high number that attracted unfavourable comment.

Slightly later, I took a German girl for a day trip to Windsor and Eton (which I did not attend). While doing this, I mentioned that the Prime Minister and several members of the cabinet had been to school there. I was later told that she had written to her mother and told her that she had been taken out by a boy who had attended the same school as more than a quarter of the cabinet. This is not relevant, but it is a nice story.

'Gentlemen, we simply must put Humpty Dumpty together again!' A cartoon by Charles George Werner. Published in the *Indianapolis Star*, 18 December 1962. Minister of Defence Peter Thornycroft, Harold Macmillan, John F. Kennedy, and US Secretary of Defense Robert S. McNamara stand on a beach looking worried. The Skybolt air-to-ground nuclear missile that the United States had agreed to produce for the UK was cancelled due to insoluble technical problems. Britain, furious with the USA, demanded some sort of compromise. Macmillan was due to meet Kennedy on 19 December. The outcome was Polaris. *Library of Congress*

45

Sir Alec Douglas-Home

1963–64

Born in 1903, Douglas-Home was the third successive Prime Minister to be educated at Eton College, and the last one to do so before David Cameron. He was remembered with liking and respect by both masters and boys, and in 1936, he married the daughter of the man who had been his headmaster. After Eton, it was Christ Church, Oxford, where he got a third-class honours BA degree.

Luncheon at the White House in honour of Sir Alec Douglas-Home, 12 September 1962, then Foreign Secretary; a year before becoming Prime Minister. *John F. Kennedy Presidential Library & Museum*

He became an MP in 1931, and five years later, he was Parliamentary Private Secretary to Neville Chamberlain, first when he was Chancellor of the Exchequer, then when he was Prime Minister. Douglas-Home's ease and charm was of considerable help to the notoriously stiff Chamberlain. He became associated with Chamberlain's appeasement policy and accompanied him to Munich. Douglas-Home warned him not to sound triumphalist on his return, but Chamberlain unwisely ignored the advice.

In 1940, Douglas-Home volunteered for the Army, but a very severe medical problem stopped him serving. He underwent a major operation and was immobilised for two years. He returned to the Commons in 1943, but lost his seat in the 1945 election. He won it back in 1950, but shortly afterwards, his father died and he moved to the House of Lords.

In 1951, Churchill appointed him Secretary of State at the Scottish Office, and in 1955, Eden made him Secretary of State for Commonwealth Relations. Macmillan chose to let him continue in this position and made him Leader of the House of Lords. In 1960, he was promoted to the position of Foreign Secretary. His performance in these roles was generally seen as unspectacular but sound.

In 1963, the ill and beleaguered Macmillan was forced to resign. There was no clear successor in place and a number of candidates disputed the succession. In very controversial circumstances, Douglas-Home renounced his title and became Prime Minister as the favoured compromise. The government was in disarray and it was not an easy inheritance. He was sometimes portrayed as an out-of-touch aristocrat and was not an enormous success, but he was competent and he turned around his party's fortunes. However, Harold Wilson won the 1964 General Election with a majority of just four over all the other parties.

A few months later, Douglas-Home stepped down as Leader of the Conservative Party and Leader of the Opposition. He was replaced by Edward Heath and became Shadow Foreign Secretary. He was then Foreign Secretary in Heath's 1970–74 government. He was the last Prime Minister to serve in the cabinet of a successor. He retired after Heath's defeat in 1974 and shortly afterwards returned to the House of Lords as a life peer. Like Eden before him, almost all his career was in the field of foreign affairs.

Sir Alec Douglas Home (1903–1995). *Nationaal Archief, [Netherlands National Archives], and Spaarnestad Photo*

Sir Alec the Cricketer

Sir Alec is the only Prime Minister to have played first-class cricket. In the 1922 Eton-Harrow match, he scored 66 in difficult batting conditions, then took 4 wickets for 47 runs. Later, he had a few games for Oxford University and Middlesex. He was of course an amateur.

In 1966, he became President of the MCC. In this role, he was criticised for not standing up to South Africa in the 'D'Oliveira Affair'. Basil D'Oliveira was black and his inclusion in the touring team led to South Africa calling off a test series. Douglas-Home advised the MCC Committee not to press South Africa for advance assurances that his selection would be acceptable.

Two Years on his Back

In 1940, an x-ray revealed a hole in Sir Alec's spine and tuberculosis in the surrounding area. Without an operation, he would have been a cripple within months. A six-hour procedure scraped out the diseased bone and replaced it with healthy bone from his shin. He was then encased in plaster and had to lay immobile for almost two years. It worked, but it was a terrible ordeal.

Flower Arranger

During the two years that he spent lying on his back, he read a lot and enjoyed arranging flowers. This was a release for him and he did it for the rest of his life. R. A. Butler disclosed:

> I will give away his secret. Whenever things became most tense he would go away on his own for half an hour and arrange a vast bowl of flowers.[1]

The 14th Mr Wilson

The opposition and Harold Wilson in particular laboured the point that Sir Alec had been a 14th Earl. The implication was that this made him out of touch with the voters. In one of his more effective television responses, he said: 'I suppose Mr Wilson, when you come to think of it, is the fourteenth Mr Wilson'.

A Mother's Frank Opinion

After Sir Alec had become Prime Minister, a newspaper reporter rang his mother for a comment. Lady Home replied, 'I think it should have been Mr Butler.'[2]

A Lot of Land

Sir Alec's stately home, The Hirsel, near Coldstream in the Scottish borders, came with a lot of land. In 1964, this and other family land amounted to 96,000 acres. Mathematically inclined readers will readily calculate that this amounts to 150 square miles.

Response at an Election Meeting

At one time, family allowances were only paid for second and subsequent children. At an election meeting, a woman asked why she did not get the family allowance for her illegitimate child. Sir Alec replied, 'Madam, you will when your next one arrives.'[3]

The front cover of *New Statesman*, 16 April 1965 with Douglas-Home sitting on top of a Polaris missile. After the cancellation of Skybolt, the UK purchased Polaris missiles for use in British-built ballistic missile submarines.

A Prime Minister not in Parliament

In 1963, it was possible but not acceptable for a Prime Minister to sit in the House of Lords. On 19 October of that year, Sir Alec became Prime Minister, and four days later, he resigned his peerage. On 7 November, he won a by-election and took a seat in the House of Commons. So, for fifteen days, he was Prime Minister without a seat in either House. He is the only person to have been Prime Minister without a seat in either House.

At a Disadvantage on Television

During the 1964 General Election campaign and just before appearing on television, Sir Alec had the following conversation with a make-up girl:

Sir Alec:	'Can you make me look better than I do on television? I look rather scraggy, like a ghost.'
Make-up girl:	'No.'
Sir Alec:	'Why not?'
Make-up girl:	'Because you have a head like a skull.'
Sir Alec:	'Doesn't everyone have a head like a skull.'
Make-up girl:	'No.'

Sir Alec and a Sex Pistol

A few years ago, I had a conversation with a London taxi driver about the people that he had carried in his cab. He volunteered the information that the two greatest gentlemen were Sir Alec Douglas-Home and Johnny Rotten (real name John Lydon) of the Sex Pistols. He said that they were both polite, considerate, interested in him, and a pleasure to be with. I could see that he meant it.

Sir Alec will not read this, but Mr Lydon is still with us and I will send him a copy of the book.

46

James Harold Wilson

1964–70; 1974–76

James Harold Wilson with his trademark pipe.

AT THE AGE of thirty-one, Harold Wilson was the youngest cabinet member of the twentieth century, and there has not been a younger one since. He was Prime Minister at the age of forty-eight, the youngest since Lord Rosebery seventy years earlier. Subsequently, John Major, Tony Blair, and David Cameron made it at an earlier age. He was very good at winning general elections, being successful four times out of five.

Born in Huddersfield in 1916, Wilson was proud of his roots in West Yorkshire. He liked to imply that he was brought up in relative poverty, but, in fact, his family was middle class. His father, who was an industrial chemist, was, however, twice unemployed. His mother's brother, Sir Harold Seddon, was an MP in Australia. Wilson went to two grammar schools and was head boy at the second one. Then it was Jesus College, Oxford, where he did brilliantly. Afterwards, he was an Oxford don at the extraordinarily young age of twenty-one.

At the outbreak of the Second World War, he was directed to war work in the civil service, where he distinguished himself and was awarded the OBE. Then he became an MP in the 1945 Labour landslide. In 1947, Attlee made him President of the Board of Trade. He did well in this cabinet post and is particularly remembered for his so-called 'bonfire of controls'. It came to an end in April 1951, when he resigned from the cabinet in protest at Hugh Gaitskell's budget.

October 1951 started what Wilson memorably dubbed 'thirteen years of Tory misrule'. They only came to an end when Wilson won the October 1964 election. During this time, he was generally seen as inclining to the left of the party, but rather an opportunist. He was not always trusted. He was Shadow Chancellor of the Exchequer for six years starting in 1955, a post that he filled with great success. Then he was Shadow Foreign Secretary until he was made party leader on the death of Hugh Gaitskell in January 1963.

Wilson and Labour won the cliff-hanger 1964 election with a majority of just four, but in 1966, another election increased the majority to ninety-six. Wilson inherited a very difficult financial situation and immediately took the decision not to devalue, but this proved to be unsustainable. A humiliating devaluation followed three years later. An attempt to join the European Community was vetoed by de Gaulle in

Harold Wilson with Barbara Castle at a Labour Party Conference.

1967, something he had already done to Harold Macmillan's earlier application. The government set up the new Department of Economic Affairs as a counterweight to the Treasury, and it instituted a prices and incomes policy. Wilson refused to let Britain have even a token military involvement in the Vietnam War.

To most people's surprise, the Conservatives won the 1970 election, and it was nearly four years before Wilson was back in Downing Street. He returned at the time of a national crisis caused by a strike called by the National Union of Mineworkers. There were two elections in 1974 and Wilson carried on for another two years. To the surprise of almost everyone, he announced his retirement in April 1976.

Mary Wilson

Mary Wilson is a Congregationalist and the daughter of a Congregationalist minister. She married Harold, also a Congregationalist, on New Year's Day 1940. She was a loyal, supporting wife, but she did not much like politics. In 1940, she thought that she was marrying an Oxford don, and this is probably what she would have preferred. She enjoyed writing poetry and was good at it. In an interview with *The Sunday Times*, she memorably said: 'If Harold has a fault, it is that he will drown everything with HP Sauce'. The interview did wonders for the product's sales.

Mary Wilson celebrated her 102nd birthday on 12 January 2018.

Gannex Raincoats

Joseph Kagan was a British-Lithuanian industrialist who invented gannex raincoats. He manufactured them near Huddersfield and became a friend of Wilson. He provided finance for Wilson's office. Wilson frequently wore the raincoats, and they became associated with him, which was good for Kagan's business.

Wilson made Kagan a knight in 1970 and a peer in 1976. In 1980, he was convicted of theft and false accounting. He was fined £375,000 and served a ten-month prison sentence.

The Pound in your Pocket

Britain operated with fixed exchange rates in the 1960s, and in November 1967, the Labour Government devalued the pound by 14.3 per cent. Shortly afterwards, in a television broadcast, Wilson said:

> From now on, the pound abroad is worth fourteen per cent or so less in terms of other currencies. It doesn't mean of course, that the pound here in Britain, in your pocket, or purse, or in your bank, has been devalued.

Critics seized on this and said that Wilson's explanation was dishonest.

Relationship with the Queen

Queen Elizabeth's views about politics and her views about the thirteen Prime Ministers who have served her are not known. Nevertheless, journalists and others sometimes look for clues and speculate. Some who have done this have expressed the view that her relationship with Wilson was good and that he was one of her favourite Prime Ministers. We do not know how true this is. The Queen honoured his resignation by dining at 10 Downing Street. She has only done this for one other Prime Minister, Sir Winston Churchill.

A Principled Resignation?

The onset of the Korean War meant that Britain needed to increase expenditure on defence. This was the main reason that Hugh Gaitskell's 1951 budget introduced National Health Service charges for dental care and spectacles. They had previously been free at the point of delivery in line with one of the founding principles of the NHS. This provoked the resignations of three ministers—Aneurin Bevan, Harold Wilson, and John Freeman. What was Wilson's motivation? Some say that it was conviction and principle, others that it was opportunism intended to help his career in the long run. Wilson's future governments did not reinstate 'free at the point of delivery'.

The Scilly Isles

Wilson had a deep affection for the islands that lie off the coast of Cornwall. He first visited them in 1952 and had a modest bungalow built there in 1958. It was the place in which he relaxed and the family enjoyed numerous holidays there. He was buried on one of the islands in 1995. Mary Wilson still owns the bungalow and visited it regularly until recently.

Harold Wilson and the Beatles at Variety Club Awards, 20 March 1964. In 1965 the Beatles were each awarded the MBE after Harold Wilson, who represented the Liverpool suburb of Huyton, had lobbied in their favour. Wilson was accused of having supported a populist agenda and several MBE holders returned their decorations in disgust. One man, Col. Frederick Wagg, even sent back 12 medals he had earned fighting in both World Wars, and resigned from the Labour Party.

White House Guards and Military Band members arrayed for the visit of Harold P. Wilson, 27 January 1970. *National Archives (USA) 194306*

Steptoe and Son

At the time of the 1964 election, it was thought that a higher proportion of Labour supporters than Conservative supporters voted in the evening. Anything that kept voters indoors late in the day was bad news for Labour. To the consternation of Labour's campaign managers, it rained in the evening of polling day, but it was too little, too late to make much difference.

The very popular television programme *Steptoe and Son* was due to be broadcast an hour before the polls closed, and Wilson believed that more Labour voters than Conservative voters would watch it. He asked the BBC to reschedule it and this was done.

Retirement and Afterwards

On 16 March 1976, five days after his sixtieth birthday, Wilson said that he would retire on 5 April. He was not under particular pressure at the time. Virtually no one was expecting it and no one knew why he was doing it. Many expected that a massive scandal would soon become public knowledge. There was no scandal, or if there was, it has not been revealed. Wilson said that he had always intended to retire at sixty.

Over the years, there have been some wild conspiracy theories, which have mostly been discounted. There have been claims that he was a Russian agent, and some thought that he was targeted by elements within MI5.

There could well have been a combination of reasons. His wife had never been keen on politics and he might have wanted to please her. It is known that he was under stress and had been drinking a lot. Old problems were coming around again and he may have come to terms with the limits of what he could achieve. His doctor had detected symptoms of what would later be diagnosed as colon cancer. Possibly he had noticed symptoms of early onset Alzheimer's disease, which would blight his later years. Perhaps he had just had enough.

Wilson remained an MP and was created a Knight of the Garter. In 1983, he went to the House of Lords as Baron Wilson of Rievaulx. He died on 24 May 1995.

The Lavender List

The awarding of honours has caused controversy both before and after Wilson's resignation, but his 1976 resignation list was especially controversial and it damaged his reputation. A hundred Labour

MPs signed a motion dissociating themselves from it. Critics seized on the fact that it was written out by his secretary, Lady Falkender (Marcia Williams), on lavender notepaper. They claimed that she had too much influence on it. She says that the colour was in fact pink, and that in any case, the names were selected by Wilson not her.[1, 2] She also says that many of the critics were snobbish and anti-semitic.[3]

There were peerages for Sir George Weidenfeld and Sir Joseph Stone. Weidenfeld was Wilson's friend and publisher, and Stone was his personal doctor. James Goldsmith, the controversial chairman of Cavenham Foods, was given a knighthood. There were a number of honours for people prominent in show business.

As already detailed in this chapter, Sir Joseph Kagan, maker of gannex raincoats and a friend of Wilson, was given a peerage. He subsequently served a ten-month prison sentence. Eric Miller, the chairman of Peachey Property Corporation and a contributor to the costs of Wilson's private office, was given a knighthood. The following year, he shot himself while under investigation for financial irregularities.

"What's he mean 'Don't rock the boat'? Are we going somewhere?"

47

Edward Richard George Heath

1970–74

EDWARD HEATH WAS born into a lower-middle-class family in 1916. He was educated at Chatham House Grammar School, and with the help of a county scholarship, he went on to Balliol College, Oxford. He was an active Conservative at the university, and in 1937–38, he was Chairman of the Federation of University Conservative Associations. In 1938, he was elected President of the Oxford Union. Prior to the war, he was very strongly opposed to the government's appeasement policy. He was conscripted in 1940 and had what is sometimes called 'a good war'.

An election poster for Edward Heath.

Afterwards, he worked in the Civil Service, then as news editor of the *Church Times*. This was followed by a period with a merchant bank. He was elected to Parliament in 1950, but it was October 1951 before Churchill and the Conservatives returned to power. Heath was the Chief Whip from 1955 to 1959, serving both Eden and Macmillan. He held this position at the time of the Suez Crisis, which was not easy. Then it was Minister of Labour, followed by Lord Privy Seal, with responsibility for negotiating Britain's entry into the European Economic Community. Heath passionately believed that this would be good for Britain and good for Europe, but de Gaulle thought otherwise and vetoed the application. Douglas-Home made him President of the Board of Trade and this was his job until Labour won the 1964 election.

Douglas-Home resigned in 1965 and Heath was elected to succeed him as Leader of the Conservative Party. His bachelor status and abrupt manner counted against him, but he was seen as young, vigorous, and a man of the future. Despite this, the 1966 election saw Wilson increase the Labour majority from four seats to ninety-six. Most people, supported by the opinion polls, thought that Labour would win the 1970 election. Heath thought differently and was proved right. The Conservatives got in with a majority over Labour of forty-three and he became Prime Minister.

It is said that Harold Macmillan, asked what he feared most, replied: 'Events, dear boy, events'. If he did say this, it was a prescient observation. Heath's government had its achievements, but it suffered badly from events. The troubles in Northern Ireland escalated. The Industrial Relations Act 1971 was

Edward Heath meets Mao Tse-tung in Mao's private residence in the Forbidden City, Beijing, 25 May 1974.

bitterly resented by some parts of the trade union movement and others, and it did not achieve the planned results. Economic problems prompted a number of controversial U-turns, reversing previous policies and commitments that had been set out in the election manifesto. Bad industrial relations and resistance to the prices and incomes policy continued to be problems.

On the plus side, as Heath but not everyone else saw it, he succeeded in getting Britain into the European Economic Community. He undoubtedly regarded this as his greatest achievement.

There was a seven-week miners' strike in 1972, which ended in what was seen to be a victory for the miners. Then, in late 1973, there was a miners' work to rule followed by another strike in early 1974. This was at the time of an oil crisis. In February 1974, Heath called an election on the issue 'Who governs Britain?' The result was close to a tie, but Wilson took office as head of a minority Labour administration. The new government gave the miners what they wanted. A further election in the same year saw Wilson continuing as Prime Minister. Heath wanted to carry on, but in February 1975, Margaret Thatcher defeated him in a leadership election.

Few of Edward Heath's supporters, let alone anyone else, thought him likeable. His manner tended to be abrupt, he often seemed ill at ease, and he had few social skills. He was sometimes respected but not loved. When he succeeded, it was usually despite his approach, not because of it. This was a shame because there was another man under the image that he projected.

Music

Throughout Heath's life, music was very important to him. Shortly after arriving at Balliol College, he won an organ scholarship, which enabled him to stay at Oxford for an additional year. He started the annual Broadstairs carol concert and conducted it numerous times. On various occasions, he conducted the London Symphony Orchestra and other great orchestras. He was an organist and a pianist. At times of stress, he would often unwind by playing an instrument. He loved music.

Morning Cloud

Heath took up yachting in 1966, relatively late, but he had great success. Given his political commitments it was extraordinary. With his first yacht, *Morning Cloud*, he won the Sydney to Hobart race in 1969, and in the same year, he captained the team in the Fastnet race. In 1971, while Prime Minister, he captained the British team to victory in the Admiral's Cup. There were five yachts named *Morning Cloud*, and he sold the last one in 1983. Tragically, in 1974, his godson was swept overboard in a freak wave and died. Significantly, a crew member once said: 'I thought he was a bit of a lonely man. I know he had his political friends, but we seemed to be a family to him. There was no politics on board'.[1]

Heath did not have a wife and family to support, but his five yachts did not come cheap.

Heath's Sexuality

Heath never married and this inevitably led to speculation, which continues to this day, about his sexuality. The lack of a wife, or at least a close female friend, almost certainly harmed him politically. In 1969, I worked for a company whose managing director was very active in the Conservative Party, and by chance, I was with him when he was told that Heath had won the Sydney to Hobart yacht race: 'Wonderful, wonderful,' he said. Then he wistfully added, 'If only they could find a woman on board.'

He had been expected to marry a childhood friend, but in 1950, she married someone else. In his memoirs, he said that he had been too busy establishing a career after the war and had perhaps taken too much for granted. When he became party leader, a journalist asked him if he thought a Prime Minister ought to be married. He replied as follows:

> I don't know. It would depend to some extent on the woman, wouldn't it? What I do know is that a man who got married in order to be a better Prime Minister wouldn't be either a good Prime Minister or a good husband.[2]

People tended to notice that he rarely engaged women in conversation. Some people think that he was asexual. Others suspect that he may have had same sex inclinations, but totally suppressed all sexual activity and perhaps thoughts as well.

War Service

Heath was conscripted, and unlike Harold Wilson, he saw military action in the Second World War. He served in the Royal Artillery and, commanding a battery, participated after the Normandy Landings in the campaigns in France and Germany. He later said that he did not kill anybody, but he saw the devastation caused by his unit's bombardments. He was mentioned in despatches and was awarded the MBE. He was demobilised in August 1946.

In 1971, the Swiss cartoonist Hans Geisen illustrated the difficult position of Edward Heath, who was in favour of the United Kingdom's accession to the European Community. *Hans Geisen*

Edward Heath with predecessors Harold Macmillan and Harold Wilson on the occasion of Harold Macmillan launching his memoirs, December 1974.

In September 1945, he commanded a firing squad that executed a Polish soldier convicted of rape and murder.

An Engaging Witticism

Heath's first book was *Sailing: A Course of My Life*. He said that his next one might be about cooking and he could call it *Cooking: Three Courses of My Life*.[3]

A Letter from Harold Wilson's Father

A few days after Edward Heath had become Leader of the Conservative Party, Harold Wilson's father wrote the following letter to his father:

> Dear Mr Heath
> Please accept my congratulations to you on the election of your son Edward to the leadership of his party. I can imagine your feelings of pride on his success as I underwent the same elation on my son's election as leader of his party a little over two years ago. I am afraid that in my case there is a difference of age of some years as I am rapidly approaching eighty-three but even so it is a great thrill to me to see and hear my son in the House of Commons. When I do so I look back on his years as a boy, a Boy Scout, etc, etc, and undoubtedly you have the same feelings at times. Trusting that you will have many years of good health to enjoy your son's success, I am,
> Yours very sincerely,
> J. Herbert Wilson.[4]

The Incredible Sulk

In a 1975 ballot for the leadership of the Conservative Party, Heath was defeated by Margaret Thatcher. He took it badly. He continued in the House of Commons and did not take the customary earldom that would have been available to him. He also did not pursue any of the important positions outside Parliament that could have been his. What he did do was sit on the back benches and glower, and criticise Mrs Thatcher and her policies. With an obvious reference to the television programme *The Incredible Hulk*, people started to refer to him as 'The Incredible Sulk'.

48

Leonard James Callaghan

1976–79

Leonard James Callaghan. *Let's Talk magazine*

In 1976, Harold Wilson (born 1916) resigned and an older man was selected to take his place. James Callaghan (born 1912) was very well qualified for the job. He remains the only Prime Minister to have held the other three great offices of state—Chancellor of the Exchequer (1964–67), Home Secretary (1967–70), and Foreign Secretary (1974–76).

He grew up in difficult economic circumstances, partly caused by the death of his father when he was just nine. He attended Portsmouth Northern Secondary School, then joined the Inland Revenue. In 1936, he became the youthful Assistant Secretary of the Inland Revenue Staff Federation, then in 1945, after war service, he was elected the Labour MP for the constituency of Cardiff South. At this time, he was on the left of the party, but over the years, he moved progressively to the right.

In October 1964, the new Prime Minister, Harold Wilson, made him Chancellor of the Exchequer. He inherited a bad economic situation, and with Wilson, he resolutely resisted the temptation to devalue the pound. However, the government was eventually overwhelmed and in November 1967 devaluation could no longer be resisted. Callaghan then swapped jobs with Roy Jenkins and became Home Secretary. It was in this position that he sent the first troops to help the police in Northern Ireland.

In 1969, Barbara Castle, with the backing of Harold Wilson, tried to reform trade union law. Her white paper was given the memorable title *In Place of Strife*. The unions were decidedly unhappy, and Callaghan with his strong links to the unions led the opposition to it and succeeded in getting the proposals dropped. This proved to be ironic because they would have made illegal some of the trade union behaviour in the so-called 'winter of discontent' nine years later. It was this that soured Callaghan's last months as Prime Minister and led to his downfall.

Callaghan wanted to be Foreign Secretary, and on returning to Downing Street in 1974, Wilson gave him this job. He had responsibility for renegotiating the terms of entry into the European Economic Community. Many people thought that not a lot was achieved, but he recommended the new terms to the electorate in a referendum—67 per cent of the voters chose to stay in.

James Callaghan lays a dedication plaque, 18 October 1976.

During the whole of his time as Prime Minister, Callaghan's party did not have a majority in the House of Commons, and by common consent, he handled this problem with skill. For part of his term, the Lib-Lab pact prevented the Liberals opposing him, and at times, he had understandings with the nationalist parties. He also showed skill in dealing with his sometimes-fractious colleagues, in particular when it was decided to take a loan from the International Monetary Fund.

Callaghan's time as Prime Minister was blighted by high inflation, other economic problems, and strikes. His responses included trying to reduce public expenditure and trying to achieve pay restraint. He had some success, but it all went horribly wrong in the winter of 1978–79. The events in that period came to be known as 'the winter of discontent'. Terrible strikes, especially in the public sector, outraged the country. Rubbish was not collected, bodies were not buried, and there were other horrors.

In March 1979, the government lost a vote of confidence in the House of Commons, and, led by Margaret Thatcher, the Conservatives won the consequent general election. Callaghan stayed as Leader of the Opposition until October 1980. In 1983, he became the Father of the House and he left the Commons in 1987. Shortly afterwards, he went to the House of Lords. He died one day short of his ninety-third birthday, which makes him the longest-lived of the Prime Ministers.

Wife and Family

His father was a seaman who turned down an opportunity to go on Scott's doomed 1911 Antarctic expedition.[1] He was a Chief Petty Officer and was wounded in the Battle of Jutland in 1916.

The future Prime Minister met his wife, Audrey, when they were both Sunday School teachers at a Baptist church. They married in 1938 and by all accounts it was a happy union. She was a Labour politician in her own right. After a period suffering from Alzheimer's disease, she died in 2005, just eleven days before her husband. The couple had three children, one of whom, Baroness Jay, had a distinguished career and was for a time the Leader of the House of Lords.

Nicknames

Three nicknames attached themselves to Callaghan, all of them complimentary. They were 'Uncle Jim', 'Big Jim', and 'Sunny Jim'. They reflect the fact that he was a large man and that he projected an avuncular image. Some people who worked with him said the image did not always match the reality. 'Sunny Jim' is a popular phrase that probably has its origins in an American advertising campaign for Force breakfast cereal. A picture of a man jumping over a fence was accompanied by the following:

VERY WELL, THEN—ALONE

A *Punch* cartoon by Trog (Wally Fawkes), 10 April 1974. On 4 March 1974 Wilson became the Prime Minister of a minority Government. He appointed Callaghan as Foreign Secretary with responsibility for renegotiating the terms of the UK membership of the Common Market. On 1 April 1974 Callaghan, outlined the position of the UK Government to the EU Council of Ministers, saying the British people should have approved the original terms of entry and that his government wished to put this right with a successful renegotiation. He referred for the first time to the possibility of a negotiated withdrawal from the EEC if the renegotiation was unacceptable. *Punch*

High o'er the fence leaps Sunny Jim
Force is the food that raises him.

War Service

Callaghan is the only Prime Minister to have served in the Royal Navy. He joined in 1942 and served in the East Indies Fleet. He was promoted to the rank of Lieutenant in 1944, but was found to be suffering from tuberculosis. He spent some time in hospital and was then assigned to shore duties.

Peter Pan

J. M. Barrie the author of the children's book *Peter Pan* assigned the copyright of it to Great Ormond Street Hospital. Under the law at the time, the copyright was due to expire in 1987, fifty years after his death. Audrey Callaghan had been Chair of the hospital's Board of Governors and she pointed this out to her husband. At the time, the Copyright, Designs, and Patents Act was under consideration in the House of Lords and the recently ennobled Lord Callaghan successfully moved an amendment. This granted the hospital a right to royalty in perpetuity, despite the lapse of copyright. After his death, Callaghan's ashes were scattered in the flowerbed around the Peter Pan statue at Great Ormond Street hospital.

The Royal Box at the Palladium

In 1978, the fiftieth anniversary of full women's suffrage was marked by a glittering televised event at the London Palladium. The performers and even the camera crews were exclusively women. There were machinations about who should have the privilege of sitting in the royal box with Princess Margaret, and due to her sex and position as Leader of the opposition, Margaret Thatcher was considered for the honour. Prime Minister James Callaghan wanted to deprive her of the publicity and he succeeded.[2] The box was occupied by Princess Margaret and a lady-in-waiting, James and Audrey Callaghan, Lord Grade (who had helped organise the event), and Lady Grade. Margaret Thatcher sat in the stalls.

My wife and I were there and we sat a short distance from Mrs Thatcher. At the end, a small group, including Mrs Thatcher, my wife, and myself, made a mistake and went down a corridor that led to a dead end. Mrs Thatcher turned to me and said, 'Is there really no way out?' I knew the answer and told her, so I have the honour of having told Mrs Thatcher the way out and seeing the advice accepted.

Crisis? What crisis?

In early 1979, during the so-called 'winter of discontent', Callaghan returned from an economic summit held on the Caribbean island of Guadeloupe. A press conference on his arrival included the following exchange:

> Question: 'What is your general approach, in view of the mounting chaos in the country at the moment?'
>
> Reply: 'Well, that's a judgment that you are making. I promise you that if you look at it from outside, and perhaps you're taking rather a parochial view at the moment, I don't think that other people in the world would share the view that there is mounting chaos'.

The Sun newspaper printed a picture of a tanned and relaxed-looking Prime Minister under the headline 'Crisis? What Crisis?' The implication was that the Prime Minister had been enjoying himself abroad and was out of touch with the problems at home. It did him great harm, though he did not quite use the words in the headline. It is probably the most remembered Callaghan so-called quote.

49

Margaret Hilda Thatcher

1979–90

Margaret Thatcher arrives at 10 Downing Street, 4 May 1979. *National Archives*

MARGARET THATCHER (*NÉE* Roberts) was born in Grantham in 1925 and grew up in that town. She was a most remarkable woman and she achieved remarkable things. Here are three of them. She was the first woman to be leader of a significant political party and the first woman Prime Minister. She held the position for an uninterrupted eleven years and 209 days, which was the longest continuous term since Lord Liverpool from 1812 to 1827. She is the only Prime Minister to have an -ism named after her. She would not have appreciated the comparison, but Thatcherism, like Marxism, is very recognisable.

Thatcher attended the Kesteven and Grantham Girls Grammar School, and was head girl in 1942–43. Then it was the all-woman Somerville College, Oxford. She graduated in 1947 with a second-class honours chemistry bachelor of science degree. Her first job was with a plastics company. At the age of only twenty-five, she was selected to be the Conservative candidate for the safe Labour seat of Dartford. She duly lost the 1950 and 1951 elections, but did creditably. She married Denis Thatcher in December 1951, and helped by his money, she qualified as a barrister in 1953. In the same year, she gave birth to twins, Mark and Carol. As a barrister, she specialised in tax law.

Thatcher became the MP for the safe Conservative seat of Finchley in 1959, and was made a junior minister by Macmillan in 1961. This ended with the Labour victory in 1964, but Heath gave her the cabinet position of Secretary of State for Education and Science in 1970. Despite the many things that she did, she is primarily remembered for ending free school milk for children over seven. Although considered to be the outsider, she replaced Heath as leader of the Conservative Party in 1975, then following the disastrous 'winter of discontent', she became Prime Minister in May 1979.

She was a monetarist and was determined that her economic policies would be very different from those of the Labour government that she replaced, and from the wishes of many of her cabinet colleagues. During her first two years in power, she was decidedly unpopular with the public. However, things started to come right, or very right depending on your point of view, and she was given an enormous boost by

Margaret Thatcher with Sir Geoffrey Howe.
National Archives

her success in the Falklands War in 1982. She achieved large majorities in the elections of 1983 and 1987.

Thatcher was Prime Minister for so long and did so much that it is only possible to mention just a very few of her policies and actions. All that follows was and is controversial. The miners had twice defeated Edward Heath and she was determined that they would not do it to her. She anticipated another strike by building up massive coal stocks, then successfully faced down a year-long strike called without a national ballot. Her government reduced the power of the trade unions, privatised many businesses and assets, and gave council tenants the right to buy their properties at a discount.

Towards the end of her period in power, the community charge (almost universally called the poll tax) was introduced. It was desperately unpopular and provoked riots and civil disobedience. Politicians and the people can be fickle and ungrateful. Despite bringing the Conservatives three successive general election victories, a revolt by her cabinet and MPs removed her from power.

Margaret Thatcher's personality and style of government were decisive and confrontational. She knew what she thought was right and she was determined to get it. Often, she did, though she sometimes respected ministers who marshalled their arguments and stood up to her. She made a lot of enemies. Attlee was another Prime Minister who secured massive changes, but the way that she operated was very different.

The Grantham Years

Thatcher was the younger of two sisters and was born in the flat over her father's grocery shop. There was an outside toilet, but no bath or running hot water. Her father was a local councillor then alderman, and he was Mayor of Grantham in 1945–46. He was a Methodist lay preacher with traditional values, and she respected him greatly. She worked hard in school, outside school, and sometimes in the shop. Sundays belonged to the Lord. She usually went to the Methodist church four times and games in the evening were not permitted.[1]

Denis Thatcher

They met at a dinner and Denis gave Margaret a lift to the station afterwards. They married in December 1951 and the rest, as they say, is history. He was divorced and ten years older than her. He was also rich and ran a family business. Over the years, he got richer still, which helped Margaret's life and career a great deal. On many issues, he had very pronounced right-wing views.

Margaret Thatcher in Falkland Islands after Argentina's surrender, 1983.

It was a love match and he helped her a lot. The help was unobtrusive and he tried to keep in the background. He was always there for her, he listened, and he gave advice. It came at a personal cost. Just one example—he sold a much-loved Rolls-Royce because he thought that his ownership of it would hurt his wife's popularity.[2]

Her First Cabinet Meeting as Prime Minister

After Thatcher's first cabinet meeting as Prime Minister, Lord Soames (Lord President of the Council) said to Jim Prior (Secretary of State for Employment): 'I wouldn't even treat my gamekeeper like that'.[3]

Three Nicknames

The first of the following three nicknames was used only at her school, and like the second one, it is uncomplimentary. The third was intended to be uncomplimentary, but she took it as a compliment and most people took the same view.

'Snobby Roberts'—This was used at Kesteven and Grantham Girls Grammar School.[4]

'Milk Snatcher'—This stuck after, when as Minister of Education, she ended free school milk for children over seven. It has been claimed that she did not want to do this, but was forced to by the Treasury.

'The Iron Lady'—This term was used by a Russian journalist writing in *Red Star*.[5] He was commenting on a speech in which she had said 'The Russians are striving for world domination'.

An Ability to Multitask

Like many barristers, Thatcher was able to move quickly from subject to subject. The late Sir Jimmy Young interviewed her fourteen times on radio and he commented as follows:

> She used to sweep in with her papers and talk animatedly when we were on air. Then when I was playing music she immediately returned to her papers only looking me up again when the music stopped and questions resumed.[6]

Mrs Thatcher's Willie

It is imperative that you note that every word in the heading has a capital letter. Mrs Thatcher famously said, 'Every Prime Minister needs a Willie.' The remark was greeted with understandable hilarity, but it was a justified tribute to her Deputy Prime Minister William Whitelaw, known as Willie.

Willie Whitelaw was loyal to Edward Heath, and when Thatcher beat him and then himself to become Party leader, he was loyal to her. He gave her frank advice behind the scenes, and helped her manage her colleagues. She relied on him a lot and it is probably true to say that she listened to him more than any other politician. Ill health forced him to retire from the cabinet in January 1988 and she missed his counsel badly.

No U-turn

Faced with rising unemployment and perceived difficulties, Edward Heath had abandoned some of his policies and gone for short-term economic growth. These changes became known as U-turns. Faced with considerable difficulties and unpopularity, Thatcher did not do this. At the 1980 Conservative Party conference, she said: 'You turn if you want to. The lady's not for turning'.

Not Popular at Oxford

Thatcher's cuts in expenditure on higher education made her unpopular at Oxford. She was the first Oxford-educated post-war Prime Minister not to be awarded an honorary doctorate by the University of Oxford. The voting against her was 738 to 319.

Dame Janet Vaughan, a contemporary at Oxford and later a Principal of Somerville College, once said:

> She fascinated me. I used to talk to her a great deal, she was an oddity. Why? She was a Conservative—she stood out. Somerville had always been a radical establishment and there weren't many Conservatives about then. We used to argue about politics; she was so set in steel as a Conservative. She just had this one line.... We used to entertain a good deal at weekends, but she didn't get invited. She had nothing to contribute, you see.[7]

Comfort for a Distressed Waitress

At a Chequers dinner, a Wren acting as a waitress accidentally dropped some food and gravy into the lap of Thatcher's cabinet colleague Sir Geoffrey Howe. Thatcher rushed to comfort the distressed Wren and said, 'Don't worry my dear, it could happen to anyone.'[8] Sir Geoffrey's reaction is not known.

Ronald Reagan and Margaret Thatcher on a sofa at Camp David, 22 December 1984. *White House Photographic Office*

Tears for her Missing Son

Margaret's son Mark was missing for six days in the Sahara Desert while competing in the 1982 Paris to Dakar rally. He was safe, but at the time, it was a big story and a big worry. Margaret was distressed and it was one of the very small number of times that she was seen to shed tears in public. Denis Thatcher flew to Dakar and a large scale and expensive aerial search was launched. This was successful, but it was not a credit to Mark who had not made adequate preparations for the demanding event. Such a large-scale hunt would probably not have been made if he had not been who he was. Margaret paid £1,800 towards the cost of the search and the celebratory dinner that was held afterwards.

The Day That She was Meant Not to See

In the early hours of 12 October 1984, a bomb, which had been planted by the Provisional IRA, exploded in the Grand Hotel at Brighton. It was an attempt to assassinate Margaret Thatcher who was staying in the hotel for the Conservative Party Conference. Margaret and her husband Denis were not hurt and were taken to Brighton Police Station. However, five people were killed, including a Conservative MP and the wife of a cabinet minister. Thirty-one people were injured including Norman Tebbit, the President of the Board of Trade, and his wife, Margaret. Norman's injuries were severe and Margaret was left permanently disabled.

At 9.30 a.m. the same morning, Margaret Thatcher delivered a rousing speech to the conference, and then she visited the injured in hospital. Her demeanour and response were magnificent.

In a television interview three days later, she referred to her visit to Ellesborough Church near Chequers on the previous day. She said: 'It was a lovely morning. We have not had many lovely days. And the sun was just coming through the stained glass windows and falling on some flowers right across the church and it just occurred to me that this was the day I was meant not to see'.

A Kal cartoon in *The Economist* for the week 4–10 November 1989, just one year before the *coup d'état* that brought John Major into office.

50

John Major

1990–97

IT WAS PREDICTABLE that some politicians would rise to the top or near the top of what Disraeli memorably called 'the greasy pole'. They came from the right families, went to the right schools and universities, and they knew the right people. Think of Arthur Balfour. The rise of others was not to be expected. Think of Disraeli and Ramsay MacDonald. John Major is an extreme example of the second category. He was Prime Minister at forty-seven, the youngest since Lord Rosebery in 1894–95, and he held the position for six years and 154 days. He is often said to rank among the well-meaning and decent Prime Ministers, but despite some notable achievements, not among the more successful.

A jubilant John Major, Friday 10 April 1992. The General Election held the previous day returned him to power with 376 seats, while Neil Kinnock's Labour Party secured only 229 seats.

Born in 1943, Major left Rutlish Grammar School at sixteen with just three O-levels. He later got three more, using the services of correspondence courses. After a short period of unemployment and two junior jobs, he joined Standard Chartered Bank and spent a short time in Nigeria. While in that country, he was involved in a serious road accident and lost a kneecap. This stopped him playing cricket and walking long distances.

At twenty-four, and for the next three years, he was a Conservative councillor in the London Borough of Lambeth, and was chairman of the Housing Committee. He was unsuccessful in the two 1974 general elections, but became an MP in 1979.

Major's rise through the ranks in the Thatcher years was swift. Starting in 1981, he progressed through ministerial roles and joined the cabinet in 1987. Less than three and a half years later, he was Prime Minister. His first cabinet job was Chief Secretary to the Treasury, and the common view is that he did it well. Then, for three months, he was Foreign Secretary.

In October 1989, the Chancellor of the Exchequer Nigel Lawson resigned with some acrimony, and Margaret Thatcher chose Major as the safe pair of hands to replace him. A year later, he persuaded Thatcher that the country had to join the ERM (European Exchange Rate Mechanism). She had resisted this for a long time, but was compelled to concede. With the benefit of hindsight, and in many people's

Bill Clinton and John Major breakfast meeting the White House Solarium, 1994. *William J. Clinton Presidential Library/ White House*

opinion without it as well, Britain joined at the wrong exchange rate. The move and the wrong exchange rate blighted Major's time as Prime Minister later.

Thatcher's spell in 10 Downing Street was the longest continuous one since Lord Liverpool in 1812–27, but it had to come to an end. As Enoch Powell wrote: 'All political lives, unless they are cut off in midstream at a happy juncture, end in failure, because that is the nature of politics and of human affairs'.[1] She was ousted and backed Major as her successor. He was again seen as a safe pair of hands and the candidate most acceptable to the different sections of the Conservative Party. So Major it was.

Major made an excellent start. The party rallied to him and he successfully led the country through the first Gulf War. Despite a recession he unexpectedly led the Conservatives to victory in the May 1992 General Election. However, it all went horribly wrong on Black Wednesday—16 September 1992. Britain was forced out of the ERM that he had been instrumental in almost forcing Thatcher to join. Even worse, the exit was botched. Ironically, the economy immediately started to improve and later some began to call the fateful day White Wednesday. Nevertheless, Major's reputation never fully recovered, even though he handed Tony Blair an economy in good shape.

The most important events in Major's term included, in Europe, the Maastricht Treaty. He secured a number of opt-outs for Britain, which many regarded as a triumph. Nevertheless, some Conservatives were against all of it on principle and thought that it was a sell-out. He scrapped Thatcher's Community Charge (poll tax) and took the first steps towards the Good Friday agreement in Northern Ireland. This was signed by the Labour government in 1998.

Major was one of the nicer Prime Ministers and he tried to reconcile many shades of opinion in his party and in the country. It worked well for a time, and then, despite some notable achievements, it did not. We should remember Aneurin Bevan's words: 'We know what happens to people who stay in the middle of the road. They get run over'.[2] Metaphorically speaking, Major did get run over. He lost the 1997 General Election by a landslide and resigned the leadership of the Conservative Party shortly afterwards. Perceived sleaze in his government and party was a factor in the defeat.

Cool Under Fire

Seventy-one days after Major became Prime Minister, the Provisional IRA launched three mortar shells at 10 Downing Street. Two overshot, but one exploded in the back garden. It was during the First Gulf War, and at the time, the war cabinet was meeting with military and civilian advisers. They ducked under the table, then Major said: 'I think we had better start again somewhere else'. The meeting resumed in another room ten minutes later. No one in the meeting was hurt, but four other people received minor injuries.

John Major's Parents

It is hard to think of a more unlikely parentage for a Prime Minister. His father was Abraham Thomas Ball, who started his working life as a bricklayer, but spent many years in the theatre as a juggler, acrobat, comedian, and trapeze artist. His stage name was Major and he became known as Tom Major-Ball. His first wife was killed in a stage accident and John Major was the son of his second wife, who also had a theatrical background. When John was born, his mother was thirty-eight and his father was nearly sixty-four.

After retiring from the theatre, John's father had a small business producing gnomes and other garden ornaments. This had financial difficulties, which necessitated a move to Brixton in South London. This is where John Major grew up.

Cricket

Major spent his early years close to the Oval cricket ground, the headquarters of Surrey County Cricket Club. He developed a lifelong love of the game, and especially of cricket in his county. Surrey won the county championship for seven consecutive seasons when he was a boy.

He cast off the cares of office by attending a match at the Oval the day after losing the 1997 General Election. He then went home and dug a fishpond in his garden.[3] After leaving office, he was President of Surrey County Cricket Club, and he has been an Honorary Life Vice-President since 2002. In 2005, he was elected to the Committee of the Marylebone Cricket Club (MCC).

John Major (left), talks with Lieutenant General Michael Walker (right), Commander, Allied Command Europe Rapid Reaction Corps (ARRC), in the Terme Hotel on Ilidza Compound in Sarajevo, Bosnia and Herzegovina, during Operation JOINT ENDEAVOR, 24 May 1996. *Photo by PFC Tracey L. Hall-Leahy, USA, U.S. National Archives*

The original depiction of John Major in the television series Spitting Image.

Bastards

Mr Gladstone did not have to worry about whether a microphone had been switched off, but modern Prime Ministers do. John Major and Gordon Brown are two who overlooked this to their cost. On a day of high drama over parliamentary approval of the Maastricht Treaty, Major was asked during a television interview why he did not sack ministers who were conspiring against him. Believing that his words were not being broadcast, he said:

> Just think it through from my perspective. You are the Prime Minister with a majority of eighteen ... where to you think most of the poison is coming from? From the dispossessed and the never-possessed. Do we want three more of the bastards out there? What's Lyndon Johnson's maxim?

It was embarrassing and provoked speculation about which of his ministers he was referring to.

Lyndon Johnson's maxim was 'It's probably better to have him inside the tent pissing out, than outside the tent pissing in'.[4] Johnson was referring to J. Edgar Hoover, who had been the Director of the FBI since its foundation in 1935. Hoover was thought to be unsackable because he was believed to have kept files on numerous leading politicians.

Back to Basics

Major twice used the phrase 'back to basics' in his speech to the 1993 Conservative Party Conference. The first mention, in context, went as follows: 'It is time to return to those old core values, time to get back to basics, to self-discipline and respect for the law, to consideration for others, to accepting responsibility for yourself and your family, and not shuffling off on other people and the state'. He did not specifically refer to sexual morality, but it was widely believed that this was one of the basics that he had in mind. Unfortunately for Major and the Conservative Party, the following years saw a plethora of, to say the least, questionable behaviour by some ministers, some Conservative MPs and some Conservatives outside Parliament. Back to basics became something of a bad joke. The press looked for, found, and revealed scandals. Others bubbled up without press enquiries. Vengeful wives, husbands, mistresses, and others were the sources of quite a few of them.

Almost immediately after Major's speech the transport minister Stephen Norris was revealed as having no fewer than five mistresses.[5] The *News of the World* published the fact that Tim Yeo had a six-month-old love child. The woman in question was a Conservative councillor.[6] Very tragically, the Conservative MP Stephen Milligan was found dead in bizarre and tragic circumstances. A pair of stockings, a cord, and a plastic carrier bag featured in the story.[7] Many other revelations of a sexual nature became public knowledge. There were financial scandals too. They included resignations by ministers and parliamentary private secretaries who had accepted payment for asking parliamentary questions.

In the shock, dismay, and general hilarity, there was quite a lot of sympathy for Major. He was a decent man, doing his best and wanting to get his country (not just his party) back to acceptable standards of behaviour. He was thinking about crime, education, respect, politeness, cycling on the pavement (endemic), and not just sexual and financial basics. Who did not, and indeed who does not? However, an unexpected bombshell would explode later.

Edwina Currie

Edwina Currie was elected to Parliament in 1983, and she held a junior position in Margaret Thatcher's government from 1986 to 1988. In 2002, the publication of *Currie's Diaries 1987–92* revealed a four-year affair with John Major starting in 1984. Both were married throughout these years, and Major has been married to his wife, Norma, since 1970. Memorable details include such comments as 'I wish my flat was filled with one big man in his blue underpants'.[8] Following the 1992 election, he offered her the job of Prisons Minister, but she turned it down and later said that it was a 'crap job'.[9]

Keeping the affair secret must have been very difficult, and the revelation came as a bombshell. In a press statement, Major said that he was ashamed by the affair and that his wife had forgiven him. It seems that Currie's motivation in making the affair public was annoyance that she did not get a single mention in Major's memoirs. However, it is fair to comment that she has written novels with salacious content, and that being in the public eye did no harm to her earnings since ceasing to be an MP in 1997.

51

Anthony Charles Lynton Blair

1997–07

A youthful Tony Blair at a Labour Party Conference.

IN HER LATER years, Mrs Thatcher is believed to have thought that Tony Blair and New Labour ranked among her achievements. Her thinking was that she had moved the centre of politics to the right and towards her way of thinking. There could only be another Labour government if its policies moved in the same direction. Neil Kinnock, John Smith, then Tony Blair (with Gordon Brown) did just that, and Blair called the party New Labour. Had Mrs Thatcher lived longer, she would have seen it under Jeremy Corbyn move back towards the left. However, at the time of writing, it has not got back into government.

Born in 1953, Blair was forty-three when he became Prime Minister, which made him the youngest holder of the office since Lord Liverpool in 1812. He served for a continuous period of ten years and fifty-six days, which, apart from Margaret Thatcher's continuous eleven years and 209 days, was the longest since the Marquess of Salisbury. He won three successive general elections, two of them with landslide majorities. It was a remarkable achievement and he was popular for a long time. So, was he a good or even a great Prime Minister? Some say that he was, but many see it differently. History will judge.

Blair was born in Edinburgh and spent his first nineteen months in the city, then the following three and a half years were with his family in Adelaide, Australia. After they returned to Britain, the rest of his childhood and adolescence was in Durham. He boarded at Fettes College, the leading independent school in Edinburgh, then graduated from St John's College, Oxford. The next step was to qualify as a barrister. Blair moved into politics and was elected a Labour MP in 1983. He became Shadow Home Secretary under John Smith in 1992, and on Smith's untimely death in 1994, party leader. The 1997 election was an overwhelming endorsement of Blair. Labour won 418 of the 659 seats in Parliament—101 of the 418 were women.

Some Prime Ministers are judged mainly by one or perhaps two defining issues. For Eden, it was Suez. For Blair, it has been his support for the American President George W. Bush, and committing troops to the 2003 invasion of Iraq. It is claimed that there was insufficient preparation for the aftermath and that the defeat of Saddam Hussein let ISIS gain a foothold in the country. Furthermore, it is claimed that the British people were misinformed about the justification for the war. They were told that Saddam Hussein had

Bill Clinton laughs with Tony Blair, 1998.

weapons of mass destruction that could be rapidly deployed. It subsequently became clear that he did not.

Some people think that the claim was a straight lie. Some people think that although he did not have the evidence, he believed that it was true and felt justified in saying that it was. Others say that Blair thought that the war was in any case justified because Saddam Hussein was an evil man who had to be removed. Put another way, the end justified the means. Regardless, the controversy has damaged Blair's reputation.

Building on John Major's work, Blair played a key part in securing the 1998 Good Friday Agreement in Northern Ireland, and this was followed by the devolution of powers to the Scottish Parliament, the National Assembly for Wales, and the Northern Ireland Assembly. Britain participated in the 2001 invasion of Afghanistan, and Blair ensured that his country took a leading military and peacekeeping role in Kosovo.

At home, the many acts of parliament secured by Blair's government included the Freedom of Information Act, the Human Rights Act, and the National Minimum Wage Act. All three remain controversial. Blair inherited a sound economy from John Major's government, but he did not pass it on. His government borrowed too much and was not in a good position to meet the worldwide economic crisis of 2008. Gordon Brown and he did not see it coming, but of course they were not alone in that.

This book's chapter on Clement Attlee states that 'he neglected presentation in favour of substance. He would have been the despair of our present day spin doctors'. This is most emphatically not true of Blair. There was a vast amount of spin. Opinions differ about the quality and quantity of the substance. In recent decades, there has been a trend away from cabinet government and towards what is sometimes termed presidential government, with the Prime Minister with centralised power being the equivalent of the president. This was noticeable during Blair's time as Prime Minister.[1]

Father Leo

Tony Blair's father, Leo, was an example and an inspiration. Born in 1923, he was the illegitimate son of two travelling entertainers, but was fostered then adopted by a working-class family in Glasgow. He worked for the Inland Revenue, then qualified as a barrister and became a law lecturer at Durham University. He had been a communist in his youth but afterwards became a Conservative Party activist. At the age of seventy-one, he joined the Labour Party. At the age of just forty, he suffered a major stroke, which left him speechless for three years. Tony Blair was eleven at the time. Leo went on to be a guest lecturer and to chair industrial tribunals. He died at the age of eighty-nine.

Baby Leo

Leo Blair was born on 20 May 2000, and was the first legitimate child to be born to a serving Prime Minister since Francis Russell in 1849. Tony Blair was forty-seven at the time and his wife, Cherie, was forty-six. In her autobiography, Cherie says that baby Leo was conceived at Balmoral when she and her husband were visiting the Queen. Knowing that her case would be unpacked for her, she decided to leave her contraceptive equipment at home. Her majesty's views on this revelation are not known. Others have said 'too much information'.

No -ism but an -ite

Blair's predecessor but one, Margaret Thatcher, was the mother of an -ism—namely Thatcherism. Tony Blair did not do that, but he fathered an -ite—namely Blairite. MPs and party members who hold to his policies are sometimes called Blairites.

Bambi

This is a nickname. It comes from Blair's perceived (by some) resemblance to the young deer in the Disney film.

The Toniblers

The Albanian people of Kosovo were very grateful to Tony Blair for his support in 1999 of air strikes on Serbian targets in Kosovo. A number of them showed this by naming boys born at the time Tonibler, a conflation of his name. In 2010, Blair visited Kosovo and met nine of his namesakes.[2]

Ugly Rumours

During his time at school, Blair was an admirer of the rock star Mick Jagger and did impressions of him. After leaving school and before going to university, with a friend and in a small way, he became a

President George W. Bush appears with Tony Blair at a press conference at Crawford High School in Crawford, Texas on 6 April 2002. *Paul Morse/White House*

President George W. Bush and Tony Blair shake hands after they conclude a joint news conference at the Camp David, 27 March 2003. *Paul Morse/White House*

promoter for bands and organised a number of gigs. Then, at university, he participated as a guitarist and lead singer for a band called Ugly Rumours. The band did not do much and it did not last.

The People's Princess

Diana, Princess of Wales died in a Paris car crash on 31 August 1997 and the country responded with unprecedented paroxysms of grief. Tony Blair, only four months in office, caught the public mood brilliantly. During the morning of her death, he spoke movingly with controlled emotion, and used the memorable phrase 'she was the people's princess'. Blair was in his honeymoon period with the British people and his popularity increased even further. The Conservative leader William Hague did not catch the public mood in this way.

After the death of the Princess, the Queen remained for a while in Balmoral with the Princes William and Harry, something that seriously upset some of her subjects. By all accounts, Blair, behind the scenes, gave her excellent advice and the problem was defused.

Religion

After a long struggle, Catholic emancipation was achieved in 1829, but Britain has never had a Catholic Prime Minister.[3] The great majority of the thirty-three Prime Ministers since 1829 have been Anglicans, and almost all of the remainder belonged to other Protestant denominations. One or two have perhaps been atheists, but did not broadcast the fact. Blair said that an Australian Priest at Oxford had helped him rediscover religion, and when he was Prime Minister, he was a practising Anglican. His wife, Cherie, was a lifelong Catholic, and towards the end of his time in Downing Street, he sometimes went to Catholic services. In December 2007, six months after ceasing to be Prime Minister, it was revealed that he had joined the Roman Catholic Church.

Relationship with Gordon Brown

Blair worked closely with Gordon Brown in opposition, and at one time, Brown had been expected to beat him to the position of Prime Minister. Brown had a uniquely powerful role in Blair's government and the two men sometimes had an uneasy working partnership. Brown felt that Blair should have stepped down earlier than he did. There is more about the Blair/Brown relationship in the next chapter.

On one occasion, Cherie Blair said something widely reported that was hostile to Brown. Blair lightened the mood by saying, 'At least I don't have to worry about her running off with the bloke next door.'[4]

A Patrick Blower cartoon for the *Evening Standard*, 13 February 2003. British public opinion was generally against involvement in Iraq.

52

James Gordon Brown

2007–10

James Gordon Brown. *The National Archives*

BORN IN 1951, Brown was brought up in Kirkcaldy, Fife. To use a Scottish expression, he was a 'son of the manse', his father being a minister of the Church of Scotland. He was fast tracked at school and started at the University of Edinburgh at the age of sixteen. He obtained a first-class honours degree in history, then upgraded it to a PhD ten years later. He was elected to Parliament in 1983, but before that, he was a lecturer in politics at Glasgow University and a tutor for the Open University. From 1980, he worked as a journalist for Scottish Television, progressing to the position of current affairs editor.

Labour was out of office but Brown became a member of the shadow cabinet after four years and shadow chancellor in 1992. Five years later, Blair headed a Labour government and made him Chancellor of the Exchequer. Brown was the most powerful person in Blair's cabinet and held the position for ten years and two months, which made him the longest-serving Chancellor in modern times. Almost immediately after taking office, he made the Bank of England independent in setting monetary policy, which included the power to set interest rates. This was generally welcomed and is regarded as part of his legacy.

Very controversially, and in the opinion of many damagingly, Brown's first budget made pension funds pay tax on their investments. This hit the viability of the funds and was a contributory factor to the so-called pensions crisis that developed later. Another very controversial step was the decision to sell part of the country's gold reserves. This was done just before a protracted rise in the price of the metal and was a costly mistake. Annoyingly, but like most recent chancellors, Brown introduced stealth taxes and made taxation more complicated. He did, however, preside over a very long benign period of expanding prosperity. It came to a juddering halt with the global financial crisis shortly after he became Prime Minister.

After more than ten years in office, Blair resigned as Prime Minister in June 2007 and Brown was the obvious person to succeed him. He hit the ground running and was initially popular. He made a mistake by not calling an early general election, which he would probably have won. After this, his popularity declined.

Gordon Brown greets President Nicolas Sarkozy and President of the European Commission, Jose Manuel Barroso before their meeting at number 10 Downing Street on 8 December 2008. The meeting was held to discuss what more could be done to stimulate the global economy.

Brown launched the inquiry into the 2003 Iraq War, which had damaged the reputation of his predecessor, and still does. He continued to keep Britain out of the Eurozone, and the wisdom of this is generally recognised. Fair-minded people might concede that he handled the global financial crisis well, though perhaps other fair-minded people might not agree, let alone the unfair minded.

His critics labelled him indecisive and he will not be remembered as a great Prime Minister—perhaps a middling one. He is widely respected as a decent man. The last two sentences sound like damning him with faint praise, but consider that it is a compliment to be called decent, and middling means much the same as average. As there have been fifty-four Prime Ministers, it implies that about twenty-seven were worse.

A Proud Scot

Brown was one of the seven Prime Ministers born in Scotland. He grew up there, went to school and university there, worked there, and represented a Scottish constituency. He went there frequently and never neglected his Scottish roots. He was a very proud Scot, but proud of Scotland within the United Kingdom. In the 2014, referendum he campaigned against Scottish independence.

Not Oxbridge

The majority of the Prime Ministers went to university, though the prominent exceptions include Wellington, Disraeli, Lloyd George, and Churchill. Of those that did go to university, only five went to establishments other than Oxford or Cambridge. Brown, who went to Edinburgh, was one of them. The others were Lord Bute (Leiden), Lord John Russell (Edinburgh), Bonar Law (Glasgow), and Chamberlain (Mason Science College, later Birmingham).

Blind in One Eye

Just before leaving school, Brown suffered a kick in the head while playing rugby. The injury cost him the sight of one eye and the rest of his career was conducted with this handicap. His handwriting and signature were sometimes untidy, which led to unfair comment. He never drew attention to the problem or sought sympathy.

As Clear as Mud

During a speech in 1994, Brown said: 'Our new economic approach is rooted in ideas which stress the importance of macro-economics, post neo-classical endogenous growth theory and the symbiotic relationships between growth and investment, and people and infrastructure'. This provoked bafflement and hilarity. Readers of this book are undoubtedly very well educated, so no explanation is provided.

The Dangers of a Live Microphone

As mentioned in the chapter about John Major, it is important to know whether or not a microphone is live. While campaigning in Rochdale during the 2010 election campaign, Brown was questioned on immigration by Gillian Duffy, a pensioner. In many people's opinion, the questions were not offensive. The following exchange in Brown's car was subsequently broadcast.

Brown: 'That was a disaster. Should never have put me with that woman. Whose idea was that? Sue I think. Just ridiculous. They will use it'.

Driver: 'What did she say?'

Brown: 'Everything. She was just a sort of bigoted woman who said she used to be Labour. I mean it's ridiculous'.

Brown was mortified when this was broadcast and it did his election campaign no good at all. He subsequently called on Mrs Duffy in order to apologise.

Relationship with Blair

Gordon Brown and Tony Blair were both elected to Parliament in 1983, and by coincidence, they shared an office. They got on well, were both ambitious, and had broadly similar views about the future of the Labour Party. Brown, who was four years older, had been seen as the more likely leader, but it was Blair who got the position first. The vacancy came sooner than expected due to the sudden death of John Smith in 1994. At the time, Blair seemed to have the better chance of winning the next election. It is believed, but never confirmed, that a deal was struck over a meal in the former Granita restaurant in Islington. Brown would not stand, and in return, Blair would make him Chancellor with a free hand in economic policy. Furthermore, after a while, Blair would stand down to allow Brown to succeed him.

It came to pass: Blair became Prime Minister with Brown as Chancellor, and Brown was the dominant figure in his cabinet. Most of the disagreements were behind the scenes, but they often had a difficult

President Barack Obama talks with Gordon Brown and President Nicolas Sarkozy prior to making a statement about Iran at the David L. Lawrence Convention Center in Pittsburgh, Pennsylvanie, 25 September 2009. *Official White House Photo by Pete Souza*

A Conservative Party poster.

Gordon Brown in conversation with Gillian Duffy, Rochdale, 28 April 2010. He was shortly afterwards caught off guard on a press cameraman's microphone saying that she was a 'bigoted woman', making sensational news. It was not a good election for Brown and his Labour party took only 258 seats while David Cameron's Conservatives took 306.

or even very difficult working relationship. If there was an agreement that Blair would step down after a while, Blair took an unconscionably long time honouring it. Brown grew more and more restless as the years rolled by. Blair was not complimentary about Brown in his memoirs.

Wife and Children

Brown had been Chancellor for three years when he married Sarah Macaulay at the late age of forty-nine. Their first child, a daughter born in 2002, arrived prematurely and only lived for a few days. Two boys followed. It was later revealed by a newspaper that the youngest suffered from cystic fibrosis, something that Brown had wanted to keep private.

There is every indication that it has been and is a happy marriage and family. When he left Downing Street, he thanked his wife and sons for their love and support and went on to say: 'And as I leave the second most important job I could ever hold, I cherish even more the first—as a husband and father'.

Life after Downing Street

Like Major, but unlike Blair and Cameron, Brown served a further parliamentary term after leaving office. He quickly wrote a book entitled *Beyond the Crash*, but unlike some prominent politicians, he has not set out to make money. He has taken a number of unpaid positions and any fees received have been donated to the Gordon and Sarah Brown Foundation to support charitable work.

53

David William Donald Cameron

2010–16

STARTING WITH WILSON in 1964, the country has had a run of progressively younger Prime Ministers. Born in 1966, Cameron is the latest to be the youngest since Lord Liverpool in 1812. He took office at the age of forty-three.

David Cameron, photographed 3 August 2010, the official Downing Street Photograph. *10 Downing Street*

Cameron came from a wealthy upper-middle-class family, and he was educated at Eton College then Brasenose College, Oxford. After that, he went into the so-called 'Westminster bubble'. For five years, he worked in the Conservative Research Department, and then in 1992, he became Special Advisor to the Chancellor of the Exchequer Norman Lamont. He was close to him, and photographed with him, during the disastrous Black Wednesday, when Britain was forced out of the ERM (Exchange Rate Mechanism). Soon afterwards, he switched to working for the Home Secretary Michael Howard.

In 1994, he became Director of Corporate Affairs at Carlton Communications. This did not prevent an unsuccessful attempt to be elected to Parliament at the 1997 election. Some of his critics (and indeed some of his admirers) have noted that his only real job out of politics was in a company with the word 'Communications' in its title. His job involved lobbying and spin.

Cameron became MP for the Witney constituency at the 2001 election, and his subsequent rise was meteoric. Labour was in power, and in 2005, at the age of thirty-nine, he defeated David Davis to become Leader of the Conservative Party and Leader of the Opposition. A very effective speech made without notes at the party conference is credited with swinging many votes his way. Leading the opposition is often regarded as a particularly thankless job, but Cameron beavered away for four and a half years.

As widely predicted, the 2010 election resulted in a hung parliament. The consequence was a coalition government, the first since the end of the Second World War. The Liberal Democrats joined the Conservatives, with David Cameron as Prime Minister and Nick Clegg of the Liberal Democrats as his deputy. Despite some inevitable difficulties, the two men appeared to get on well and work together effectively. Some people believe that a coalition suited Cameron personally because his views on some issues were more liberal than those of many of his followers.

David Cameron speaks to British troops at Camp Bastion, Helmand province, Afghanistan, 3 October 2014. Cameron spoke with British troops and met with International Security Assistance Force and Afghan National Army leaders in charge of the region. *Official U.S. Marine Corps photo by Cpl Darien J. Bjorndal*

Cameron and the Conservatives inherited a very difficult economic situation. Government borrowing was disastrously high and the need to get it down cast a shadow over his time in Downing Street. He made progress, but not as much as he wanted and it is still a problem at the time of writing this book. Civil servants appreciate Prime Ministers who are good administrators, are efficient, and give clear decisions at the right time. Not all Prime Ministers do this, but Cameron generally did.

It was widely expected, including some say by Cameron, that the 2015 General Election would result in another hung parliament, with Labour perhaps having the most seats. This did not happen and Cameron formed an exclusively Conservative administration with a working majority of twelve. This was his opportunity to deliver a purely Conservative programme, unhindered by the constraints of a coalition. He did not have long to do this because his previously promised in/out referendum about membership of the European Union dominated his brief second term. From his point of view, it went disastrously wrong.

Cameron's attempt to renegotiate changes in Britain's relationship with the European Union resulted in only very minor concessions. Nevertheless, he pronounced himself satisfied and recommended continued membership. He was backed by most of his cabinet, most of his MPs, and most of the Labour, Liberal Democrat, and Scottish Nationalist MPs. As the fateful date approached, increasingly dire and dreadful warnings were given about the consequences of a vote to leave. They included an emergency budget and a big increase in tax. Nevertheless, on 23 June 2016, 51.89 per cent of the electorate voted to come out. Cameron immediately signalled his intention to resign and left office on 13 July.

Royal Lineage

Cameron is the fifth cousin, twice removed, of Queen Elizabeth II.[1] George III is their common ancestor. His son, George IV, died leaving no legitimate children, so the throne passed to his brother, William. The new king had no legitimate children, but before his marriage, he had ten illegitimate ones with his mistress Dorothea Jordan. One of these, a daughter, married the 18th Earl of Errol. Cameron is descended from the couple.

Wife and Children

Cameron is married to Samantha, who is the daughter of Sir Reginald Sheffield, 8th Baronet. Her mother is now Viscountess Astor. Samantha has been involved in a number of charitable organisations, and until her husband became Prime Minister, she was the Creative Director of the stationery business Smythson of Bond Street. She is now involved in fashion.

The Camerons have had four children. The first, Ivan, was born with a rare combination of cerebral palsy and severe epilepsy. He died in 2009 at the age of six. The couple were admired for their care and commitment to him. The fourth child, a daughter, was born shortly after Cameron became Prime Minister. She was the second legitimate child to be born to a serving Prime Minister since 1849. Leo Blair was the first.

Photo Opportunities

In 2006, while Leader of the Opposition, Cameron sometimes cycled to Westminster. He may well have wanted to and thought it a good thing to do, but happily for him, it portrayed an image of a healthy young man doing his best for the environment. The effect was somewhat marred by the realisation that he was often followed by a car carrying his papers. Like many politicians, he was not averse to photo opportunities. Hugging huskies in Norway while visiting a glacier to see the effects of global warming was an example.

The Bullingdon Club

The Bullingdon Club is an unofficial all male club based at Oxford University. Founded in 1780, it was originally a sporting club, particularly for cricket and horse racing, but club dinners are now the main activity. Unfortunately, it has a tradition of what might kindly be called boisterous activity, but would otherwise be termed vandalism. Its members have damaged restaurants, though afterwards promptly paid for what they have done.

The members tend to be privileged and wealthy. At the annual dinner, they wear tailcoats in navy blue with a velvet collar, ivory silk lapels, brass buttons, and a mustard-coloured waistcoat. The present-day cost of the outfit is around £3,000.

The long list of famous members includes David Cameron, Boris Johnson (ex-Mayor of London and current Foreign Secretary), and George Osborne (ex-Chancellor of the Exchequer). It is not suggested that any of these three took part in the disreputable behaviour described above. It is, however, suggested that their past membership is an embarrassment to them. Cameron and Johnson were members

David Cameron, President Barack Obama, Chancellor Angela Merkel of Germany, José Manuel Barroso, President of the European Commission, President François Hollande of France and others watch the overtime shootout of the Chelsea vs. Bayern Munich Champions League final, UEFA, in the Laurel Cabin conference room during the G8 Summit at Camp David, Maryland, 19 May 2012. Angela Merkel does not look so happy. *Official White House Photo by Peter J. Souza*

The 'Plebgate', 'Plodgate', 'Gategate' scandal resulted from an altercation between Andrew Mitchell, the Conservative Chief Whip at the time, and the police, which took place on 19 September 2012. First published in *The Sun*, 2012. *Courtesy Andy Davey*

together and appear in a photograph wearing the dress described. The men in the photograph appear to be adopting a rather supercilious pose.

Honours and the House of Lords

It is a commonly held opinion that several modern prime Ministers have been complicit in the awarding of honours to unsuitable people, and in elevating too many people to the House of Lords. Cameron is in the frame on both counts, though not matching the excesses of Lloyd George in the early twentieth century. Although they may be worthy, donors to party funds, friends, and people who have done favours somehow get recognised.

The House of Lords has expanded to more than 800 members, which is far too many. Blair created 374 peers in ten years, and Cameron created 244 peers in six years. Some of Cameron's creations were Labour and some were Liberal Democrats. None were from UKIP, although that party secured 12.6 per cent of the vote (but just one seat) at the 2015 election. UKIP has three peers, all of them having defected from the Conservative Party.

A Dignified Resignation

Cameron was admired for the great dignity that he showed when it became known that the country had rejected his recommendation and voted to leave the European Union. The poll was on 23 June 2016, and the next day, he announced his intention to resign. On 13 July, he received a standing ovation from MPs. His final comment was 'I was the future once'. He submitted his resignation to the Queen later that day.

Although he is still very much alive and hopefully has many more years still to live, a quote from Macbeth by William Shakespeare seems appropriate: 'Nothing in his life became him like the leaving of it'. In the play, the words are spoken by Malcolm to King Duncan and refer to the execution of Cawdor. If a second literary quotation can be tolerated, we might add an extract from Andrew Marvell's poem on the execution of Charles I:

He nothing common did or mean
Upon that memorable scene.

54

Theresa Mary May

2016–

BORN IN 1956, Theresa May doubled the number of female Prime Ministers and the number of female leaders of the Conservative Party. Margaret Thatcher had previously held both positions. Her predecessor but one, Gordon Brown, was a son of the manse (Scottish term) and she was a daughter of the vicarage (English term). Her father was a Church of England vicar.

May briefly attended an independent Catholic school, and then a state grammar school at Wheatley. While she was at the school, it changed its status and became a comprehensive. Afterwards, she read geography and obtained a second-class BA degree at St Hugh's College, Oxford. The college was all-women at the time.

Theresa May is clapped into 10 Downing Street for the first time, 13 July 2016. *Tom Evans, Official 10 Downing Street Photograph*

From 1977 to 1983, May worked at the Bank of England, and from 1985 to 1997, for the Association for Payment Clearing Services. During this time, she was for eight years a councillor in the London Borough of Merton, and twice unsuccessfully contested safe Labour seats in parliamentary elections. In 1997, at the age of forty, she became the Conservative MP for the Maidenhead constituency.

The Conservative Party was in opposition for the next thirteen years, and during that time, she served in the shadow cabinets of William Hague, Iain Duncan Smith, Michael Howard, and David Cameron. For a talented and ambitious woman, such a long time in opposition must have been dispiriting. It came to an end when Cameron formed his coalition government in 2010. Despite not having held the shadow brief for the department, she was appointed Home Secretary.

May was Home Secretary for just over six years, and was the longest holder of the position since Chuter Ede served Clement Attlee in the post-war Labour government. There was no shortage of problems. She confronted the Police Federation about some of its perceived failings, and she had to fight crime within the limits of financial constraints. Overall recorded crime fell, but there were nevertheless very pressing and labour-consuming difficulties. Prisons were at bursting point and supplied a succession of problems and scandals, and there was the ever-present threat of terrorism.

Illegal drugs are, like the poor, always with us. In 2013, Abu Qatada the radical cleric, or hate preacher as the press called him, was finally deported after many years of trying. This was a May triumph, and she was not reluctant to tell us. Human rights laws hampered this and other actions that she tried to take. She even had to deal with a backlog in dealing with passport applications.

Perhaps May's biggest problem was immigration, including border control. Cameron's government was committed to getting net immigration down to the tens of thousands. She (and her government colleagues) never got anywhere near achieving this. In the year to September 2016, net immigration was 273,000. However, given membership of the European Union, human rights laws, the problems of illegal immigrants, and other difficulties, it is very hard to see that the commitment was ever realistic.

Theresa May delivers her Brexit speech at Lancaster House, 17 January 2017. *Jay Allen, Official 10 Downing Street Photograph*

In the referendum held on 23 June 2016, the UK voted to leave the European Union. Like most of her cabinet colleagues, May had advocated that the country should stay in, but she had done so in a noticeably lukewarm manner. Perhaps this was because she had doubts about the benefits of staying in, or perhaps she privately thought that the country should come out. Perhaps she thought that her lack of enthusiasm would help her chances of becoming Prime Minister if the vote was to come out and Cameron resigned. In the event, she was well placed to take the top job. She won the first and second ballot of Conservative MPs and a vote of the party members was not required.

How and when the United Kingdom leaves the European Union has dominated the early part of May's premiership. She has consistently taken a firm line with doubters, and said that it will definitely happen and that her government will get the best possible deal. She has repeatedly enthused or irritated the citizenry by firmly stating 'BREXIT MEANS BREXIT'.

Is she a good Prime Minister? Time will tell. I recall that in my youth, a Chinese student was asked what were the consequences of the French Revolution. His much-publicised reply was, 'It's too soon to tell'. Ask me the question in a few years' time and I will give you the answer.

The Loss of her Parents

May endured a double tragedy at the age of twenty-five. Her father died in a car accident, and a few months later, her mother's battle with multiple sclerosis ended with her death.

Husband Philip

Theresa and Philip May met at Oxford and they married in 1980. They have no children, which Theresa has said is for medical reasons and a matter of regret. By all accounts, it is a very happy marriage.

Being the spouse of a Prime Minister is not easy, and being the spouse of a female Prime Minister is perhaps particularly hard. Philip, like Denis Thatcher before him, copes well. He is a great support behind the scenes and is happy to let his wife take the limelight. Unlike Denis, he still has a career. He works in the city in client relations for the Capital Group. He is successful, respected, and does not take advantage of the May name.

Theresa May in conversation with President Donald Trump at the White House, 27 January 2017. *Jay Allen, Official 10 Downing Street Photograph*

Religion

The children of ministers of religion sometimes renounce their parents' beliefs. This did not happen to Theresa. She is a Christian and regularly attends church with her husband.

Health

In 2012, May was diagnosed with diabetes mellitus of Type 1 and takes insulin injections daily. There were fears that this would be a significant handicap, but she seems to cope very well.

Recreation

Modern Home Secretaries and Prime Ministers do not have much spare time, but she and her husband enjoy hiking. They have spent several holidays hiking in the Swiss Alps. She is keen on cricket and is said to be an admirer of the greatest living Yorkshireman, Geoff Boycott. She enjoys cooking and has more than a hundred cookery books.

Mistaken Identity

Theresa May shares a name with a porn star. She has said: 'We do get calls from people who want to book me to do programmes which are perhaps not about politics'.[1]

Clothes

May is always careful with her dress and takes an interest in fashion. In 2014, when she was the guest on *Desert Island Discs*, she chose a subscription to *Vogue* magazine as her luxury item. She is particularly noted for her distinctive shoes and trousers.

The Nasty Party

May was chairman of the Conservative Party at the time of its 2002 party conference. She stunned the delegates by including in her speech the words: 'There is a lot we need to do in this party of ours. Our base is too narrow and so, occasionally, are our sympathies. You know what some people call us—the nasty party'. At the time, the party had lost two successive elections and was in a bad way. There had been many scandals.

She told the listeners that the party needed more women and more from ethnic minorities. In a hard-hitting speech, she said that the party had indulged in 'petty feuding, personal sniping, had demonised minorities and twice gone to the country unrepentant, just plain unattractive'. A lot of Conservatives did not like it, but it was an effective wake-up call. The phrase 'nasty party' is indelibly linked to her name.

A Brutal Cull

When May became Prime Minister, nine of Cameron's ministers resigned or were sacked. *The Daily Telegraph* called the process 'a brutal cull'. The excluded ministers included the Chancellor of the Exchequer George Osborne, a man who for many years had nursed an ambition to be Cameron's successor. His sacking was said to have been done swiftly and unceremoniously. Another casualty was Nicky Morgan who had been Secretary of State for Education and Minister for Women and Equalities. In December 2016, her invitation to a meeting in Downing Street was revoked after she expressed concern about the Prime Minister's expenditure of £1,000 on a pair of leather trousers.

A good Prime Minister needs to know when to dismiss colleagues and be able to do it, a point made in this book's chapter on Clement Attlee. Nevertheless, she made some hostages to fortune and put some disgruntled colleagues on the back benches.

An Adam Zyglis cartoon for the *Buffalo News*, 12 June 2017. *Adam Zyglis: Cagle Cartoons*

Endnotes

Chapter 1

1. Thomson, G. M., *The Prime Ministers* (Martin Secker, 1980), p. 1.
2. *Ibid.*, p. 2.
3. *Ibid.*, p. 3.
4. Douglas Home, W., *The Prime Ministers: Stories and Anecdotes from Number 10* (W. H. Allen, 1987), p. 29.
5. *Ibid.*, p. 24.
6. Thomson, *The Prime Ministers* (1980), p. 1.

Chapter 2

1. Thomson, G. M., *The Prime Ministers* (Martin Secker, 1980), p. 11.

Chapter 3

1. Eccleshall, R., and Walker, G., (eds), *Biographical Dictionary of British Prime Ministers* (Taylor & Francis Ltd, 1998), p. 26.

Chapter 4

1. Thomson, G. M., *The Prime Ministers* (Martin Secker, 1980), p. 18.
2. *Ibid.*, p. 20.
3. *Ibid.*, p. 18.
4. *Ibid.*, p. 18.
5. Parker, R. J., *British Prime Ministers* (Amberley Publishing, 2013), p. 19.
6. Douglas Home, W., *The Prime Ministers: Stories and Anecdotes from Number 10* (W. H. Allen, 1987), p. 38.
7. Thomson, *The Prime Ministers* (1980), p. 22.
8. *Ibid.*, p. 18.
9. *Ibid.*, p. 18.

Chapter 5

1. Fraser, A., *Perilous Question: The Drama of the Great Reform Bill 1832* (Orion Publishing Co., 2013), p. 57.

Chapter 6

1. Eccleshall, R., and Walker, G., (eds), *Biographical Dictionary of British Prime Ministers* (Taylor & Francis Ltd, 1998), p. 37.
2. Thomson, G. M., *The Prime Ministers* (Martin Secker, 1980), p. 29.

Chapter 7

1. Douglas Home, W., *The Prime Ministers: Stories and Anecdotes from Number 10* (W. H. Allen, 1987), p. 46.

Chapter 8

1. Eccleshall, R., and Walker, G., (eds), *Biographical Dictionary of British Prime Ministers* (Taylor & Francis Ltd, 1998), p. 53.

Chapter 9

1. Douglas Home, W., *The Prime Ministers: Stories and Anecdotes from Number 10* (W. H. Allen, 1987), p. 53.
2. Wilson, Sir H., *A Prime Minister on Prime Ministers* (Weidenfeld & Nicholson, 1977), p. 12.
3. Douglas Home, *The Prime Ministers* (1987), p. 53.

4. *Ibid.*, p. 56.
5. Thomson, G. M., *The Prime Ministers* (Martin Secker, 1980), p. 43.

Chapter 10

1. Eccleshall, R., and Walker, G., (eds), *Biographical Dictionary of British Prime Ministers* (Taylor & Francis Ltd, 1998), p. 61.
2. Douglas Home, W., *The Prime Ministers: Stories and Anecdotes from Number 10* (W. H. Allen, 1987), p. 59.
3. Parker, R. J., *British Prime Ministers* (Amberley Publishing, 2013), p. 33.
4. Thomson, G. M., *The Prime Ministers* (Martin Secker, 1980), p. 47.
5. *Ibid.*, p. 47.
6. Holy Bible, Luke Chapter 15 Verse 7.

Chapter 11

1. Thomson, G. M., *The Prime Ministers* (Martin Secker, 1980), p. 49.
2. Mason, R., *Great Railway Journeys London to Sheffield* (Amberley Publishing, 2016), p. 77.
3. Thomson, *The Prime Ministers* (1980), p. 51.
4. Douglas Home, W., *The Prime Ministers: Stories and Anecdotes from Number 10* (W. H. Allen, 1987), p. 61.
5. *Ibid.*, p. 61.
6. *Ibid.*, p. 63.

Chapter 12

1. Wilson, Sir H., *A Prime Minister on Prime Ministers* (Weidenfeld & Nicholson, 1977), p. 15.
2. Thomson, G. M., *The Prime Ministers* (Martin Secker, 1980), p. 56.
3. *Ibid.*, p. 55.
4. Eccleshall, R., and Walker, G., (eds), *Biographical Dictionary of British Prime Ministers* (Taylor & Francis Ltd, 1998), p. 74.
5. Thomson, *The Prime Ministers* (1980), p. 56.

Chapter 13

1. Douglas Home, W., *The Prime Ministers: Stories and Anecdotes from Number 10* (W. H. Allen, 1987), p. 67.
2. Thomson, G. M., *The Prime Ministers* (Martin Secker, 1980), p. 58.
3. Bastable, J., *Prime Ministers* (David & Charles, 2011), p. 113.

Chapter 14

1. Johnson, P., (ed.), *The Oxford Book of Political Anecdotes* (Oxford University Press, 1986), p. 90.
2. Thomson, G. M., *The Prime Ministers* (Martin Secker, 1980), p. 65.
3. Mason, R., *The Struggle for Democracy: Parliamentary Reform, from the Rotten Boroughs to Today* (The History Press, 2015), p. 17.
4. Johnson, *Political Anecdotes* (1986), p. 92.

Chapter 15

1. Thomson, G. M., *The Prime Ministers* (Martin Secker, 1980), p. 72.
2. *Ibid.*, p. 72.
3. *Ibid.*, p. 69.
4. Eccleshall, R., and Walker, G., (eds), *Biographical Dictionary of British Prime Ministers* (Taylor & Francis Ltd, 1998), p.96.

Chapter 16

1. Thomson, G. M., *The Prime Ministers* (Martin Secker, 1980), p. 74.
2. Eccleshall, R., and Walker, G., (eds), *Biographical Dictionary of British Prime Ministers* (Taylor & Francis Ltd, 1998), p. 99.
3. Thomson, *The Prime Ministers* (1980), p. 76.
4. Bastable, J., *Prime Ministers* (David & Charles, 2011), p. 35.

Chapter 17

1. Thomson, G. M., *The Prime Ministers* (Martin Secker, 1980), p. 80.
2. Bastable, J., *Prime Ministers* (David & Charles, 2011), p. 20.
3. Douglas Home, *Stories and Anecdotes from Number 10* 1987), p. 82.

Chapter 18

1. Eccleshall, R., and Walker, G., (eds), *Biographical Dictionary of British Prime Ministers* (Taylor & Francis Ltd, 1998), p. 115.
2. *Ibid.*, p. 107.
3. Douglas Home, *The Prime Ministers* (1987), p. 86.

Chapter 19

1. Taylor, A. J. P., *British Prime Ministers and Other Essays* (Penguin Books Ltd, 1999), p. 61.
2. Johnson, P., (ed.), *The Oxford Book of Political Anecdotes* (Oxford University Press, 1986), p. 104.

Chapter 20

1. Wilson, Sir H., *A Prime Minister on Prime Ministers* (Weidenfeld & Nicholson, 1977), p. 37.
2. Thomson, G. M., *The Prime Ministers* (Martin Secker, 1980), p. 94.
3. *Ibid.*, p. 92.
4. Douglas Home, W., *The Prime Ministers: Stories and Anecdotes from Number 10* (W. H. Allen, 1987), p. 94.
5. *Ibid.*, p. 96.
6. *Ibid.*, p. 96.

Chapter 21

1. Hibbert, C., *Wellington A Personal History* (HarperCollins, 1997), p. 57.
2. *Ibid.*, p. 162.
3. *Ibid.*, p. 162.
4. Parris, M., *Great Parliamentary Scandals* (Robson Books Ltd, 1995), p. 37.

Chapter 22

1. Douglas Home, W., *The Prime Ministers: Stories and Anecdotes from Number 10* (W. H. Allen, 1987), p. 107.
2. Thomson, G. M., *The Prime Ministers* (Martin Secker, 1980), p. 103.

Chapter 23

1. Eccleshall, R., and Walker, G., (eds), *Biographical Dictionary of British Prime Ministers* (Taylor & Francis Ltd, 1998), p. 138.
2. Thomson, G. M., *The Prime Ministers* (Martin Secker, 1980), p. 110.
3. Douglas Home, W., *The Prime Ministers: Stories and Anecdotes from Number 10* (W. H. Allen, 1987), p. 116.
4. Thomson, *The Prime Ministers* (1980), p. 112.
5. *Ibid.*, p. 111.
6. *Ibid.*, p. 109.
7. *Ibid.*, p. 112
8. Douglas Home, *The Prime Ministers* (1987), p. 118.

Chapter 24

1. Wilson, Sir H., *A Prime Minister on Prime Ministers* (Weidenfeld & Nicholson, 1977), p. 45.
2. Douglas Home, W., *The Prime Ministers: Stories and Anecdotes from Number 10* (W. H. Allen, 1987), p. 120.
3. Thomson, G. M., *The Prime Ministers* (Martin Secker, 1980), p. 116.
4. Douglas Home, *The Prime Ministers* (1987), p. 120.
5. Wilson, *A Prime Minister on Prime Ministers* (1977), p. 59.

Chapter 25

1. Parker, R. J., *British Prime Ministers* (Amberley Publishing, 2013), p. 66.
2. Douglas Home, W., *The Prime Ministers: Stories and Anecdotes from Number 10* (W. H. Allen, 1987), p. 126.
3. Mason, R., *The Struggle for Democracy: Parliamentary Reform, from the Rotten Boroughs to Today* (The History Press, 2015), p. 60.
4. Thomson, G. M., *The Prime Ministers* (Martin Secker, 1980), p. 119.
5. Eccleshall, R., and Walker, G., (eds), *Biographical Dictionary of British Prime Ministers* (Taylor & Francis Ltd, 1998), p. 160.

Chapter 26

1. Eccleshall, R., and Walker, G., (eds), *Biographical Dictionary of British Prime Ministers* (Taylor & Francis Ltd, 1998), p. 163.
2. Douglas Home, W., *The Prime Ministers: Stories and Anecdotes from Number 10* (W. H. Allen, 1987), p. 129.
3. Eccleshall and Walker, *Biographical Dictionary of British Prime Ministers* (1998). p. 162.

Chapter 27

1. Douglas Home, W., *The Prime Ministers: Stories and Anecdotes from Number 10* (W. H. Allen, 1987), p. 135.
2. Bastable, J., *Prime Ministers* (David & Charles, 2011), p. 119.
3. Douglas Home, *The Prime Ministers* (1987), p. 134.

Chapter 28

1. Wilson, Sir H., *A Prime Minister on Prime Ministers* (Weidenfeld & Nicholson, 1977), p. 84.
2. Thomson, G. M., *The Prime Ministers* (Martin Secker, 1980), p. 132.
3. *Ibid.*, p. 134.

Chapter 29

1. Taylor, A. J. P., *British Prime Ministers and Other Essays* (Penguin Books Ltd, 1999), p. 24.
2. Johnson, P., (ed.), *The Oxford Book of Political Anecdotes* (Oxford University Press, 1986), p. 123.
3. Douglas Home, W., *The Prime Ministers: Stories and Anecdotes from Number 10* (W. H. Allen, 1987), p. 145.
4. *Ibid.*, p. 143.
5. *Ibid.*, p. 148.
6. Jenkins, R., *Gladstone* (Macmillan, 1995), p. 418.
7. Thomson, G. M., *The Prime Ministers* (Martin Secker, 1980), p. 146.

Chapter 30

1. Jenkins, R., *Churchill: A Biography* (Pan, 2001), p. 912.
2. Jenkins, R., *Gladstone* (Macmillan, 1995), p. 35.
3. Mason, R., *The Struggle for Democracy: Parliamentary Reform, from the Rotten Boroughs to Today* (The History Press, 2015), p. 219.
4. Douglas Home, W., *The Prime Ministers: Stories and Anecdotes from Number 10* (W. H. Allen, 1987), p. 153.
5. *Ibid.*, p. 160.
6. Bastable, J., *Prime Ministers* (David & Charles, 2011), p. 23.
7. Parris, M., *Great Parliamentary Scandals* (Robson Books Ltd, 1995), p. 50.
8. Jenkins, R., *Gladstone* (Macmillan, 1995), p. 106.
9. *Ibid.*, p. 470.
10. *Ibid.*, p. 513.
11. *Ibid.*, p. 514.
12. *Ibid.*, p. 618.
13. *Ibid.*, p. 631.

Chapter 31

1. Johnson, P., (ed.), *The Oxford Book of Political Anecdotes* (Oxford University Press, 1986), p. 135.
2. Wilson, Sir H., *A Prime Minister on Prime Ministers* (Weidenfeld & Nicholson, 1977), p. 128.
3. Douglas Home, W., *The Prime Ministers: Stories and Anecdotes from Number 10* (W. H. Allen, 1987), p. 165.
4. *Ibid.*, p. 162.
5. *Ibid.*, p. 163.

Chapter 32

1. Churchill, Sir W., *Great Contemporaries* (Thornton Butterworth Ltd, 1937), p. 10.
2. *Ibid.*, p. 9.
3. *Ibid.*, p. 14.

Chapter 33

1. Churchill, Sir W., *Great Contemporaries* (Thornton Butterworth Ltd, 1937), p. 183.
2. Dampier, P., and Walton, A., *The Wit and Wisdom of British Prime Ministers* (Book Guild Publishing, 2008), p. 66.
3. Douglas Home, W., *The Prime Ministers: Stories and Anecdotes from Number 10* (W. H. Allen, 1987), p. 177.
4. *Ibid.*, p. 178.

Chapter 34

1. Mason, R., *The Struggle for Democracy: Parliamentary Reform, from the Rotten Boroughs to Today* (The History Press, 2015), p. 122.
2. Bastable, J., *Prime Ministers* (David & Charles, 2011), p. 51.
3. Douglas Home, W., *The Prime Ministers: Stories and Anecdotes from Number 10* (W. H. Allen, 1987), p. 181.
4. *Ibid.*, p. 183.
5. Parker, R. J., *British Prime Ministers* (Amberley Publishing, 2013), p. 83.

Chapter 35

1. Johnson, P., (ed.), *The Oxford Book of Political Anecdotes* (Oxford University Press, 1986), p. 175.
2. Thomson, G. M., *The Prime Ministers* (Martin Secker, 1980), p. 184.
3. Jenkins, R., *Asquith* (HarperCollins, 1964), p. 19.
4. *Ibid.*, p. 179.
5. *Ibid.*, p. 78.
6. Feely, T., *Number 10: The Private Lives of Six Prime Ministers* (Sidgwick & Jackson, 1982), p. 130.

Chapter 36

1. Douglas Home, W., *The Prime Ministers: Stories and Anecdotes from Number 10* (W. H. Allen, 1987), p. 193.
2. Johnson, P., (ed.), *The Oxford Book of Political Anecdotes* (Oxford University Press, 1986), p. 190-192.

3. Feely, T., *Number 10: The Private Lives of Six Prime Ministers* (Sidgwick & Jackson, 1982), p. 159.
4. *Ibid.*, p. 159.
5. Dampier, P., and Walton, A., *The Wit and Wisdom of British Prime Ministers* (Book Guild Publishing, 2008), p. 78.
6. *Ibid.*, p. 78.
7. *Ibid.*, p. 79.
8. *Ibid.*, p. 79.
9. Parris, M., *Great Parliamentary Scandals* (Robson Books Ltd, 1995), p. 88.
10. *Ibid.*, p. 90.
11. *Ibid.*, p. 91.

Chapter 37

1. Bastable, J., *Prime Ministers* (David & Charles, 2011), p.79.
2. Douglas Home, W., *The Prime Ministers: Stories and Anecdotes from Number 10* (W. H. Allen, 1987), p. 203.
3. *Ibid.*, p. 202.
4. Bastable, *Prime Ministers* (2011), p. 79.

Chapter 38

1. Powell, J. E., *Joseph Chamberlain* (Thames & Hudson Ltd, 1977), p. 151.
2. Douglas Home, W., *The Prime Ministers: Stories and Anecdotes from Number 10* (W. H. Allen, 1987), p. 205.
3. *Ibid.*, p. 205.
4. Bastable, J., *Prime Ministers* (David & Charles, 2011), p.98.
5. *Ibid.*, p. 77.
6. Douglas Home, *The Prime Ministers* (1987), p. 208.
7. Thomson, G. M., *The Prime Ministers* (Martin Secker, 1980), p. 199.

Chapter 39

1. Taylor, A. J. P., *British Prime Ministers and Other Essays* (Penguin Books Ltd, 1999), p, 107.
2. Douglas Home, W., *The Prime Ministers: Stories and Anecdotes from Number 10* (W. H. Allen, 1987), p. 212.
3. *Ibid.*, p. 213
4. Dampier, P., and Walton, A., *The Wit and Wisdom of British Prime Ministers* (Book Guild Publishing, 2008), p. 85.
5. *Ibid.*, p. 86.
6. Feely, T., *Number 10: The Private Lives of Six Prime Ministers* (Sidgwick & Jackson, 1982), p. 193.

Chapter 40

1. Ward, R., *The Chamberlains: Joseph, Austen and Neville 1836–1940* (Fonthill Media, 2015), p. 121.
2. Wilson, Sir H., *A Prime Minister on Prime Ministers* (Weidenfeld & Nicholson, 1977), P. 220.
3. *Ibid.*, p. 220.
4. *Ibid.*, p. 214.

Chapter 41

1. Jenkins, R., *Churchill: A Biography* (Pan, 2001), p. 647.
2. Parris, M., *Great Parliamentary Scandals* (Robson Books Ltd, 1995), p. 115.

Chapter 42

1. Douglas Home, W., *The Prime Ministers: Stories and Anecdotes from Number 10* (W. H. Allen, 1987), p. 237.
2. *Ibid.*, p. 237.
3. *Ibid.*, p. 237.
4. *Ibid.*, p. 238.
5. Bastable, J., *Prime Ministers* (David & Charles, 2011), p. 107.
6. Douglas Home, *The Prime Ministers* (1987), p. 236.
7. Bastable, *Prime Ministers* (2011), p. 102.
8. Parris, M., *Great Parliamentary Scandals* (Robson Books Ltd, 1995), p, 117.

Chapter 43

1. Douglas Home, W., *The Prime Ministers: Stories and Anecdotes from Number 10* (W. H. Allen, 1987), p. 241.
2 *Ibid.*, p. 240.

Chapter 44

1. Douglas Home, W., *The Prime Ministers: Stories and Anecdotes from Number 10* (W. H. Allen, 1987), p. 248.
2. Thomson, G. M., *The Prime Ministers* (Martin Secker, 1980), p. 237.
3. Dampier, P., and Walton, A., *The Wit and Wisdom of British Prime Ministers* (Book Guild Publishing, 2008), p. 107.

4. *Ibid.*, p. 107.
5. *Ibid.*, p. 108.
6. *Ibid.*, p. 108.

Chapter 45

1. Bastable, J., *Prime Ministers* (David & Charles, 2011), p. 109.
2. Douglas Home, W., *The Prime Ministers: Stories and Anecdotes from Number 10* (W. H. Allen, 1987), p. 251.
3. Thomson, G. M., *The Prime Ministers* (Martin Secker, 1980), p. 239.

Chapter 46

1. Parris, M., *Great Parliamentary Scandals* (Robson Books Ltd, 1995), p. 182.
2. *Ibid.*, p. 184.
3. *Ibid.*, p. 183.

Chapter 47

1. Bastable, J., *Prime Ministers* (David & Charles, 2011), p. 32.
2. Douglas Home, W., *The Prime Ministers: Stories and Anecdotes from Number 10* (W. H. Allen, 1987), p. 259.
3. *Ibid.*, p. 260.
4. *Ibid.*, p. 258.

Chapter 48

1. Douglas Home, W., *The Prime Ministers: Stories and Anecdotes from Number 10* (W. H. Allen, 1987), p. 261.
2. Macqueen, A., *The Prime Ministers Ironing Board* (Little, Brown Book Group, 2013), p. 226.

Chapter 49

1. Douglas Home, W., *The Prime Ministers: Stories and Anecdotes from Number 10* (W. H. Allen, 1987), p. 265.
2. Deedes, W., *Brief Lives* (Macmillan, 2004), p. 204.
3. Hennesy, P., *The Prime Minister: The Office and Its Holder Since 1945* (Palgrave Macmillan, 2000), p. 400.
4. Eccleshall, R., and Walker, G., (eds), *Biographical Dictionary of British Prime Ministers* (Taylor & Francis Ltd, 1998), p. 361.
5. Bastable, J., *Prime Ministers* (David & Charles, 2011), p. 71.
6. *Daily Express*, 14 November 2016.
7. Douglas Home, *The Prime Ministers* (1987), p. 265.
8. *Ibid.*, p. 266.

Chapter 50

1. Powell, J. E., *Joseph Chamberlain* (Thames & Hudson Ltd, 1977), p. 151.
2. *The Guardian*, 6 December 1953.
3. Bastable, J., *Prime Ministers* (David & Charles, 2011), p. 85.
4. *The New York Times*, 31 October 1971.
5. Parris, M., *Great Parliamentary Scandals* (Robson Books Ltd, 1995), p. 309.
6. *Ibid.*, p. 312.
7. *Ibid.*, p. 317.
8. Bastable, *Prime Ministers* (2011), p. 77.
9. *Ibid.*, p. 76.

Chapter 51

1. Eccleshall, R., and Walker, G., (eds), *Biographical Dictionary of British Prime Ministers* (Taylor & Francis Ltd, 1998), p. 398.
2. Bastable, J., *Prime Ministers* (David & Charles, 2011), p. 123.
3. Mason, R., *The Struggle for Democracy: Parliamentary Reform, from the Rotten Boroughs to Today* (The History Press, 2015), Chapter 2.
4. Dampier, P., and Walton, A., *The Wit and Wisdom of British Prime Ministers* (Book Guild Publishing, 2008), p. 151.

Chapter 53

1. Bastable, J., *Prime Ministers* (David & Charles, 2011), p. 81.

Chapter 54

1. *Daily Express*, 20 March 2017.